Language Assessment in the Early Years

Language and Learning for Human Service Professions

A Series of Monographs
edited by

Cynthia Wallat, Florida State University
and
Judith Green, The Ohio State University

Language
Assessment in the
Early Years

CELIA GENISHI
University of Texas at Austin

ANNE HAAS DYSON
University of Georgia

Ablex Publishing Corporation
Norwood, NJ 07648

Material reprinted from *Language in Early Childhood Education, Revised Edition*, edited by Courtney B. Cazden. From Chapter 7, ''Making It and Going Home: The Attitudes of Black People Toward Language Education,'' by Courtney B. Cazden, Betty H. Bryant, and Melissa A. Tillman, p. 98. © 1981 by the National Association for the Education of Young Children, 1834 Connecticut Avenue, N.W., Washington, DC 20009.

Material reproduced from *Talking and Learning* by J. Tough, 1977, pp. 162–163, by permission of The Schools Council, London, England.

Material from *A First Language* by R. Brown, 1973, p. 54, reprinted by permission of the publisher, Harvard University Press, Cambridge, MA.

Printed in the United States of America.

Library of Congress Cataloging in Publication Data

Genishi, Celia, 1944–
   Language assessment in the early years.

   Bibliography: p.
   Includes index.
   1. Language acquisition.   2. Children—Language.
I. Dyson, Anne Haas.   II. Title.
P118.G38   1984   401′.9   84-3074
ISBN 0-89391-176-3
ISBN 0-89391-246-8 (pbk.)

Ablex Publishing Corporation
355 Chestnut Street
Norwood, New Jersey 07648

To Mary and Hiroshi Genishi, Athleen Haas, and Millie Almy

Table of Contents

Preface to the Series Language and Learning for Human Service Professions

This series of monographs is intended to make the theories, methods, and findings of current research on language available to professional communities that provide human services. From a theoretical and practical point of view, focus on language as a social process means exploring how language is actually used in everyday life.

Communication between and among adults and children, professionals and clients, and teachers and students, as well as the effect of changing technology on communication in all these contexts, has become the object of study in disciplines as varied as anthropology, cognitive psychology, cognitive science, education, linguistics, social psychology, and sociology. The series provides a forum for this research analyzing talk in homes, communities, schools, and other institutional settings. The aim is to shed light on the crucial role of language and communication in human behavior.

The monographs in the series will focus on three main areas:

- Language and Social Relationships
- Language and Helping Professions
- Language and Classroom Settings

We hope that these books will provide rich and useful images of and information about how language is used.

Cynthia Wallat and Judith Green

Acknowledgments

Most authors are indebted to various people. Because we present many examples of conversations and activities that took place in homes, centers, and schools, we have a myriad of friends, children, colleagues, and students to acknowledge. We know only some of their names, but they have all contributed substantially to our work. We are grateful to Irma Arteaga and staff, Erin and Jay Baxter, Susan Bennett, Patty Boyd, Cynthia Ann Cuevas, Linda Daugherty, Colleen Duffy, Lois Gamble and staff, Deborah, Elaine, and Michael Horwitz; Karinna and Patrick Hurley, Alfred James, Julie Jensen, Sandra Johnson and staff, Melanie Lee, Sara Madera, Sandra Ríos, Stewart Robertson, Nancy Roser, Meredith Saunders, Mary Scott, and Gale Spear and staff, in Texas; and Hugh Agee, Jan Bell, Joan Bond, Cathy Dunaway, Carol Fisher, Lee Galda-Pellegrini, Carol Garbin, Barbara McConnell, Eleanor Miller, Cindy Pifer, Lynn Saunders, Joel Taxel, Dee Ward, and Hsiu-li Wu, in Georgia.

We thank Cynthia Wallat and Judith Green for their very promptly done and helpful editorial suggestions.

Typing in Georgia, done by Kim Jackson, and typing and bibliographic assistance, provided by Jim Patterson in Texas, were much appreciated.

CHAPTER 1

Introduction: Purposes and Perspectives

Purposes

This volume was written to encourage you, the reader, to appreciate, foster, and assess the language and communication of young children in the years between birth and eight. Whether you are a parent, student, teacher, paraprofessional, researcher, or interested individual, we hope that your perspective on language will broaden as you read these pages. There is much to appreciate about language: how each language is different from others, how language can be used for multiple purposes, how speakers learn language in a short time when they are very young. At a time of life when we credit them with little intelligence, children master a most complex and sophisticated system of sounds and meanings, their first language.

We have only to try to learn a foreign language in adulthood to appreciate what children accomplish as preschoolers. The first author, who speaks her second language, English, as if it were her first, recently started to relearn her first language, Japanese. She "lost" this language, which is stubbornly different from English, by the age of 4 when she began to speak English. Her relearning task has been difficult but illuminating, especially in light of the content of this book. While writing about the processes of first language acquisition, she envied young children who don't need classes, audiotapes, or extra hours in the day to become fluent communicators. Neither do they ask a tutor exactly how each word in a sentence is related to the other words. (Adult learners might like to see the words written down, since some adults cannot say what they cannot see in print.) If you have mastered more than one language, particularly in a formal school setting, you may already appreciate the feat that language acquisition is. As a course in music appreciation may change the way you respond to music, we hope the following chapters enhance your sense of language, so that you hear and see meaning, structure, beauty, and style that you may have missed before.

Perspectives

Both authors are teachers in colleges of education and former classroom teachers, Dyson in preschool and the primary grades and Genishi at the preschool and secondary levels. We, therefore, have an interest in going beyond appreciating to the fostering and assessing of young children's language. The way we view *fostering* and *assessing* is shaped by the theoretical framework we take—introduced here and elaborated upon in Chapter 2. *Interactionist* is the term that best describes the theory. Language development—and development in general—are accounted for by the interaction of the active, thinking child with her genetic makeup and the nature of her environment.[1]

The general term *interactionist* implies other points of view that underlie our choice of content. Our way of looking at children is *developmental*; what happens in the first weeks or years of life is the foundation for what happens later. Experiences accumulate and in complex ways affect future changes and growth. To understand language acquisition, then, we take the long view. We assume that the gradual process of becoming a communicator begins at birth.

Interaction further implies that the context of development matters. Students of language need to know not only what happens that advances development within the child, but also what happens in her surroundings. Language specialists have become increasingly attentive to aspects of the social context of development, concerning themselves with the contexts of adult-child interaction and child-child interaction in home and out-of-home settings. We call this focus on context *sociolinguistic* in order to establish early on that, when studying children's language, we take into account both linguistic and social abilities. Our notions of fostering and assessing are based on the premise that the social situation can have powerful effects on the kinds of language a

---

[1]We have chosen to use both the feminine and masculine pronouns in our writing. To avoid the awkwardness of *she/he*, *his/her*, etc., we use feminine forms in odd-numbered chapters and masculine forms in even-numbered chapters as generic pronouns.

child produces. To learn how children use language we need to see them in a variety of contexts, using a range of sociolinguistic abilities.

Given the premise that language varies from situation to situation, we can summarize our approach to fostering and assessing language. If children can learn to use language in varied ways, adults can facilitate that versatility by providing opportunities for talk (and later, for reading and writing) in many different settings and activities. Fostering language, then, depends heavily on adults' willingness to arrange and change contexts for interacting and learning. The term *integrative* captures our perspective on curricula that foster young children's language. Especially with respect to language, we see little justification for separating one subject matter area from another. Language is used as a tool for thinking, learning, and expressing in all areas of the curriculum.

Our definition of *language acquisition* includes written language, although some may disagree. In a literate society, the abilities to read and write are part of one's competence in communicating. Literacy is not acquired universally as spoken language is, but children are expected to acquire it. We, therefore, want to foster and assess it. As children become literate, the traditional facets of language use—speaking, listening, writing, and reading—are integrated. For young children, the most effective language "program" occurs when the boundaries between these facets are blurred. The child in such a program can use language as she has previously experienced it, as a unified whole.

So far we have presented our general purposes and identified an interactionist framework which implies developmental, sociolinguistic, and integrative perspectives on language acquisition and education. In identifying our framework we acknowledge our biases. We are biased in favor of fostering productive language in all settings and in favor of assessing that language informally. By *informal* we mean methods of assessment based on observation and teacher documentation, not on standardized tests. We do not condemn the use of these tests, but urge you to supplement them by noticing—hearing and seeing—what your children do with and by means of language across varied situations. We believe careful observation and documentation of development and progress are the most effective ways of assessing language in young children, for they are still becoming the listeners, speakers, readers, and writers that some formal language tests expect them already to be. Adults who live and work with children know that scores on one or two tests cannot represent all a child does or can do. The individual capabilities, strengths, and weaknesses of children are best depicted over time and in diverse settings by those who know them well.

Organization

We present a dual emphasis on research and practice. You will note, for example, a focus on research in Chapter 2, and an equally important focus on real-life interactions in Chapter 3. In Chapter 2 we elaborate upon the interactionist framework, citing many recent studies related to the acquisition of oral language and literacy. The "researchers' tone" of this chapter reappears occasionally in later chapters but is in its most concentrated form here. We draw on the results of research as we later make suggestions for classroom practice. At the end of each chapter, we suggest readings that are sources of related research, activities, or assessment methods.

Chapter 3 presents the first of several sets of examples of interaction or children's products that we have observed, audiotaped, or received from students, colleagues, and friends. Most examples throughout the book appear in print for the first time; some are from other publications; and all are based on real-life interactions and conversations. In Chapter 3 the emphasis is on appreciation of what happens spontaneously in the home, rather than on what can be deliberately fostered or assessed.

Chapter 4 is about communication in day care settings. The effects of day care on development, the use of nonstandard and standard dialects, the importance of caregiver talk to children, and peer interaction are topics of this chapter. The kinds of language functions caregivers can encourage, as well as ways for them to observe and document infants' and preschoolers' communication, are presented. In this and later chapters we include guidelines and checklists, along with more formalized researchers' techniques that have been unavailable to the general public. The issues and methods we discuss are not limited to the day care setting, and the basic ways of assessing language are also applicable to later chapters.

Chapter 5 is a look at language in preschools for children from 3 to 5 years old. Its central theme is the effect of situations on the kinds of language children use. A significant feature of the situation is activity, which supports and promotes talk between child and child and adult and child. We portray several children—most monolinguals and two learning English as a second language—as they engaged in various activities. The relationship of play to language and learning is discussed, as well as the role of teacher talk in preschools.

Chapter 6 maintains the focus on using language for a variety of purposes: to ask questions, share experiences, direct others' behavior, and so on, this time in the kindergarten classroom. Many of the activities are also typical of the day care and preschool settings, but there is a shift to assessing what children learn about print: how they talk about stories and how they tell their own. The emergence of writing is discussed as a process firmly linked to children's oral language. Lists of predictable and wordless books for kindergarteners are included.

In Chapter 7, children from age 6 to 8 are depicted in classrooms as they become increasingly skilled communicators. Their competence is sampled across a range of situations, including sharing time, a science lesson, a play written by children, and teacher-led discussions. Because the business of schooling in the primary grades often centers on children's becoming literate, reading and writing receive more emphasis. Chapter 7 reflects a shift away from the diverse activity centers of preschools and kindergartens toward curricula that are more prescribed, predictable, and teacher-directed. The lessons and interactions we present are intended to show that, regardless of age or grade level, children can be enthusiastic speakers and, later, readers and writers when the curriculum is both varied and integrated. Finally, Chapter 8 presents a brief summary.

Glossary

behaviorist–referring to a psychological theory that emphasizes the importance of the environment, rather than a person's thought processes, in shaping learning. According to strict behaviorist theory, people learn largely through responding to stimuli. Responses are positively or negatively reinforced; positively reinforced responses are likely to recur, or be learned. Classical behaviorist theory is associated with B. F. Skinner.

bilingual–a person who is ideally able to understand and speak two languages with ease. In reality, many bilinguals are fluent in one language and have varying degrees of fluency in the other.

communication–the sending and receiving of meaning in a given context, through verbal and/or nonverbal means.

communicative competence–a person's unconscious knowledge of both linguistic and social rules that enable her to use language appropriately in different social contexts. When a speaker applies these rules in talking or interacting, she is engaged in *communicative performance*.

complexity–sometimes called cumulative complexity. As children's utterances increase in length, the rules they must unconsciously know to form them increase in both number and difficulty; what they can do with language becomes more complex. This use of *complex* is related to, but not the same as, that in *complex sentences,* which are formed by combining two or more ideas or propositions in one sentence.

comprehension–understanding; the receptive aspect of language.

dialect–a variant of a language. A single language is spoken in different ways in different geographic regions and social groups (community, social class, or ethnic group). Language specialists say that a dialect contains systematic deviations from the standard form of the language—in phonology, semantics, and syntax.

ethnographic–referring to research that involves participation in and observation of the daily lives of a particular social group. By describing in detail behaviors in a variety of contexts, the researcher aims to understand the patterns and meanings of group members' lives.

form–an element of language often named in grammatical terms, such as verb, noun, adjective. Sometimes form is a synonym for structure: a focus on language form refers to a concern with correct (standard) structure, for example, using a singular verb with a singular noun.

function–a purpose for which speakers use language, for example, to make requests, to give information, to tell stories, to ask questions.

grammar–a description of language structure, of the parts or elements of the language (sounds, words), and how those elements are combined to form spoken utterances.

grammatical rules–rules that enable speakers to combine the sounds and words of their language to convey meaning. Linguists traditionally refer to three aspects or levels of these rules: phonological, semantic, and syntactic. They are learned by all speakers of a first (native) language without formal instruction.

interlocutor–a person who participates in a conversation or interaction.

language–for purposes of this book, a system for human communication that relates sounds to meanings.

language arts–the producing and receiving of both oral and written language, generally referred to as speaking, listening, reading, and writing.

linguistic competence–a person's unconscious knowledge of the grammatical rules of one's language. When a speaker applies these rules to use language for thinking, understanding, or communicating, she is engaged in *linguistic performance.*

linguistics–the study of the structure or grammar of language.

monolingual–typically a person who can understand and speak one language.

morpheme–the smallest unit of meaning in the syntax of a language. It may be a word or a part of a word, for example, *story* is one morpheme, but *bluebirds* is made up of three: *blue, bird,* and *-s.*

nonstandard–referring to a dialect that is different from the one found in textbooks or generally used by educated speakers. In English, a well-known nonstandard dialect is black English, used by some black and nonblack speakers.

phonology–the aspect of grammar that has to do with speech sounds and the ways they can be combined and spoken in a given language.

pragmatics–sometimes referred to as the fourth aspect or level of grammar, it has to do with rules of language usage, or how language is used in different social contexts.

prelinguistic–referring to the period of time before a child uses words or language to communicate.

production–speech or referring to speaking; the expressive aspect of language.

psycholinguistics–the study of the cognitive or mental processes involved in learning and using a language; a marriage of psychology and linguistics.

semantics–that aspect of grammar that has to do with the meanings of words and sentences.

social context–the situation in which communication occurs. It consists of various factors: number of participants, their relative social status or rank, degree of familiarity with each other, topic, nature of the physical setting, the communicative purpose, and so on.

sociolinguistics–the study of how language is used in particular social contexts, or of how social structure is related to linguistic structure: sometimes used as a synonym for pragmatics.

standard–referring to a dialect that is generally used in print and is considered the "correct" form of a language by most speakers. The rules of standard English, for example, are found in school textbooks and textbooks for those learning English as a second language.

syntax–the aspect of grammar that has to do with how speakers systematically arrange elements of language (words and morphemes) to form utterances or sentences that are acceptable to native speakers, those who consider a given language to be their first (native) language.

CHAPTER 2

Language Acquisition Research: An Interactionist View

Introduction

> Yes, the one thing that we know with some clarity from the last decade of intensive research on language acquisition is that the child requires some knowledge of the world and how it is arranged socially, and something as well about the human intentions that will be encoded in speech acts, before he is able to use his "innate knowledge" . . . to search for, or invent, linguistic forms. . . . It is impossible to doubt that there is some kind of bioprogram for language that steers the searching and the invention. But that program cannot begin to work until the child is inducted into a social world where language has already made a deep impression in shaping and even in constituting the reality to which speech will refer. (Bruner & Feldman, 1982, p. 36)

In this short paragraph, Bruner and Feldman summarize what research in language acquisition has shown over the last 10 or so years. They conclude that children become language users through interaction, and that viewpoint underlies the remainder of this book. Our theoretical framework is best described as *interactionist,* whether we consider the way children learn spoken language or the way they learn to read and write. Interaction may be defined in several ways: in the everyday sense, there is interaction when people engage in social activity together. Conversing at home, school, or work is interacting. In a more general sense, different aspects of our experience interact with, or have an effect on, each other. What happens in our social lives can affect how we learn or perform cognitively; how we think affects how we feel, and vice versa. In a scientific sense, chemicals in our bodies constantly interact with each other; characteristics that are genetically determined interact with aspects of the environment to produce unique individuals. For example, a person with inherent musical ability needs exposure to music and opportunities for training for the inborn ability to develop. Similarly, language development occurs through these different kinds of interaction. To understand how it occurs, we need to take a comprehensive view that incorporates the child and his capacities to think, feel, and act; what his genes have provided; and what his physical and social environment contribute (see Figure 2–1).

Many current views about early language acquisition rest on the theories of Chomsky (1965), Piaget (Piaget & Inhelder, 1969), and Bruner (1975). Although neither Chomsky nor Piaget focused primarily on child language development, both emphasized the child's ability to engage in rule-governed behavior. According to Chomsky, children learn language by unconsciously figuring out how language works. They somehow internalize a set of grammatical rules that enable them to produce an unlimited number of sentences in a given language. They can do this without having heard or practiced, according to behaviorist principles of repetition and reinforcement, most utterances before. Since all normal children develop language in the first few years of life, Chomsky believes that human beings have an inborn ability to learn it. Piaget has been less concerned with the study of language than with the development of logical thinking. However, the Piagetian principle that children develop through activity, by acting upon their environment, has motivated child language researchers' recent focus on the context in which children learn language. The ''here-and-now''—what the child sees, touches, hears; who the child interacts with—are sources of development in all areas, including language.

One of the clearest spokesmen for the interactionist perspective on

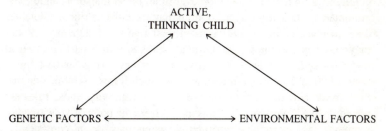

Figure 2–1 The child, who is capable of acquiring language, is at the top of this triangle. The arrows show that genetic and environmental factors interact with each other, as well as with the child.

language itself is Bruner, who has studied the connections between infants' actions and the beginnings of language. His writing and research have also supported the view of the young child as inherently sociable. This sociableness provides motivation for attempts to communicate well before children say their first words.

We agree that the process of language acquisition is based on inborn abilities to formulate rules, act physically upon the environment, and seek social interaction. Acquiring language is a prime example of the interaction of nature and nurture. Human beings are biologically prepared to use language in ways that no other organism does. What is with us at birth, however, must be cultivated by an environment consisting of people, objects, and actions, the essentials of interaction and bases of development. The studies that we summarize next are among those that provide initial answers to these questions: What is the nature of young children's language? When and how does the process of language acquisition begin? What do we know about the cultural and social aspects of the process? How do children learn to read and write?

Young Children's Language: Early Syntax

Due largely to the work of Chomsky (1965), linguists and psychologists interested in child language in the 1960s focused first on rules of *syntax,* which guide the ways we combine words to form grammatical utterances. Researchers sought to describe the nature of children's early utterances by discovering what their internalized rules might be. Pioneers in this effort included Brown and his collaborators (Brown, Cazden, & Bellugi, 1969) and Ervin and Miller (1964). These and other psycholinguists recorded thousands of utterances to induce the rules children used to combine their first words. They came to speak of children's grammars that develop over time, rather than of a single fixed grammar. In the early stages children may formulate a rule that enables them to place nouns before verbs in their two-word statements. Later they may apply a rule to add *-ed* to all verbs to form a past tense, as in *walked, goed,* or *hided,* even to verbs that have irregular past forms (*went, hid*). When children regularly use such forms, we conclude that they speak as if they know rules of syntax, even when those rules are not adult-like. What we call "mistakes" from the point of view of adult grammar, are especially informative when they occur consistently, since they tell us what the child's own rules are.

In addition to noting spontaneous child utterances like, "two feet*s*," "Bubba eat*ing*," or, "Daddy go*ed*," researchers have tested children's syntactic rules experimentally. Berko (1958) created an imaginative test for tapping children's knowledge of specific aspects of syntax, their rules for combining morphemes, or parts of words, to form other words. Berko used nonsense words, such as *wug, gling,* and *spow,* to see whether children aged 4 to 7 years could look at a picture related to the word and then form an appropriate new word. A child might respond, then, that a picture of more than one *wug* (drawn like an animal in a cartoon) was a picture of *wug-s.* Or the experimenter might show a picture of a man doing something he called *spow-ing* to see if the child could say that the man *spow-ed* yesterday. Berko inferred that children who were able to produce plural, progressive, past, etc. forms with nonsense words also knew rules for combining the specified morphemes with ordinary English words. (English and Spanish versions of this test are included in Chapter 5.)

Partly in reaction to the earlier focus on syntactic rules, researchers in the 1970s shifted from syntax to a concern with meaning, or *semantics.* The concern was not just with how children combined words but what those combinations meant. One syntactic structure could have multiple meanings, for example, "Daddy juice," could mean, "Daddy's juice," or "Daddy, give me juice," etc. Describing "Daddy juice" or "Kitty sleep" as a noun + noun and noun + verb combination, respectively, was inadequate. Instead both syntax and possible meanings of the combinations needed consideration. A more satisfactory description would be based on Brown's "rich interpretation," by which one credits the child with the ability to convey a variety of basic meanings and relationships (R. Brown, 1973). Some of these are the ability to use language to name things (nomination), to remark on the disappearance of a person or object (nonexistence), or to comment on who is performing an action (agent and action).

These categories of meaning are indications of what children are attending to and thinking about, in other words, what they experience and know. Believing that there is a close tie between the child's thinking and what he can say, investigators turned their attention to younger—prelinguistic—children, to a focus on infancy as the critical period in the development of both language and cognition.

Infancy and the Cognitive Bases of Language

A rich interpretation of children's early utterances raised fundamental questions: If children are conveying a variety of meanings in their early speech, how did the meanings develop? What enabled the child to convey those meanings through speech? How did the process of language acquisition begin? Psycholinguists, building on Piaget's studies of the first two years of life (Piaget, 1954), proposed cognitive prerequisites, certain abilities and understandings a child must have before he can use speech for communication:

> The child must be able to perceive, analyze, and store verbal messages; he must conceive of a stable world, with objects and events and human participants; and he must be able to engage in social interaction for the achievement of various personal and interpersonal goals. (Slobin, 1979, p. 80)

The child needs to be mature enough to understand and process language and to remember the combinations of sounds (words) that refer to elements of his environment. He knows that things and people in that environment exist apart from himself and that objects have a certain permanence. According to Slobin, these abilities and understandings emerge along with the infant's capacities for symbolic representation and tool use. That is, he can hold things in mind or mentally represent events and objects, even when they are absent. And he perceives that other people can be used for particular purposes. In this sense, people are tools that can be manipulated through communicative means, through both gestures and vocalizations. The factors that account for the onset of language, then, are *intra*individual, within the child and his cognitive capabilities, as well as *inter*individual, dependent upon experiences and social interactions with caregivers that begin at birth.

Spoken language is only one part of adult-infant communication; nonverbal elements are equally important. Stern (1977) is one of those who documented in detail the ways that mothers and infants became acquainted and communicated with each other during the first six months of the infants' lives. He suggested that infant and mother perform a "dance," in which each accommodates to the other. By adult standards, an infant can perform a limited number of actions that are fundamental for the establishment of communication. His gaze, for example, is the link to his caregiver, who spends about 70 percent of feeding time facing and looking at the infant. Facial expressions are another means for early communication. Newborns' facial muscles are mature enough to enable a range of expressions of pleasure and displeasure, including anger, sorrow, and joy. Though these expressions are elementary, they provide a base for more complex nonlinguistic and linguistic interaction in the future.

In addition to the first months of life, researchers attended to the next period when children make the transition from prelinguistic to linguistic communication. The interest was not only in what words were uttered first, but also continued to be in what kinds of interactions took place at that time between caregiver and infant. To follow this transition Bruner (1975) studied six mother-child dyads. He concluded that what facilitates the child's entry into speech is the match between the structure of action and the structure of language. Even at 2 months of age, for example, some infants can follow the adult's direction of gaze, especially if pointing and verbal exclamations accompany the gaze (Scaife & Bruner, 1975). The possibility for caregiver and infant to focus on a single object or event exists early on. Caregiver and infant both notice who is engaging in specific actions, what is affected by the actions, when it happens, and so on. That action-based information is eventually encoded in language: our utterances contain subjects (agents), verbs (actions), objects (recipients of action), places (locatives). The synchronization or dance that Stern (1977) described continues, but now the child begins to verbalize with words such as *juice, sleep, car, up*—words that refer to his concrete world.

Nelson (1973) documented what children's first 50 words were likely to be. In her study of 18 1- to 2-year-olds she found that most of those words were general nouns like *car, sock,* and *key,* which named things that were not only common but also often mobile and handled by the children themselves. Other researchers (Clark, 1973; Barrett, 1982) propose refinements to Nelson's approach. For various reasons, including frequent use, children may first name common objects in their environments. But for children to acquire the full meaning of a word, they may need to go through an unconscious but progressive analysis of its features. The child notes features that are functional (how is a *shoe* used?) and perceptual (what is its shape, size, texture, and so on?). At first he may refer only to *his* shoes as shoes; then he may focus on features that are salient to him, for example, the shoe's shape. For a short while he may call both shoes and slippers "shoes," but over time he is finally able to identify the features that set shoes apart from boots and slippers. At this point, he has acquired the appropriate bundle of features and concepts that define the word.

Interested in communicative functions rather than acquisition of words, the linguist, Halliday (1975), studied his son from 9 to 18 months of age. In keeping with the work of Bruner and others, Halliday stressed the social and interactive functions of language and its precursors. Learning language is a crucial element in the process of socialization through which children become members of their families, communities, and cultures. In Halliday's terms, as infants are socialized they first learn to *mean,* not to speak. There are functions and a range of possible meanings well before there are linguistic forms to specify those meanings. The prelinguistic child, then, may use sounds and nonverbal means to express biological needs, regulate others' behavior, assert one's own importance, and so on. By the time the first words are uttered, the child has a good understanding of what language is for—in other words, how it functions in human interaction. (For further explanation and application of Halliday's functions to children's speech, see Chapter 4.)

Later Syntactic and Semantic Development

The bulk of research on language acquisition has focused on children under 5 years old, and most recently on children under 2 years of age. Nevertheless, there is much "complexification" that develops after the early stages. Somewhere between 2 and 4, for example, children not only use multi-word utterances, they also begin to use complex sentences that include more than one idea or proposition. Instead of saying in two separate sentences, "I see the toy. The toy is new," the child can say, "I see the toy, and the toy is new," or—using more advanced rules for combining ideas in a single sentence—"I see the toy that is new." "I'm going to sleep. Then my mom's going out," later can be stated, "Before my mom goes out, I'm going to sleep." In order to accomplish these combinations, the child must master certain rules of syntax that enable him to eliminate some words, add others, and change the word order when necessary. By learning a few rules about embedding one sentence or idea within another (or subordinating one clause to another), the child can eventually produce countless numbers and varieties of sentences that he could not before. (For a brief, technical discussion of complex sentences, see Bowerman, 1979.)

In addition, children acquire rules for forming other types of sentences. When they can consistently say, "Does Dan have the book?" instead of, "Dan has the book?" they speak as if they know a basic rule for question formation. That is, to verbalize certain questions they must use a form of *do* and invert the order of subject and verb. Similarly, a 6-year-old's utterance, "I don't want to sleep any more," shows mastery of adult-like rules for negative sentence formation, whereas his earlier, "I not sleep," does not. Since the late 1960s researchers have come to realize that such rules may develop over a period of several years. In the case of special structures, requiring the use of *ask* and *tell,* for instance, children may not master adult-like constructions until age 9 or 10 (C. Chomsky, 1969). In experimental settings, children under 9 years may confuse the meanings of *ask* and *tell,* so that they interpret, "Ask Joan what her address is," the same way as, "Tell Joan what her address is." Part of the dialogue between experimenter and child might sound like this:

> Adult: Ask Joan what her address is.
>
> Child (addressed to Joan): 4 Maple Street.
>
> Adult: Now tell Joan what her address is.
>
> Child (addressed to Joan): 4 Maple Street

The child here responds to *ask* as if it means the same as *tell.* Until children reach about 8 years of age, they also do not completely understand the differences in meaning between the articles *a* and *the* in experimental interviews (Karmiloff-Smith, 1979).

In the cases of *ask/tell* and *a/the,* children are working out semantic as well as syntactic puzzles. Semantic development in the school years occurs gradually and, like the acquisition of first word meanings, is bound up with the development of concepts. Children learn new vocabulary through instruction in school and through unplanned exposure in conversation. Semantic refinements learned by school-aged children have been studied infrequently. An old and interesting study is Asch and Nerlove's investigation (1960) of "double function" words, such as *bright, sweet,* and *cold.* By interviewing children between 3 and 12 years, they found that the youngest subjects could talk about the physical definition of such words but not the psychological one. Objects could be *bright* or *sweet,* but people could not. Almost all 12-year-olds, in contrast, understood both meanings. If the definitions of these dual function words develop over a period of years, full understandings of subtler distinctions must also take time. A first grader, for example, might understand that *skinny* and *thin* are synonyms, but for a period of time may not understand what distinguishes a skinny person from a thin one, as an adolescent or adult may only gradually learn, without instruction, the distinctions among *fashionable, faddish,* and *trendy.*

Whether our topic is the development of complex sentences or the understanding of dual function words, we know that children's linguistic abilities grow through interaction. Their language is affected in part by what adults say to them. We focus next on the specific features of adults' talk to children.

Adult Talk to Children

Because for children a major source of learning about human interaction is adult talk, researchers have begun to analyze what caregivers say to children. What ways of talking to children are associated with positive language development later? The answers to this question are very tentative. At the same time that she studied children's first words, Nelson (1973) asked what features of a child's environment might be associated with rapid language development. Among other things, she noted mothers' behavior in response to their children. Mothers of children developing vocabulary, comprehension, and length of spoken utterance more quickly than others shared two characteristics: they were less directive in their speech, gave fewer commands, and asked more questions; and they were accepting of whatever the child said and behaved as if the child's utterances were meaningful.

Caregivers modify their speech in other ways, as if they are tailoring it to fit the linguistic capabilities of their young children. Adults use utterances that are short and grammatically simple, hardly more complex than what the child can say. They also repeat or paraphrase themselves, and their pitch and intonation are high and varied enough to capture and maintain the child's attention (Snow & Ferguson, 1977). Researchers have found, in addition, that children learn to talk more quickly if the meaning of their mothers' conversational responses depends on, or is contingent upon, what the children say. The children, then, have opportunities to "guide" conversations with a receptive adult (Cross, 1978).

Special ways of talking to young children have been termed "motherese" and "baby talk," although researchers are aware that "fatherese" also exists. As parents reconsider and negotiate traditional sex roles and as the number of single-parent families increases, the father-child relationship deserves and receives more attention. Evidence so far shows that fathers can be as nurturant as mothers (Parke, 1979). Despite the recent discovery of fatherhood, mothers are still the primary caregivers in the first years of life, and investigators interested in fathers' behaviors often study mother-father-child interactions. Two major differences have been found between mothers and fathers. First, fathers treat sons, especially first-born sons, differently from daughters. They vocalize more to sons and are more physically active with them (Lamb, 1977). Second, fathers are more typically playmates than caregivers (feeders, diaper changers, and so on), regardless of the sex of the child. Fathers' playfulness is also reflected in their talk, which includes affectionately insulting nicknames, such as "dingaling" and "nutcake." Gleason (1975) notes this and other differences between men's and women's talk in a paper called, "Fathers and other strangers: Men's speech to young children." In this exploratory study, fathers' talk was compared with that of mothers and male and female day care teachers. Fathers used more imperatives (direct commands) and threats with children, whereas male day care teachers talked in ways similar to female teachers.

The "strangeness" of fathers, according to Gleason (1975) and Masur and Gleason (1980), can be beneficial to children's language development. If the father is an infrequent listener or interlocutor, the child may need to be more verbally explicit in conversations with him. The father may be unable to fill in gaps that the mother can because of her greater familiarity with the child. Further, Masur and Gleason found that fathers interacted differently from mothers in a task situation. When talking about toy cars with their 2½- to 5-year-old children, fathers provided more different terms than mothers and were more demanding, asking for more labels and functions than mothers. Children's responses to fathers subsequently contained more varied vocabulary than their responses to mothers. Thus, even in traditional families in which fathers are absent for much of the day, fathers may have a more direct and positive effect on children's language development than was previously suspected.

More generally, Wells (1981) found that adults' responsiveness to children's speech may be associated with both rapid oral language development and a higher level of reading achievement. The way adults responded to 3-year-olds' speech was closely associated with such measures as length of utterances, variety of uses of language, and reading achievement at age 7. Adults responding to the 20 children in the study were considered the most effective if they made "developing" responses. They added new information or encouraged the child to add to a previous utterance, for example, by means of appropriate questions.

Cultural Variation

Much of what we know about first language acquisition in English is based on studies of white middle-class children. Anglo-American or British families in this social group tend to value highly children's verbal abilities, including their ability to provide information when others ask questions and to engage in conversation to the extent possible. Consequently, studies like those mentioned earlier by Wells (1981) and Nelson (1973) highlight parental responsiveness, a general ability to understand what the novice speaker is communicating, to respond positively, and to maintain the dialogue. In some studies (Howe, 1981; Wells, 1981), responsiveness is defined in terms of informativeness, so that adding or exchanging new information is a much desired goal in interaction. Clearly, information exchange is important, and adults want to be responsive to children's communications. But because American society is heterogeneous, we realize that not all groups within it share the same values with respect to language and how it is used. We might also look at cultural variation and consider the contrasting values that underlie normal processes of language acquisition in different groups of people. Some social groups, for example, emphasize information exchange far less in early childhood than middle-class Anglo-Americans.

Miller (1982) reports in her study of three working-class white children in South Baltimore that her 2-year-old subjects—Amy, Wendy, and Beth—showed developing abilities to use language in ways appropriate to their social group. Their mothers valued and encouraged not only information-giving, but also functions such as teasing, asserting themselves, and defending what was theirs. They also stated their belief that children are taught to speak and engaged in direct instruction, primarily of names of people and things. There were many aspects of language that were not taught in this way, but Miller points out the importance of exploring the processes of acquisition among nonmiddle-class populations to see what diverse beliefs and practices exist.

Heath (1982a), investigating a working-class black community of the Piedmont Carolinas, describes how children are socialized to show verbal adroitness that is valued in their own culture. Adults or older children on occasion asked accusatory questions of younger children who could respond in two ways. They could quietly wait for a scolding for their behavior, or they could say something so clever that the questioner would forget the misbehavior. A mother that Heath observed said to her 3-year-9-month-old son, "What'd you do with that shoe? You want me to tie you up, put you on the railroad track?" This was the child's response:

Railroad track

Train all big 'n black

On dat track, on dat track, on dat track.

Ain't no way I can't get back.
Back from dat track,
Back from dat train,
Big 'n black, I be back.

(Heath, 1982a, p. 118)

After that performance, the mother forgot about her earlier annoyance. Examples like these show that responsiveness in social interaction may be defined in a variety of ways, not only in terms of informativeness.

Other groups stress spoken language in their family interactions far less than Anglo-Americans or blacks. Some native Americans, for example, say very little to child learners, even in situations that white middle-class speakers would find information-laden, for example, when teaching a child to weave (Scribner & Cole, 1973). The native American child observes adult weavers and learns by watching and later doing. In this case, spoken language is not the primary means of transmitting and obtaining information.

Further evidence of differences in patterns of language acquisition and use comes from non-Western cultures. The Kokwet, a Kipsigis community in Kenya, differ from middle-class Anglo-Americans in at least two major ways with respect to early language (Harkness, 1977). First, the child is more often in the company of peers and siblings than adults. Second, caregiver talk to young children contains fewer expansions, which are contingent responses that repeat parts of or elaborate upon the child's utterances. Thus, there are fewer exchanges of this type:

Child: Kitty?
Adult: Yes, that's a nice kitty.
Child: My kitty?
Adult: Yes, it is your kitty.

Kokwet mothers used expansions in only 3 percent of their utterances, whereas R. Brown (1970) found them to occur in 30 percent of his data from American mothers.

Interactions among adults and children of the Kaluli in Papua New Guinea also differ significantly from those of Anglo-Americans (Schieffelin, 1979). In this society adults believe that they teach children to speak through conscious repetition, not through casual interaction. The child is told to repeat what the adult has just said—"say like that'' (*"elema"*)—in a variety of situations. Further, Kaluli adults consider a child a beginning speaker only after he can say the Kaluli words for *milk* and *breast*. Words spoken before these two do not count as speech.

Those who have studied cultures abroad and diverse ethnic groups in the United States have seen that people in all these groups acquire language. Though Kokwet and Kaluli caregivers may use few expansions or "developing" responses (Wells, 1981), their children become able speakers in their own communities. It seems presumptuous to assume, then, that the Anglo-American model of adult-child interaction is a universally effective or desirable one. The fondness of many of us for informativeness in speech and increased speed of learning may tell something about language acquisition in a segment of our society, but it may detract from a full understanding of general processes of acquisition.

Individual Differences and Individual Uniqueness

When the early studies of language acquisition were done in the 1960s, very little was said about cultural variation; nor was there an attempt to discover individual differences among children as they developed language. This second lack was explained partly by linguists' concern with rules of syntax that all speakers acquire and partly by the newness of the field of child language research. So few children had been systematically studied that researchers did not focus on the differences among them. Recently, there has been discussion of individual differences in both adult and child language learners. Investigators tend to categorize those differences in terms of contrasting styles. In this sense, individual differences resemble group styles. Nelson (1973), for example, observed a referential versus an expressive style. Referential children, from 1 to 2½-years old, used a large proportion of object names when they spoke, whereas expressive children had more varied vocabularies, containing a number of social routines ("stop it," "don't do it," and so on). Referential children appeared to be object-oriented in their speech, but expressive children seemed to be socially or person-oriented. This distinction has been elaborated upon (Nelson, 1981) and supported by recent studies. What is significant for us is the care that Nelson takes to point out the fluidity of these styles. Children may be both expressive and referential, or they may exhibit one style at age 2 and another at age 4.

Individual differences in second language acquisition have been studied by Fillmore (1976), in her study of five Spanish-speaking 5- to 8-year-olds learning English. She found that the girl who learned English the most rapidly also had the most outgoing and confident personality. She had the ability to place herself in social situations where she could practice what she knew about English. More recently Fillmore and Ervin-Tripp (1979) have suggested that personality type is only one of many complex factors contributing to second language learning. They have identified two global variables as sources of difference: first, social style, or the learner's interactive and communicative preferences, including personality characteristics, social orientation, and social competence; and, second, language learning style, or the learner's aptitude for language learning, including verbal memory, ability to induce patterns from language, ability to infer meaning from contextual information, and verbal playfulness.

All of these factors can also be sources of differences in first language learners. We introduce them to demonstrate again how complicated the process of developing language is. With such things as personality, verbal memory, quality of adult input, and cultural expectations always interacting, we know that children will differ in their approaches to learning language and in their rates of acquisition. Although it may sometimes be useful to speak in terms of the opposites like object-oriented versus person-oriented, we are aware that most people are better captured somewhere in between. In the chapters that follow, we underscore the value of individual differences and encourage a view beyond general styles to individual uniqueness, to a set of characteristics that parents, caregivers, and teachers come to know through repeated interaction. Rather than a verbal child versus a quiet child, we describe individuals who may vary from conversation to conversation, task to task, and setting to setting. In the next section, we summarize studies of how varying social goals and situations influence language use and development.

Sociolinguistic Development

Regardless of their style or rate of language acquisition, we credit children with two kinds of competence. They develop *linguistic competence,* the unconscious knowledge of phonological, syntactic, and semantic rules; and *communicative competence,* the knowledge that language is used differently in different situations (Hymes, 1972).

Children gradually learn to use varied styles of speaking—formal, informal, colloquial—and they learn to adjust what they say to suit their listeners and the occasion. In other words, they learn rules for differentiating among social situations. As an infant, the child responded nonverbally in different ways to family and strangers. Later as a speaker, he demonstrates social rules for talking or not talking—to varied categories of people. The bilingual child who has learned two languages in the preschool years acquires additional rules as to when he speaks one language or the other (Lindholm, 1980). The acquisition of rules for language choice appears to be well-grounded by the time the child is 3 or 4 years old. Like monolingual speakers, bilinguals make inferences about social and linguistic appropriateness, based on continued interaction in diverse social settings. For all children knowledge of the forms of language develops simultaneously with knowledge of uses and functions. Language functions are as important as forms. (See Figure 2–2.)

Research focused on how linguistic forms are used in different communicative situations is often called sociolinguistic. More technically, sociolinguists study the relationship between linguistic structure and social structure. An aspect of sociolinguistic competence that children show in infancy is their ability to participate in routines (Snow, Dubber, & De Blauw, 1982). Before they utter their first words, infants are partners in repetitive and predictable game routines like "peek-a-boo." Once they begin to speak, adults involve them in instructional routines ("Where's your nose? Where's your mouth?" and so on.) The situation of book reading, more common in some social groups than others, is the basis for other routines. The child easily fills in dialogue "slots," for example, by repeating the last word of each sentence read by the adult or by answering a question after the adult reads each page. These routines have the potential for teaching the child about both language and appropriate social responses. A more restricted routine is the politeness routine (Gleason & Weintraub, 1978). An example, that of waving "bye-bye," can be seen in the first year of life. Others, including "thank you" and "you're welcome," do not become routines until well after the preschool years. Learning such forms may seem trivial in comparison with learning conceptual or academic content, but politeness routines gain significance in the school setting when adults may rightly or wrongly consider them to be characteristics of good students.

Sociolinguists investigate language as part of general social or interactional competence that, like the routines it encompasses, has been developing since birth. Cook-Gumperz (1981) sees language as a powerful social resource, which the child adds to his existing nonverbal

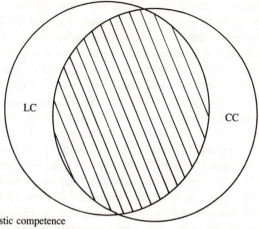

LC = linguistic competence
CC = communicative competence

Figure 2–2 When speakers use language for communication, their linguistic competence (LC) overlaps their communicative competence (CC) (shaded area). At other times they may use language without communicating for talking to themselves or thinking with language, or they may communicate nonverbally without language.

resources for communicating. In this view, children use talk primarily as a tool for influencing others' behavior. Talk can be a means of asserting one's own importance and controlling self and others. Children, like other people, can have more than one purpose when speaking: they can provide information at the same time that they "say" who is in charge of a situation.

Over time, children learn to use language in specific social contexts, for example, in narratives, arguments, and instructional situations (Ervin-Tripp & Mitchell-Kernan, 1977; Wilkinson, 1982). A sociolinguist who has investigated a similar range of situations in different dialects of English is Labov (1970). He called attention to the validity of the forms of black English, which he has analyzed as a dialect separate from standard English. Equally important is his emphasis on the diversity of functions language serves.

Along with others, Labov countered the myth that poor children are nonverbal and "culturally deprived." He did this by examining contexts outside of the school. In the black community of New York City, he gathered samples of speech from adults and children who he found to be both verbal and knowledgeable about their own culture. In one well-known study, Labov placed an 8-year-old black child, Leon, in three different situations. In the first, a white male adult interviewed the child about a toy airplane. Leon was not responsive in this test-like setting and gave the impression that he was not talkative. In the second situation, a black male adult interviewed Leon about a popular television show and prompted more language. Still the child's speech was not fluent. The third time, the same black adult brought with him a bag of potato chips, along with Leon's best friend. The adult also sat on the floor and turned the situation into a party. Finally, he began to joke with the boys about taboo topics. In this last setting, Leon talked easily and quickly and appeared to be highly verbal while using black English dialect. By manipulating participants, topic of talk, and purpose of the encounters, Labov supported his view that "the social situation is the most powerful determinant of verbal behavior" (Labov, 1970, p. 163). Not only do linguistic forms vary from dialect to dialect, the way speakers use those forms will vary, according to the situation or context.

Eisenberg and Garvey (1981) studied variations in a single conversational context, the argument, in 3- to 5-year-olds, who played in pairs in a laboratory setting. The researchers were concerned with specific sequences of discourse, or conversation, which they also termed an adversative episode or conflict. This was defined as "the interaction which grows out of an opposition to a request for action, an assertion, or an action" (Eisenberg & Garvey, 1981, p. 150). The episode ended with a resolution of conflict, and resolution seemed to be the children's interactive goal. Thus, an argument was primarily a problem jointly solved through talk. This perspective was both sociolinguistic and cognitive, since solutions to arguments could be analyzed as more or less adaptive, depending on how able a child was to take the viewpoint of his listener and to reach a compromise.

According to Eisenberg and Garvey, the structure of a conflict can be described by the nature of the "initial opposition" (the utterance that begins the conflict) and the "strategies" that follow the opposition. Examples of strategies that children could follow were: (a) insistence— support for a previous utterance that adds no new information; (b) reasons; (c) compromise—proposal for some form of sharing; and (d) physical force. Eisenberg and Garvey concluded that their preschool subjects did not rely only on simple strategies, such as insistence. They also used reasons and requested explanations or justifications for behavior. More than any other, the strategy of giving reasons led to successfully ending conflicts.

Contrasting results were reported by Genishi and Di Paolo (1982) who studied the arguments of seven 3- to 5-year-olds. These children tended not to resolve conflicts by means of reasons or compromises. Of 189 arguments, only 41 contained attempts at resolution. Children often seemed to argue to establish their own authority, not to reach a resolution. The researchers concluded that features of the social situation contributed to the simplicity of the arguments. Whereas Eisenberg and Garvey's subjects were recorded in pairs in a laboratory setting, Genishi and Di Paolo recorded theirs in the naturalistic preschool setting. A child arguing could be distracted by other children, the teacher, or events. On the other hand, subjects interacting in pairs might find it necessary to resolve a conflict so that their interaction could continue.

The argument demonstrates why language is best analyzed from an interactionist point of view. It embodies clearly the cognitive and social complexity of all kinds of talk. As they argue, children have particular social purposes. They may want an object that someone else has, they may disagree with what someone has said, or they may be asserting their own importance. Children also apply strategies that reflect their cognitive abilities, whether their strategy is to repeat what they have already said or to offer a reason to support their argument. Finally, the nature of the situation affects the kinds of social purposes children have and cognitive strategies that they will employ. The presence of an adult or of other children, the availability of desired objects, the number of ongoing activities all contribute to children's social goals and how they accomplish them.

In addition to children's spontaneous talk with each other, researchers have studied how teachers and children interact during classroom lessons (Erickson, 1982; Mehan, 1982). They point out that participating effectively in lessons involves both academic and social understandings. Thus, teachers' ability to teach individual children, and their assessment of what those individual children know, is dependent upon the children's ability to participate appropriately in the interactional structure of classroom lessons. This three-part structure has been repeatedly observed: (a) teacher's initiation (I); (b) child's reply (R); (c) teacher's evaluation (E). This is referred to as the IRE sequence (Mehan, 1979). Another element typical of lessons is the use of "pseudoquestions" (Barnes, 1969), or questions to which the teacher already knows the answer.

Recently, researchers have become concerned with the relationship between the interactional demands of such lessons and those of the home. As Cazden (1982) puts it, researchers ask if the interactional strategies children acquire at home interfere with, positively affect, or simply coexist with those demanded by school contexts. With reference to this issue, Maclure and French (1981) stress the continuity that sometimes does exist between parent-child and teacher-child exchanges. They discuss data collected in the Bristol study of language development (Wells, 1981), demonstrating that preschoolers from varied social backgrounds participated in three-part lesson-like exchanges at home and also answered pseudoquestions. However, researchers who have studied children from other cultural groups have documented in detail how home and school interactional rules may differ and, in addition, how those differences may affect both school instruction and assessment.

For example, Philips (1972) studied native Americans, reared on reservations, at home and at school. She found that the children did not participate verbally in large group lessons. However, they did participate in small student-controlled groups in which they worked cooperatively and spoke voluntarily. The latter setting was the one most compatible with the interactional style in their home community. Heath's study (1982b) of communities in the southeastern United States is another example of research which has examined the continuity in interaction patterns between home and school. Her work demonstrated that the ways community members interact with print has a differential effect on children's ability to grasp both the interactional and the academic demands of the school.

Shultz, Florio, and Erickson (1982) point out that, by simply acknowledging that students may have different notions of "interactional etiquette," teachers may find children to be "more sensible than might be thought if observed only in their interactional performances in limited classroom situations" and classroom lessons to be "more complicated and demanding events than we might have thought" (p. 120), events which demand both cognitive and social skills.

By using insights from research on cultural interactional styles, teachers may be able to ease children's transition to school. For example, in her study of interaction between first grade teachers and black children during reading group lessons, Piestrup (1973) documented the instructional effectiveness of "Black Artful" teachers. These teachers adopted a rhythmic, playful interactional style with their children, building on the children's ability to engage in verbal games. In addition, they listened to their children's responses, acknowledging and building upon their comments—a strategy which would seem beneficial to all children.

However, teachers deal with children displaying a range of interactional styles. Shultz et al. (1982) suggest that, although teachers may lack the knowledge to decide which interactional strategies may benefit particular children, they can observe how individual children interact and then make decisions about the kinds of assistance they may require. Teachers may consequently redefine children who are discipline problems as children who have different strategies for carrying out interactions. These children may benefit from changes in the ways tasks are organized or, perhaps, from more explicit and consistent directions about the teacher's expectations.

Features of the interactive context affect the outcome of all verbal interactions, including school lessons that were once defined as purely cognitive. Reading and writing have traditionally been thought of as cognitive activities, though we now believe that we understand them better when we place them in their social contexts and consider how young children might become literate in the foundation of social interaction. We turn now to research related to early literacy and its foundations.

Becoming Literate: An Active Process

The major concepts applied to oral language development appear to apply to written language development as well. Children actively develop their own models of how written language works by purposefully interacting with people and objects in their environment. This view of written language as actively acquired by the child over time is relatively new. The vast majority of research on literacy has treated written language as a set of skills taught by adults in the context of school lessons. Researchers and practitioners alike have worried about whether or not the first-grade child is "ready" for books and paper and pencils. Vigorous debates, epitomized by Jeanne Chall's book *Learning to Read: The Great Debate* (1967), have focused on whether the child's first reading lessons should emphasize sound/symbol correspondences or whole words. Of course, many educators still worry about these matters. Early childhood curricula today reflect that worry; for example, basal reading series publish kindergarten programs which frequently focus on the names and formations of the letters and on sound/symbol correspondences. In discussions of such issues, it is hard to find the lively child who often—long before school entry—has already begun to explore the written language that exists and is used in his environment.

A strong spokesperson for the active child has been Frank Smith

(1978). Smith describes children learning to read as they do everything else, through purposeful interaction with their environment. Smith stresses children's reliance on their language competence—their understanding of how language works to make sense—as they uncover the rules of written language. The selected literature review in the following sections reflects this view of children actively becoming literate as they interact with written language in a variety of contexts over time. We begin by discussing the research that called attention to children who became competent readers and writers with no formal schooling.

Early Readers and Writers

An early focus of research was children who read and/or write in a conventional manner before instruction in school begins. Most of this research is labeled "early reading research," although it could more accurately be labeled "early reading and writing research." Investigators have frequently found—to quote Durkin (1966)—that early readers are "pencil and paper kids" (see also Clark, 1976; Plessas & Oakes, 1964; Torrey, 1969).

Durkin, whose *Children Who Read Early* (1966) is a classic, found that these "paper and pencil kids" initiated their own exploration of written language through questioning readers in their environment: "when families of early readers were interviewed, it became clear that none of the subjects learned to read early 'all by himself.' What also became apparent was the wonderful productivity of a young child's questions—when they get answers" (p. 26). Questions concerning the identification of words, the spellings of particular words, and the formation of letters were most often reported. In contrast to parents of early readers, parents of children who were not early readers often were reluctant to respond to such questions, fearing that their children might become confused or bored in the first grade. Similarly, Clark (1976) reported that, in 25 of her 32 home interviews, parents stated a belief that the initial interest in written language had come from the child; as parents, they had responded to requests for help in a casual, non-systematic manner.

Both Durkin and Clark noted that homes of early readers made available a wide range of print, not only storybooks, but everyday print as well, including cookbooks, food can labels, newspapers, and maps. Clark pointed out that different children approached reading through different materials due to different interests. Not only was print available, but it was used. Parents of early readers were themselves avid readers and, in addition, they read to their children.

Hildreth (1936) was the first researcher to conduct a systematic, developmental study of preschool writers. She charted the development of name-writing ability in children between the ages of 3 and 6. Interviews with parents of these early writers revealed that children acquired writing skill by "begging to know how to write when seeing others write;" parents responded to requests with suggestions as to letter formation and the spelling of the child's name. Similar findings were reported by Hall, Moretz, and Statom (1976). In their study of early writers, they also found that the majority of parents reported that help with writing was given at the child's request. Most frequently, help was requested with letter formation, spelling of words, or recording of a child's dictation.

The researchers discussed in this section have all agreed that early readers and writers come from homes where reading and writing are done and where someone responds to the children's questions about print. They have all highlighted the active child in a responsive environment. Recently, Wells (1981) has provided additional support for the importance of a supportive environment for literacy growth. One focus of his longitudinal study of language development was to identify possible causes of variation in both oral and written language development by examining features of children's home environment. Wells' data indicated that, for a sample of 20 children, the best single predictor of reading achievement at age 7 was the extent of the child's understandings about the conventions of literacy. For example, did the child know that the print (not the picture) tells the story? That the print is read from left to right? Could the child name any letters? Explain the purposes of punctuation marks? Match capital and lower-case letters? The extent of the children's knowledge about such conventions of print was, in turn, associated with characteristics of their preschool home environments, specifically, with the degree to which parents had engaged in extended conversations with their children and, in addition, had shared literacy experiences with them (for example, read to them, answered their questions about print). Sharing in such literacy experiences appeared to be associated as well with writing achievement at age 9 (Kroll, n.d.).

Researchers are just beginning to focus on young children in the process of becoming readers and writers. These researchers are not concerned so much with whether or not children are reading and writing in a conventional manner, but with the process through which young children figure out for themselves how print works. As we turn to this research, we focus first on reading, and then on writing to accurately reflect the nature of the literature. This does not imply that the processes are independent of each other. Reading and writing are complementary processes. Further, the process of writing messages involves reading as well as listening and speaking.

Early Reading and Writing in Process

Children appear to approach reading and writing as they do most human skills—globally. They experiment and approximate, gradually becoming aware of the specific features of written language and the relationships between symbols, sounds, and meaning. They form their models of how written language works as they encounter it in specific settings. Researchers of early reading have focused particularly on children encountering print in one type of print setting—storybooks.

Clay (1966, 1979b) carefully observed the reading and reading-like behaviors of 5-year-old New Zealand children as they became literate in the school context. Clay identified concepts about both the visual and linguistic aspects of reading which children become aware of in their preschool or early school years. She described the first stage of learning to read books as one in which the child understands that print can be turned into speech. Children initially invent sentences for texts which reflect their own colloquial speech styles. Then, the language of books emerges. Children begin to "talk like a book." As they are learning about the language of books, children are also beginning to grasp concepts about the visual aspects of print, including that of directionality (that print moves from left to right) and voice-print correspondence (that there is a specific relationship between spoken and written words). Clay stresses that children acquire these concepts as they explore books on their own and with others—not as a result of isolated training on specific skills. In this regard, Clay noted in her study that children's performance on the *Metropolitan Reading Readiness Test* (which tests such skills as naming letters, matching figures, and copying patterns) improved *concurrently* with their mastery of the actual reading task, with their ability to make sense of print.

Holdaway (1979) has focused on children who are reared in homes in which books and reading to children are significant parts of daily life. He has described children's behaviors as they "read" well-known books. Their reading reflects knowledge about the language of books and the processes of reading. Children become able to "read," to reproduce the meaning of a book, because of their ability to predict words and plots and to self-correct in an effort to read "correctly"—to match the book's language. Prediction and self-correction are aspects of the mature reading process just as they are aspects of young children's early reading (Smith, 1978). In Holdaway's work, as with Clay's, we see children's independent reading growing out of social experiences with adults and their own active exploration of print.

Certain researchers have drawn attention to the literacy knowledge that children gain from interacting with print in their physical environment, in addition to the book environment. For example, Harste, Burke, and Woodward (1982) asked 48 preschool children (ages 3 through 6) to perform varied reading and writing tasks, such as, reading a commercial label, dictating and reading a story, and writing or pretending to write a letter. Their findings demonstrated children's hypotheses about how written language works in specific settings. In one task, the children read a post office logo. The children's responses were varied and included "a birdie flew" (from a 3-year-old), "American picture sign" (a 4-year-old), "Put in mail" (a 5-year-old), and "U.S. Mail" (a 6-year-old). Although the 6-year-old's answer was most controlled by the graphic information, Harste et al. point out that all of the children followed a similar process of associating what they saw with what they knew about their world.

Of the researchers who have focused specifically on writing, Clay (1975) provided a seminal work on the beginnings of written communication. She analyzed writing samples spontaneously produced both in the home and in the school by New Zealand children between the ages of 4;10 and 7;0 years. In her analysis of writing samples, Clay noted two key features of the learning-to-write process which provide developmental insight:

1. The initial writing products are gross approximations to be refined later: letter-like forms, invented words, and make-believe sentences.

2. Individual letters and words are first known in a very specific way; for example, Jenny writes her name as "Jehhy" and does not acknowledge "Jenny" as her name.

In her study of the progressive refinement of these early approximations, Clay identified certain principles, which children appear to follow in their early writing. The most critical of these principles are the *sign* concept: letters and letter-like shapes carry some unknown message; and the *message* concept: messages the child speaks can be written down. Other principles reflect children's increasing "perceptual awareness of those arbitrary customs used in written language" (p. 2); for example, children discover the *recursive* nature of print (that the same basic forms recur repeatedly) and its *directional* orientation.

These concepts, of course, serve children's reading as well as their writing, a point which Clay has emphasized. Children beginning to read, as we have seen, tend to rely primarily on language cues—on their sensitivity to and memory for language; for example, they "read" familiar picture books by recalling the way the book "sounds." In writing, children must develop strategies for attending to visual cues—particular arrangements of specific graphic forms.

Ferreiro (1978, 1980) is another researcher who has focused on both the reading and writing processes. Her major concern is how children come to understand the alphabetic nature of the written language system and—like Clay—she emphasizes the value of early exploration of writing. Ferreiro studied a group of 30 children between the ages of 3 and 6 years in Mexico City. She interviewed them regularly over a 2-year period. During the interviews, she asked each child to perform particular reading and writing tasks. She found that, regardless of social class, children initially hypothesized a concrete and direct relationship between graphic features and their referents. For example, one child, Marianna, a 4-year-old, asked for four letters to write her own name, seven letters to write her mother's name (which has two syllables), and "as much as a thousand" to write her father's name (which also has only two syllables)—someone as big as her daddy should certainly have many more letters than someone as small as herself! During this early literacy stage, the children believed that only referents for concrete entities are actually written in a written sentence, although one reads the "complete" sentence. Thus, when asked to read the printed sentence "Delfino vendió tres gatitos" ("Delfino sold three little cats"), 5-year-old Javier identified *Delfino* as the first word and the three remaining words as the three little cats. At a later point in development, the children's writing and reading behaviors reflected an understanding that a relationship exists between print and the formal characteristics of oral language. Like Clay's, Ferreiro's work suggests that we accept and value children's writing, even before the children know the alphabetic system. Through their own active exploration of the writing act, children reinvent our written language system.

Like Ferreiro, Dyson (1981) was interested in children's conceptions of the relationship between oral and written language, but she was interested in child-initiated writing, rather than researcher-structured tasks. She used participant observation methodology to examine how children use oral language during writing. Data collection took place daily over a 3-month period in a public school kindergarten classroom of 22 children. The group was academically, ethnically, and socially balanced. She set up a writing center in which children were asked simply to write, according to their own definition of writing. She observed and interacted with the children to gain insight into their perceptions of writing and their reasoning about writing behaviors, focusing particularly on five children selected as case studies.

Dyson found that, for the children in the observed classroom, writing most frequently did not involve encoding lengthy messages into print. The children frequently wrote just to write, with no specific intended message (for example, "I'm gonna do it how my Mama does it."). The most common type of representational writing was to write labels for people and objects. Thus, rather than trying to encode speech into graphics, most of the children made meaningful graphics about which they could talk, much as they talked about their drawings (that is, "This is a *dog* [a written word] and this is a house [a drawn object]). Writing, like drawing, was a means of symbolizing significant people and objects in the child's world.

Certain children in the room did attempt to encode spoken messages into specific graphics. These children used a variety of methods, including requesting spellings from others, writing a certain number of letters per syllable, and writing letter names heard in the spoken word. Like Ferreiro, Dyson documented children writing outside the alphabetic system. But she found more variation in writing strategies than Ferreiro had. She also found certain children who simply did not want to write. Many factors appeared to influence a child's approach to writing besides the kinds of knowledge discussed by Clay and Ferreiro. These included individual style of functioning, risk-taking ability, and the particular purposes for which the child chose to write.

Much interest in children's writing strategies has centered on young writers who are already operating within the alphabetic system and who, in addition, have an operational knowledge of letter names or letter sounds. Researchers have focused on children's early invented spellings, and their systems for relating sounds to letters. In a classic study, Read (1971, 1975) studied 20 selected preschool children from professional families who invented their own spelling system for English. He documented the systematic nature and the phonetic basis of their spelling. Interestingly enough, the children all arrived at roughly the same spelling system. While noting the children's active role in their own learning, Read also cited the apparent importance of their supportive environment; Read noted in particular parents' willingness to accept incorrect spellings from their children.

In the next section, we turn from a consideration of the earliest readers and writers to research which has focused on school-aged children.

Literacy in the Primary Grades

The popular conception is that children in the primary grades learn reading during reading lessons, and they learn writing during handwriting, English, or language arts lessons, and perhaps during writing, a "subject" which has been neglected in the primary grades (Graves, 1978). However, several researchers, including Clay (1975), Graves (1975, 1983), Griffin (1977), and Florio and Clark (1982) have countered this view. A picture is emerging of what children actually do as they read and write and of how what they do changes over time. Research findings demonstrate that children use all the language arts, oral and written, in an integrated fashion as they carry out a range of tasks throughout the school day.

Clay (1979a and b) has carried out descriptive studies of New Zealand children, from 5- through 7-year-olds, learning to read in school. Her work, as discussed earlier, has indicated that children begin to "read" books by relying on their knowledge of language in that context—they know how books "talk." As children gain experience in reading, they begin to attend to the fine details of the visual or graphic aspect of text. They differentiate the significant features of print which allow meaning to be uncovered. To become mature readers, children must integrate information from both the language and the graphic aspect of print; they must monitor their reading in order to see if what they are saying sounds correct and seems also to match what is written. Clay noted that the ability to self-correct, to engage in this active monitoring behavior, was a predictor of good reading progress in these early school years.

A researcher who has focused our attention on the behaviors of primary-grade children writing is Graves. In his study (1975) of second graders' writing, he not only gathered written products, but he also observed children actually writing, and he talked to them about their own views of writing. Among his tentative conclusions was the identification of two composite profiles of general types of child writers. Reactive writers, whom Graves considered developmentally less advanced, struggled with the basic task of getting the individual words on the page. Since these children often had to spend their time coming up with a spelling, they had to reread their work often to recall their intended message or to decide what word came next. For reflective writers, spelling was less of a problem. Thus, these children wrote quickly, and were freer, in this sense, to reflect upon their writing, to think about its content. In comparison to reactive writers, they seemed to have a greater sense of what they intended to write before they began and, in addition, they were more apt to review or contemplate their products when done. Another conclusion of the Graves' (1975) study was that varied factors affected the way a child approached writing, including home and family, peers, teacher, and developmental level as a writer.

The themes of increasing reflectiveness and the effect of environmental factors on one's writing are also present in Graves' (1981, 1983) more recent study. With Sowers and Calkins, he studied 16 children over a 2-year period. He noted that the children became increasingly more conscious of their control over the writing process. For example, they evidenced greater thoughtfulness about the topic they might write about, the way they might begin their particular piece, and the reactions their audience might have to their work. Much of this growth in conscious control over the writing process is no doubt attributable to the instructional context in which the children worked. It was a context in which children interacted with both their peers and their teachers about their work and, in addition, a context in which the focus of the interaction was on the meaning the individual child was attempting to communicate.

Descriptions of the interactions which took place in one small group of first graders are provided by Dyson and Genishi (1982). The analysis focused on two children, Peter and Tambrea, at the beginning of the school year as they began officially to learn how to write. Of interest was the way in which the two children's interactional styles complemented each other. Tambrea wrote quickly, rarely seeking assistance with her own writing, although she freely gave help to others in the group. Peter, in contrast, wrote very slowly—writing was a struggle for him. He frequently requested help from the other children with his spellings. He needed their help to persevere, and his peers were responsive. They modeled writing behaviors for him and provided assistance and encouragement. Thus, Peter's sociolinguistic skill—his ability to request information in a pleasant and effective manner—was supporting his academic growth.

A few researchers have focused specifically on the varying school contexts for literacy. For example, Griffin (1977) collected audio and video tapes and observational notes in order to learn how reading occurred naturally throughout the school day. She noted that a great deal of what went on during the official reading lessons had little to do with learning to read, but more to do with learning how the group was organized and managed. On the other hand, a great deal of reading went on throughout the curriculum as children read, not only primers, but trade books, math worksheets, bulletin boards, each other's writing, and so on.

Florio and Clark (1982) were also interested in the social situations in which literacy occurs in school. But, in contrast to Griffin's focus on reading, they wondered about the purposes or functions which writing serves in the school lives of young children. In a year-long descriptive study in a second/third grade classroom, Florio and Clark found that writing did not take place just during writing time, but served varying functions during the day. For example, children wrote class rules, kept a diary, wrote letters and cards, and completed a science workbook. Florio and Clark comment that only the writing done on worksheets or in workbooks was evaluated by the teacher; it seemed to be the writing which "counted." Their findings lead to concern regarding the attitude towards writing functions being fostered in the school context.

In the next section, we step back and take a broader look at context. We consider research on how children's initiation into literacy may vary across cultures.

Sociocultural Variation and Written Language

Cook-Gumperz and Gumperz (1981) argue that the transition from oral to written language, often associated with the transition from home to school, is a significant change for all children. Cook-Gumperz and Gumperz are concerned with linguistic/cognitive strategies which children must acquire in order to make use of written language in a range of school situations. They point out that children acquire language within an oral culture: children learn language through hearing and speaking in information-rich settings. Written language, and much of the oral language used in school, is decontextualized. That is, language exists apart from a familiar social and physical setting and must convey meaning primarily through words alone.

Despite this change for all children, particular types of initiations into literacy in the home may ease children's transition to written language as it is used in the school. We know that exposure to books and varied forms of print is valuable. The researcher's questions here go beyond exposure. They include: What styles of interaction do parents and children establish when they focus on books and other kinds of print? How do particular styles reflect different social groups' values, related to written language and its uses?

Ninio and Bruner (1978) conducted one of the first studies which drew researchers' attention to this question of how adults initiate children into literacy. They studied interactions during book reading between a mother and her infant, a white, English, middle-class male, from the time the child was .8 to 1.6 years. Ninio and Bruner point out that the book-reading experience had a ritualized structure; it was, in effect, a dialogue. In this dialogue, another form of Stern's (1977) dance, the central activity was to name the object pictured in the book. The routine consisted of four types of utterances: attention-getting ("Look"), query ("What's that?"), labeling ("It's an X."), and feedback ("Yes."). The mother eased her infant into the book-reading experience by providing "scaffolding;" that is, she reacted to his verbal and nonverbal behaviors as though they were appropriate turns, as though he were requesting a label or providing one. In this social game the child was learning to label simultaneously with learning about books. It is within the context of such social events that children are initiated into literacy (Teale, 1981).

Heath (1982b) has attempted to identify variations in such socialization events. Her research on working-class communities in the Piedmont Carolinas is based on ethnographic fieldwork in a mainstream middle-class (Maintown), a white working-class (Roadville), and a black working-class (Trackton) community. One aspect of her study was cultural variation in the acquisition of oral language. Another was the manner in which parents in the three communities introduce children to literacy. Focusing particularly on story-reading events, Heath documented striking differences in the three communities' styles of literacy socialization. She showed that the way in which each community uses and talks about print has a differential effect on the children's school success.

Children in Maintown, who perform well in school, are socialized to become members of a society in which books and information gained from books play a significant and ongoing role in helping one learn about the world. From as early as age 6 months, parents interact with children during book-reading events in ways which parallel primary grade reading lessons. Parents ask children information questions about items in books. They also help children to relate the content of books to situations occurring in their daily lives. In addition, parents encourage children to tell their own narratives, both fictional and factual.

Roadville children are also involved in book-reading events, but they have a significantly different introduction to literacy. Book-reading events center on alphabet and number books, "real-life" stories, Bible stories, and nursery rhymes. In both conversations about such books and children's and adults' oral stories, the focus is on factual recounting of events. Parents ask their children information questions about the content of books but do not relate the characters and episodes of literature to events in daily life. In that sense, the content of books stays in the books; it is not shifted to new situational contexts. Although Roadville children do well in the early grades, where attention is given to such specifics as alphabet, colors, and the answering of literal recall questions, they have difficulty after the third grade. In these higher grades, a greater emphasis is put on analytic, predictive, and evaluative questioning, which requires children to think in flexible, abstract, and independent ways.

For Trackton children, book-reading events are rare. Further, the types of questions they are asked by adults differ from those asked in Maintown or Roadville. Children are not asked to name or describe features of their environment ("What's that?") but, rather, to compare in general ways situations or items ("What's that like?"). In addition, the type of oral stories told differs from those told in the other two communities. The stories are fictional and put familiar events into new contexts. Trackton children have trouble in the early primary grades where the emphasis is on such "basics" as the alphabet and literal recall of facts. Thus, these children are unsuccessful in school despite the fact that they have advanced skills, such as analogical reasoning and fictional narration, which are rewarded in the upper grades. Like the Roadville children, Trackton children would benefit from teachers who are sensitive to the ways in which their use of language differs from that of mainstream children.

In an earlier study, Clay (1976) also suggested that the role of written language in the child's culture affects the acquisition of literacy. While not based on observations of parents with children, her study is significant. It demonstrated that the popular assumption of a close relationship between competence in the standard language and success in school literacy is not necessarily true. She studied white, native Maori, and immigrant Samoan children in New Zealand between the ages of 5 and 7 years. She found that, while the Samoan children had the poorest average scores on language tests, the Maoris had the poorest reading scores. Clay points out that, while neither the Maoris or the Samoan children had homes filled with print, Samoan children are exposed to oral Bible reading in the home. In addition, writing letters to relatives is a valued activity. For these reasons, Clay suggests, the Samoan children manage to progress well in the early years of school.

Another example of research related to both literacy and sociocultural variation is the work of Teale, Estrada, and Anderson (1981). Their in-home studies of low-income families depend heavily on naturalistic observation and combine description of social contexts with some data from controlled tasks and interviews. Studying 24 Mexican-American, Black, and Anglo children, the researchers are investigating parents' ideas about literacy, children's awareness of print, the nature and frequency of print-related interactions in the home, and cognitive tasks associated with literacy. Preliminary analysis shows many differences among families with respect to frequency and length of literacy activities. No single factor, such as sex of child, ethnic background, or education of parents, seems to account for the variation. Complex domains (parents' work that involves literacy, interpersonal communication, religion, and so on) are being investigated as possible sources of differences.

Teale et al.'s finding concerning variability among families brings us back to the complexity of language acquisition, oral and written, and the need for us to come to know children as unique individuals. In the next section we discuss research which has focused on the relationship between the individual child's style of functioning and the manner in which he goes about learning to read and write.

Individual Uniqueness

Studies designed to identify intraindividual patterns focus intensively on a small number of children across a range of activities and settings. Such case study research documents the diversity of paths to literacy. An example of such a study is the ETS Collaborative Research on Reading (Bussis, Chittenden, and Amarel, 1978). A major goal of this longitudinal study was to describe how a child's overall functioning style influences exactly how and when the child becomes a reader. Researchers and teachers jointly investigated individual children's changing behaviors over time and across various classroom contexts. Although this was called research on "reading," it was research on all the language processes. The findings of the study have documented a consistency between the way a child approaches reading and his approach to other types of learning (including writing) in the classroom. As Bussis et al. stress, a sensitivity to such patterned variation in children allows teachers to make instructional decisions for individuals, rather than for groups.

The uniqueness of each child learner is a theme of Bissex's (1980) description of her son Paul's growth as a writer and reader. As she details his progress from age 5 to age 11, she does discuss how his development was similar to that of other young writers and readers. At the same time, however, she shows that Paul's behavior over the years consistently reflected continuity in particular interests and in his inventive and independent style of functioning. Bissex points out that Paul's growth as a reader and a writer came about as a result of qualitative changes in reading and writing strategies. He didn't simply learn to read more and to write more, but he developed new and increasingly effective and flexible ways of approaching these tasks. Like that of Bussis et al., her research suggests the importance of observing closely how children go about reading and writing. Observation reveals more about the learning process than can standardized achievement tests.

Summary

The portrait of the child language learner is hard to envision without including the people who are his partners in communication. The infant, for example, performs a "dance" with his caregivers, who accommodate to his actions as readily as he responds to theirs. The toddler, able to use words, may convey basic meanings through simple two-word utterances. Since he is more mobile than the infant, he may be surrounded by a variety of adults and children. The preschooler, whom we can imagine in a group setting with other children, begins to use complex sentences that serve a variety of functions. He may speak differently in different situations, and he may also begin to show interest in books. Parents, as well as teachers, may read to him, anticipating the time when he will be expected to read and write on his own. The primary grade child retains and builds on all the linguistic and sociolinguistic abilities that he has already developed as he becomes a reader and writer, a more skilled communicator.

Regardless of the form children's language takes, spoken or written, we have tried to show by reviewing many studies that the process of acquiring language does not occur solely within the mind of the child or in repetitious "lessons" between an adult and a child. Investigations of child language have over the last two decades placed the child in an increasingly broad context. Early studies had their focus on the syntactic forms young children used. Later both syntax and semantics were considered, as psychologists asked what within the child's mind enabled him to learn language. Recently, researchers of oral language acquisition have asked what factors outside the child—and particularly features of the infant's social context—make a difference to the acquisition process. Finally, some investigators of literacy acquisition have taken the broadest view, studying what happens to young children in the home context, in relation to how they become readers and writers in the classroom.

Language, then, develops in different social contexts; at the core of these is the active child, who unconsciously formulates rules—phonological, syntactic, semantic—about language. He is aided by the genetic endowment that enables him, in a period of only 5 or 6 years, to learn much of his first language as he interacts verbally and nonverbally with people and objects. In the following chapters we elaborate on this portrait of the young learner and on ways of assessing his language. We refer occasionally to studies already discussed and add others as we consider the contexts in which he becomes a communicator. The first and most fundamental of these contexts is the home, the setting for Chapter 3.

Suggested Readings

de Villiers, P. A., & de Villiers, J. G. *Early language.* Cambridge, MA: Harvard University Press, 1979. This is a brief and readable overview of research, written for a general audience. The authors discuss the sequential course of language development, how researchers figure out what a child knows about language, and the importance of adult-child interactions in the first years of life.

Fletcher, P., & Garman, M. (Eds.). *Language acquisition: Studies in first language development.* New York: Cambridge University Press, 1979. A collection of readings that surveys the field of language acquisition research, this book is thorough and detailed. It is also technical and written for readers, graduate students and researchers, with some background in language study.

Lindfors, J. W. *Children's language and learning.* Englewood Cliffs, NJ: Prentice-Hall, 1980. This is an excellent and comprehensive introduction to processes of acquisition and language structure, functions, and variation. As a readable textbook for both undergraduate and graduate students, it takes an interactionist perspective and provides suggestions for classroom practice that are grounded in research findings.

Suggested Readings for research related to the acquisition of literacy are included in Chapters 6 and 7.

CHAPTER 3

Where It Begins: Communication in Home Settings

Introduction

> I talk to her all the time—while feeding her, bathing her, changing her bed, just walking around her room. I try to make her aware that I'm in the same room. I talk to her even if I'm at a distance and while I'm doing my housework. I think it's comforting for her to know that mother is close by. I did the same thing with my son. I think she realizes that I'm talking to her because she says something back to me and then I respond to that and then she responds, and it goes on like that. When parents talk to them it makes them want to talk. She cries and you respond. Crying is a form of language. (Mother)

We began Chapter 2 with a quotation that summarizes many researchers' beliefs about the language acquisition process. In this chapter we use one parent's view of the process as the starting point for a sampler that depicts communication primarily in homes between parents and child and child and child. Family interactions illustrate that, regardless of the child's age, a parent's description of interaction at home is often: the child does or says something, "then I respond to that and then she responds, and it goes on like that." The families we present reflect a range of socioeconomic backgrounds, and the children exhibit a range of communicative abilities, from the newborn whose main means of communication is crying, to school-aged children who can vividly create a fantasy in outer space, using a variety of verbal skills. The examples of interaction are an introduction to children as communicators, seen first with mothers and fathers and then with siblings and peers.[1] Like other social contexts, the home consists of many subcontexts, or conversational settings that support interaction in different ways. Our focus is on appreciating what children in different kinds of settings can communicate, rather than on the deliberate fostering or assessing of specific types of communication. At the end of the chapter we briefly discuss what parents and others might do if they believe that their children's language is not developing normally.

Parents with Their Children

Example 3–1: Mother and infant have a "conversation" as they go from diapering to feeding.

Mother: I think it's a good time for changing and sucking. You think it's a good time for changing and sucking? Oh, you're all wet! Changing and sucking, OK?

Dinah: (Crying.)

Mother: Oooooh (sympathetic sounds). Now you're better. Now you're better. Now you're better.

Mother: We're gonna have sucking. You like sucking. You like sucking. Remember sucking? Remember sucking? Remember sucking? OK? Sucking? Sucking? Mmmmm, sucking. Did you get scared? Did you get scared? You found yourself on the changing table? Aaaaw. Mommy's here. You don't have to worry. Mommy's here. You don't have to worry. (Time passes as Dinah nurses.)

Mother: Why don't you try burping? Why don't you try burping, OK? We're gonna try burping.

Communication between the infant and those around her, the "dance" mentioned in Chapter 2, begins at birth. In Example 3–1 the mother of 2-month-old Dinah talks with her as if she were silently comprehending the one-sided conversation. Our picture of Dinah's contribution is incomplete since it is nonverbal, but we can imagine that she occasionally moves her arms or legs, maintains eye contact with her mother, and occasionally vocalizes or makes sounds that are interpreted as attempts to communicate. Dinah's mother asks many questions

---

[1]The examples were audiotaped, mainly by parents who are colleagues and students, and often transcribed by the first author. Conventions, or a key, for the transcriptions are found at the end of this chapter.

("Remember sucking?"); gives comfort ("Now you're better"), describes the situation ("Oh, you're all wet!"), and makes suggestions ("Why don't you try burping?") All parents may not be this talkative, but they generally provide a linguistic environment for the prelinguistic child, anticipating the time when her sounds become words.

A contrasting family interaction occurs when mother, father, and 10-month-old Julie play and talk before dinner. Julie's growing ability to walk and coordinate her movements provides a focus for action and talk, though the talk is still the parents'.

Example 3–2:

Mother: Throw the ball to Daddy. Whee. Throw it to Daddy.

Father: Throw me the ball. Throw it here. (Julie throws the ball.) That's the girl.

Mother: Wheeee.

Father: No. (Julie walks toward father.) Stay there. Here you go. Yeah. ( )

Mother (to Julie): Here's a piece of paper for you.

Father: Pick it up.

Mother: Get the ball for me.

Father: Pick it up and do some walking for us.

Julie: Wawawoo.

Father: Stand over here. Stand over there. (He picks her up.)

Mother: Come on, Julie.

Father: Now walk over here to Dad. Come on. Come to Dad.

Julie: Yadahaha.

Father: Yeah! Good girl!

Mother (to Father): I read a new book today and it said that once they start walking you should put shoes on them.

Julie: Ummmmmm.

Father: Throw me the ball, Julie.

Julie: Yahahaha.

Mother: Throw it to Daddy.

Father: Throw it here. (Julie throws ball.) That's a girl. Thank you. Thank you.

Julie: Dadada.

In this three-person interaction both parents use language primarily to direct Julie's actions, which are her contributions to maintaining the play session.

The next three examples were recorded in 19-month-old Karen's home. Each situation has a different focus that engages parent and child in conversation.

Example 3–3: Karen and her mother sit next to a table in their family room. Mother is ready to draw something with a pen.

Mother: What should I draw first?

Karen: Bi goggie

Mother: A big doggie, all right. Is that big?

Karen: Oggie bi. Bi gog.

Mother: What's this? What's this part of the doggie? Is that a big enough doggie?

Karen: Bi goggie.

Mother: Well, I did make a big doggie, look.

Karen: Bi goggie.

Mother: You make a big doggie. Make a kitty.

Karen: Kiki.

Mother: Well, you make it. (Mother keeps trying to draw.) I'm not sure I know how to make a kitty. Does that look like a kitty a little bit?

Karen: Goggie.

Mother: That looks like a doggie too? I don't know how to make a kitty different from a doggie. Here, maybe that's good. Here, what is that?

Karen: Goggie.

Mother: Well, I guess. No. I'm not very good at that. Your daddy's the one who draws good.

The dialogue in Example 3–3 shows well how conversations with young children center on concrete activity, in this case, drawing together, and of how even a novice at language can help build conversations that lead from one topic to another. Karen is just beginning to use words in combination, as in, "Big doggie." With several variations on this two-word utterance, along with changes in intonation and stress, this 19-month-old takes part in—and directs—a dialogue that leads from drawing a dog to drawing a cat to the mother's suggestion that Daddy may draw a better cat than she can.

Example 3–4: Karen again, this time with her father, who is watching television and attending to his daughter and an adult visitor at the same time.

Karen: Mommy tape. Mommy tape. Mommy tape. Mommy tape. Mommy tape.

Father: Invisible mending tape. (''Translating'' for other adult.)

Adult: Oh!

Father: You can have *this* much (shows with his thumb and index finger how long the piece of tape can be).

Karen: Daddy knee (pointing toward his face).

Adult: Daddy's knee?

Father: That's not Daddy's knee. Daddy's knee's down here. Is this your knee?

Karen: Mommy tape.

Father: All right, one more (piece) and that's all.

Karen: Knee. Knee.

Father: You want it on your knee?

This time Karen's main interlocutor is her father and the focus of talk is an object, the mending tape, rather than an activity as in Example 3–3. Though mother and father are different conversationalists, both construct dialogues with Karen through their comments and questions. They provide major social and linguistic support, the scaffolding, for their child's communicative growth.

Example 3–5: A third example of Karen. Her mother is asking her to label pictures in one of her books.

Mother: What's that? (pointing to part of the picture.)

Karen: Turtle!

Mother: A turtle. What's this thing?

Karen: Cow.

Mother: And what's this thing? Are you gonna clap when you get it right? And what's this thing?

Karen: Turtle.

Mother: Yeah, that's a turtle, too. What's this?

Karen: Tree.

Mother: A tree. What's this?

Karen: House.

Mother: And what's this?

Karen: Box.

Mother: You knew that was a box? (Surprised.) How'd you know that was a box? What's this?

Karen: Turtle.

Mother: Yeah, turtle. What's this?

Karen: Kiki. (Kitty.)

Mother: Yeah, what's this?

Karen: Flower. Flower.

Mother: All right, now here's a hard one. What's this?

Karen: Fork.

Mother: Spoon. What's this?

Karen: Fork.

Mother: And what's this?

Karen: Wawa (water).

Mother: Wawa. You should get a clap. You got them all right! What's this thing?

Karen: Chooo!

Mother: A choo choo.

Another object, a picture book, is the basis for this quickly moving dialogue. As recent research in middle-class homes indicates, book "reading" can begin early, and a book is just one of many objects and activities that become topics of talk.

Up to this point our examples have come from recordings in three white middle-class homes. In contrast, the next two mother-child dialogues come from a white working-class and black middle-class family, respectively.

Example 3–6: Amy, a 20-month-old, and her mother are reciting favorite nursery rhymes.

Mother: Say, "Pattycake, pattycake, baker's man. Bake me a cake as fast as you can. Roll it. Pat it. Mark it with an A, and put it in the oven for Amy." (Mother guides Amy through the accompanying gestures.) Went around the world. Say, "I went around the world. Shot me a bear."

Amy: Bear. (Amy sitting on mother's lap, poking at mother's belly, looking at mother.)

Mother: Guess where I shot him at?

Amy: On.

Mother: Right in—. (Amy continues to poke at mother's belly, looking at mother.)

Amy: There.

Mother: There! (Mother pokes Amy's belly. Amy pokes mother's belly.)

Amy: Shoot a oo.

Mother: Okay. Say it. "Went around the world."

Amy: Shot a bear. (Amy still poking at mother's belly.)

Mother: Guess where I shot him at?

Amy: There.

Mother: Right in there. (Mother pokes Amy's belly.)

(Based on Miller, 1982, pp. 114–115)

Example 3–6 recalls the question-answer structure of Karen and her mother's book reading. The distinctive phrase that Amy's mother uses is, "Say it," as if this game has an instructional purpose. The nursery rhyme is to be both enjoyed and learned, even if Amy repeats only short bits of it.

The example that follows is similar to Amy and her mother's dialogue in its instructional and gamelike quality:

Example 3–7: Two-year-old Sari and her mother are talking about a picture of a turtle in water and a girl swimming.

Mother: Where's the water?

Sari: Right there.

Mother: Who else is in the water?

Sari: The turtle in the water too.

Mother: The turtle's in the water, too?

Sari: Yeah.

Mother: What are they doin'?

Sari: Put their hand (the turtle's "hand") in here.

Mother: Put his hand in here?

Sari: Yeah.

Mother: Yeah??

Sari: Yes, ma'am. The girl put his head in there.

Mother: Why do you think she put her head in the water?

Sari: 'Cuz.

Mother: Is she swimming?

Sari: Yeah.

Mother: Yeah??

Sari: Yes ma'am! The girl put her head in the water.

Mother: She did what?

Sari: Put her head in the water.

Mother: She put her head in the water?

Sari: Yeah.

Mother: Oh, I see. You wanna swim?

Sari: No.

Mother: Why not?

Sari: 'Cuz.

Mother: 'Cuz why?

Sari: 'Cuz no.

Sari and her mother keep up a quick pace as Sari answers a series of questions. Sari's mother playfully interjects reminders about speaking politely when she says, "Yeah??" which prompts Sari's, "Yes ma'am."

Example 3–8 shows a middle-class Mexican-American father talking to his 4½-year-old daughter Eloisa about Bemelmans' book *Madeline* (Bemelmans, 1977), in which Madeline is in a boarding school, directed by a Mother Superior.

Example 3–8:

Eloisa: Where's Madeline? Her? (Pointing at the picture of a girl.)

Father: Probably this one, the one that's looking behind and smiling at everybody.

Eloisa: Why?

Father: Why is it Madeline?

Eloisa: Uh huh.

Father: Because she knows that the story is about her. And not very many little girls get stories told about them. So she is probably very happy. . . .

Eloisa: But it's about her mommy (referring to the Mother Superior) and the other kids too.

Father: No, this one's not her mommy. She is a person who takes care of them while they are in school. She's sometimes called Mother.

A short time later, the same father and daughter have this exchange:

Example 3–9:

Father: Yes, because they (kids in boarding school) are used to having mothers and sisters and fathers and brothers and things like that in their homes and when they go to school, they have to stay in the school for a few months at a time, weeks at a time. And they don't get to see their family. And they get lonesome. They get homesick.

Eloisa: You know what?

Father: What?

Eloisa: What if I had to stay at school and it would be my home for a couple of days, that wouldn't make me feel bad about you. But it probably would make you feel bad about me and make (you think?) I'm never coming home. But I would.

Father: Well, it probably would make me feel homesick, make me miss you very much when the time comes for you to go away to school. But when you do go away to school, you'll be a lot older than you are right now.[2]

Examples 3–8 and 3–9 demonstrate how the content of books can elicit questions from children and, further, be the basis for conversations about feelings that one has or might have in the future.

Children's growing understanding of language is reflected not only in their talk about books, but also in their artwork. Figures 3–1 and 3–2 are the work of 4-year-olds, drawing, writing, and talking at home with their parents. Figure 3–1, written on a piece of scratch paper, is a letter to God. At the top the boy has written, "For God," and below, "Up in the sky, stop that thunder lightning boom." The girl who created Figure 3–2 drew and wrote around her mother's drawing of a whale. For these two children, both "words" and drawings seem like equally important forms of expression. During a car ride, Ginny, a 5½-year-old, produced Figure 3–3, a sample of "Indian writing" for her grandmother, the driver. Ginny's recollection of a kindergarten lesson about Indians and writing prompted her activity.[3] She is not yet a reader in the conventional sense, but she "writes" as if she knows that marks on paper systematically represent words that she can say. That knowledge will underlie what she learns in the future as she begins to read.

In this section, adult family members have been receptive and constructive conversational participants, with children whose ages have ranged from 2 months to 5 years. Next, children from 2 to 7 years show how they interact with each other as their communicative competence increases further.

---

[2]We are grateful to Miriam Martínez for Examples 3–8 and 3–9, which are based on data from her dissertation.

[3]One concise source of information about Indian writing, or pictographs, is Scholastic *Let's Find Out* (Part A: Language Arts), 1982, *17* (2), 3. Many teachers make up their own pictographs.

Figure 3–1 Four-year-old boy's letter to God.

Figure 3–2 Four-year-old girl's drawing. It shows a whale, drawn by her mother, and the girl's initials, E. T.; her nicknames Bebop and Beth; the name of the musical, "Annie"; her brother Michael's name, and her additional illustrations and letters.

One morning	one family	in their teepee	there were five of them	one of them heard	a bear.	They went hunting	for two days and two nights

It rained	for two days and two nights.	All of them got on their horses	they found the bear	in the grass	down by the sea

They shot the bear.	There was plenty of meat for all.	That evening	they smoked a smoke pipe.	That morning again all of the Indians were hungry again.

One of them heard	two bears.	They, he hunted	through the woods.	He found two bears in the grass and killed them.	There was plenty of meat for all

Next, at evening	they smoked a smoke pipe.

Figure 3–3 Indian writing by Ginny, 5½ years, who orally interpreted the symbols for her grandmother.

53

Children and Other Children

Example 3–10: Six-year-old Eric puts on a puppet show for his 2-year-old sister Sari, whom we introduced earlier with her mother.

Eric: Hi, Sari. Hey, Sari—I'm Bobby the Bear. (Eric has a puppet on his hand.)

Sari: No!

Eric: How are you doing today?

Sari: No.

Eric: Don't say no—I'm Bobby the Bear. How you doing today?

Sari: No.

Eric: My name is Koalery.

Sari: Rocka my baby in the rock—

Eric: Sari, hi lo.

Sari: Hi lo.

Eric: Hello. My name is Bobby the Bear. Do you know, do you like cheese?

Sari: Yeah.

Eric: Well, I have a story about cheese. Once upon a time, there was a little cheese. It was walking down the little road. (Said in slowly and clearly enunciated, book-like tones.) Also ( ) came a little wolf. Oooh, woof, woof, woof.

Sari: Woof, I'm a wolf.

Eric: You a wolf?

Sari: I'll whup you.

Eric: No, don't whup me, please. Please don't whup me.

Eric, unlike his mother, needs five turns to talk to induce Sari to cooperate in his puppet play. Despite the 4-year difference in their ages, both exert control over the topic and direction of conversation.

Example 3–11: Beth, 27-months-old, and her 5-year-old cousin Lori are active as they talk.

Beth: Shake a boogie! (Lori sings, holding Beth's hands. They swing their arms back and forth.)

Lori: Shake your boogie!

Beth: (laughs)

Lori: Hello in there! (Beth and Lori approach mike. Lori speaks into mike.)

Beth: Hello. Hello. Hello.

Lori: Hello sweetheart!

Beth: Hello my kitty cat. (Beth sits up, smiles.)

Lori: Hello sugar roll.

Beth: Hello. (Beth leans over again and speaks into mike.)

Lori: You like to see my Nora (Beth's mother's) boyfriend!

Beth: Yea boyfriend!

Lori: OK. Get ready. Get on my back.

Beth: Yeah. (Lori begins to talk to Nora.) Yeah ah ah. Mm mm.

(Based on Miller, 1982, pp. 117–118)

The two children of working-class families in Example 3–11 play a verbal game that incorporates repetition of some forms (''Hello. Hello. Hello''), as well as changes (''Hello sweetheart.'' Hello my kitty cat,'' and so on).

Example 3–12: Punkin, Meka, and Hunk, all 4-year-olds, are sitting on the front porch of a house, talking and playing. The children are from black working-class families and use black English dialect.

Punkin: Come here, girl.

Meka: Look at her. Get up of that seat now, 'fore I get mad with you and slap you.

Punkin (to
Hunk): That boy just like a clumsy booger.

Hunk: You the clumsy booger.

Meka: Sit down! Y'all leave that boy alone. Come on, pass a lick. Give him a hard one. Give him a hard lick. (Playing a pretend game.) You 'pose to start crying.

Hunk: An, han! (Pretends to cry.)

These children, like Beth and Lori in Example 3–11, use language as the basis of a verbal game. Punkin and Hunk exchange insults before Meka starts to pretend she is hitting Hunk. Pretending is also the basis of the following exchange:

Example 3–13: Brother and sister, Jack, 7 years old, and Emmy, 5 years old, play in Jack's bedroom, creating a fantasy in space, while they sometimes refer to a model spaceship they built earlier.

Jack: Fire! Pew pew pew! (Sound effects.)

Emmy: Uh, sir, that Spider (the enemy) did some damage to us. He tore out the whole back.

Jack: Damage report. Lieutenant!

Emmy: Yes, sir!

Jack: Damage report. What is it?

Emmy: All the levels have been blown off.

Jack: (Sighs.)

Emmy: I wanna get that one guy out of there. (Refers to plastic man in model ship.)

Jack: He's third, and, um, also, he's third and captain of the guards.

Emmy: Yes, sir.

Jack: Would you quit lounging around?

Emmy: Sir, there's nothing to command. You're not moving. I might as well take a nap.

Jack: Why take a nap? Go to your headquarters.

Emmy: But, sir, this is my headquarters.

Jack: Go to your headquarters (firmly).

Emmy: Yes, sir.

Jack: I want a damage report on paper. You have 11—

Emmy: But, sir, I already brought you the damage report on paper.

Jack: Oh, you did? You don't know how to spell!! (Jack's intonation changes here, as if he's no longer pretending.)

Emmy: Yes, sir.

Jack: I want it right. I want a report on everything the Spider did, what it was, what damage it did, and all that.

Emmy: OK, 2 hours later. Sir, I've got it made up. Here.

Jack: It's about time.

Emmy and Jack are middle-class children whose experiences have included movies, books, television, and innumerable conversations in standard English. Although their lives have been different from those of Beth, Lori, Punkin, Meka, and Hunk in Examples 3–11 and 3–12, all these children use language to serve many purposes, appropriate to their families and communities. The forms of speech they use differ, for example, "You 'pose to start crying" contains no form of *to be* as does, "You're not moving"; functions also differ. Sometimes language is part of a verbal game or routine; at other times children use it to create their own scenario. At the same time, they negotiate a variety of social goals. One child in a pair or group (for instance, Meka in Example 3–12 or Jack in 3–13) may stand out as the one who verbally regulates what others do, in fantasy play or in reality. The desire to assert one's authority or to resist another's is expressed again in contrasting forms that are appropriate in each child's respective culture (''Come on, pass a lick,'' versus, ''Why take a nap? Go to your headquarters.''). Questions related to different groups' ways of speaking are considered in the next chapter. The final focus of this chapter is the rare case of the child whose linguistic forms and functions do not develop normally.

If Development Lags

This book is about fostering and assessing language in normally developing children. We say little about recognizing and treating delayed or abnormal development, but because parents and teachers are concerned that their children develop language in a normal way, we include this brief section. Parents may begin to worry about their child's language when they compare her ability to understand and produce language with other children's. Our first suggestion is to try to avoid such comparisons, especially in the first 2 years of life, since children develop language at such different rates.

To indicate when you might become justifiably concerned, we recount a recent experience. A preschool teacher asked the first author about remediation for a child whose speech was hardly ever understandable. Lily, a 4-year-old in Ms. Stein's classroom, seemed to have difficulty responding to others' questions or comments; her responses were often unrelated to what preceded them. The teacher's hunch was that Lily had a hearing problem and that this problem was affecting her speech. Ms. Stein had already talked with Lily's mother, who was eager to call doctors or agencies as long as they could make allowances for low-income families. Together, we discussed sources of help. The problem has not been fully resolved, but Lily's mother and Ms. Stein eventually will have the advice of the following people: a university graduate student in special education, who gave a general assessment of Lily's communicative abilities and suggested an audiologist; an audiologist, who can diagnose hearing problems; and a speech pathologist, who can diagnose and treat language-related problems and will be available at little or no cost through a university department of speech communication. If therapy is needed, one of the specialists can provide it or will refer the parent to other sources.

In general, parents may want to consider these guidelines:

1. Expect young children's language to be different from adults'.

Especially at the early stages, pronunciation and sentence structures are only approximations of adult-like talk. Correction of what adults consider to be mistakes is hardly ever effective. Attentiveness and acceptance of children's speech as meaningful are apt to be the best facilitators of language development.

2. Expect continual development of language forms and functions. Although much of language is mastered by the time children start elementary school, they develop their abilities to pronounce words clearly and combine them in more complex ways throughout the primary grades. In fact, people become increasingly sophisticated language users—orally and in writing—throughout life.

3. Take a relaxed attitude toward your child's (language) development, unless you notice speech or hearing problems that lead to breakdowns in communication, or language-related behavior that causes embarrassment to the child and that calls attention to itself.

4. By age 4 most children are able to comprehend and produce language so that others in their family and community understand them with ease. At any age—but especially by age 3 or 3½—if you believe your child's language is not developing normally, consult a specialist or someone who knows about community resources—for example, a day care director, teacher, school nurse, or doctor.

5. If your community lacks resources, this is an association that provides information about sources of help, related to language problems:

Prevention
American Speech-Language-Hearing Association
10801 Rockville Pike
Rockville, Maryland 10852[4]

We emphasize that almost all children develop language impressively well without problems or special treatment. Most likely you will judge your child's communications to be similar to—or better than—those presented in this chapter.

---

[4]We are grateful to Dr. Anne van Kleeck of the Department of Speech Communication at The University of Texas at Austin for providing us with general information, which we have freely adapted, about communication disorders and with information about the American Speech-Language-Hearing Association.

Summary

In this chapter we have tried to show how children's communicative competence, given a supportive social context, rapidly grows from birth to the early school years. Building on the child's innate abilities to learn language, adults first provide all or most of the linguistic portion of interaction. Children gradually supplement their many nonverbal contributions with words, so that even as 2-year-olds they may determine topics of talk with peers and adults. By the time children are of school age, they generally talk as their parents do, in ways appropriate to their families and communities.

Though most of our examples illustrate interactions in middle-class families of three ethnic groups (black, Mexican-American, and white), a few come from black and white economically poor families. We make no claim that the examples are typical of each socioeconomic group. We suspect the children whose language we present are more talkative and verbally advanced than the "typical" child; but our examples do depict varying forms and functions of language as these are used by different groups. More importantly, the examples reflect a range of communicative purposes: there is adult talk that is soothing and constant to an infant, adults' and children's talk to direct another's behavior, reminders about polite speech, playful talk in verbal games, adults' pseudoquestions to see what children know, talk about feelings. All of the examples, regardless of participants' group membership, share two characteristics: first, a fluency that indicates the children and adults are comfortable communicating with each other and, second, a strong interest in communicating. Parents are major contributors to the growth of communication in their children, particularly because of their role in focusing and maintaining interaction. Siblings and peers, the child's equals, are also important since she is apt to use language differently with them than with adults.

Five of our examples, including Figures 3–1 through 3–3, involved writing and print. Years before children learn to read, many parents and other caregivers talk about children's drawings and wordless or regular books. Dialogues focusing on pictures or books differ from family to family. One parent may correct children's mistakes more than another, while some prefer to present as much information as possible. Others are less concerned with content than with maintaining a warm relationship with the child. The reading and writing processes are not central at first. There may be an interest in identifying pictures, but there is little concern for identifying letters or words. For these families a drawing or book seems to be just another thing to talk about. As such, it can be the basis of unpressured and affectionate, informative, or playful conversations at home. We turn next to an out-of-home context for early communication, the day care setting.

Suggested Readings

Brazelton, T. B. *Infants and mothers: Differences in development.* New York: Delacorte Press, 1969. Of the many books on parenting and the first years of life, we suggest this one, not for its focus on infants, but for its focus on differences among them. A major theme is that the range of normal development in children is surprisingly broad, a point we also emphasize here. Brazelton illustrates the point by presenting absorbing case studies of the first year of life of three strikingly different children, one average, one active, and one quiet child. Comments and advice to parents are interspersed.

Appendix

The following conventions are used in transcripts of examples throughout the book:

1. Speaker or participant is identified on the left.
2. Ends of utterances or sentences, usually indicated by slight pauses on the audiotape, are marked by conventionally used punctuation (periods, question marks, exclamation points). Dashes (—) mark interrupted utterances.
3. Words stressed by the speaker are italicized.
4. Intonation is not marked.
5. Contextual and nonverbal information is enclosed within parentheses.
6. Translations are enclosed in brackets, [ ].
7. Empty parentheses, ( ), indicate an unintelligible word or phrase.
8. (. . . ?) indicates the word or phrase in parentheses is our best guess.

CHAPTER 4

Communication in Day Care Settings

Introduction

Gee, I must confess convenience to where I work was the first thing I thought about. Then I could go down a list. The next thing was amount of space and cleanliness. The next thing's how nurturant the teacher was. Oh, and then if they took them outside. And then I guess the next thing was the kind of food. The last thing is the kind of toys they have. (Day care mother)

I guess I thought the interactions between the children and teacher were the most important. Did the teacher ignore the kids, or did she try to get involved with them? Secondarily I considered cleanliness. (Day care father)

The ideal day care for Terry? That's a hard one. The most important thing would be the training. They should have certified teachers, not just certified teachers, but teachers who get trained while they're working, you know. But that's ideal. If you're talking about the resources available, and I've done lots of shopping around, it's the culture and the language. That's the main thing. Terry just didn't like the place I took her out of. She'd come home and say, "Mommy, they don't even have tacos, not even once a week." And then she said the teacher says to her, "She tells me to say it in English." (Day care mother)

What parents would like to find in a day care setting for their children is as broad-ranging as the criteria in these three quotations. All parents are concerned with the quality of the caregiver, but beyond that their requirements diverge. Only one parent specifically mentioned language, but implicit in caregiver-child interaction is the kind of language that caregivers use with children. How adults and children use language and how day care might affect its growth are topics of this chapter as we move from interactions in the home to those outside the home.

For some children the transition to nonfamily care takes place in infancy; for others it happens much later when they enter kindergartens or first grade classrooms. The day care setting is usually defined as out-of-home care that is available for a full day, often to children whose parents work. In practice there is a great variety of settings that are referred to as day care, from the center that serves 300 suburban middle-class children to the home of an elderly housewife who cares for four neighborhood children. These four children's parents earn the minimum wage. Along with variations in size, there are variations in quality. Some day care is ideal; the staff are concerned and knowledgeable about children, have a reasonable amount of equipment and space, and maintain effective communication with the children's parents. Others, often unlicensed by governmental agencies, are dreary and unsafe, perhaps with a television set that substitutes for a curriculum or program (Keyserling, 1972).[1]

Laypeople familiar with both day care and nursery schools may distinguish the two institutions by saying that day care is a necessity whereas nursery school is an optional form of enrichment for preschoolers. From this point of view, parents who must work place their children in relatively inexpensive day care, and substitute care of this kind is less desirable than having the children at home with their mothers. This attitude is changing because an increasing number of mothers now work to provide or bolster family income. In March 1981, 8.2 million, or 45 percent of all children under 6 years old had working

[1]Guidelines for day care programs are just that: guidelines. These are difficult to enforce unless individual states inspect centers and homes in keeping with their own regulations. In Texas, the Department of Human Resources has established minimum standards that include qualifications for the director, staff-child ratios, amount of space per child, equipment and facilities, and fire and safety regulations. The guidelines related to center program or language curriculum are of this general nature:

b. Indoor and outdoor periods shall provide for:
  (1) Alternating active and quiet activities.
  (2) Opportunity for individual, small, and large group activities (State Advisory Committee on Child Care Facilities, 1980, p. 16)

and "Infants shall be talked to, held, and played with by the staff" (p. 16). These are minimum standards, and centers vary widely in their implementation. Some go far beyond the minimum. Licensed day care centers are inspected in Texas approximately once every six months. In Georgia "Daily experience with music, science, literature, dramatics, art, language, manipulative activities, large muscle activities, etc." are required (Rules and Regulations for Group Day Care Centers, p. 12). Other minimum requirements, unrelated to language itself, resemble those of Texas.

mothers (Grossman, 1982). The resulting increase in the use of day care by families from all socioeconomic backgrounds blurs the traditional distinctions between day care and nursery school environments.

Any setting in which growing numbers of children spend many, sometimes most, of their waking hours can be a major influence in their development, including their language. Although the conventional belief that there is no substitute for mother's care may still prevail, more families are employing substitute care and hoping that its effect on their children will be positive. In this chapter we begin by addressing an issue of concern to parents and caregivers: the effects of out-of-home care on development, especially language development. We then turn to the nature and importance of caregiver talk to children, children's talk among themselves, and the use of nonstandard dialects in the day care setting. Next we consider the kinds of language functions caregivers can foster and, finally, ways for caregivers to observe and document children's productive language so that they can maintain their own records of children's development.

Effects of Day Care

In a recent study (Fosburg, et al., 1981) parents were asked what they wanted most in day care for their children. The reliability of the caregiver was mentioned most often, and the acquisition of cognitive and linguistic skills was named almost as frequently. Whether day care benefits children cognitively and linguistically is still unknown. Because children's thought processes, or cognition, and language are interdependent, it's hard to separate the development of one from the other, especially in young children. Tests of cognitive development, therefore, often include abilities to understand and use language. When researchers ask whether children who attend day care do better on such tests than children who do not, they find mixed results. What seems to make a difference in most cases is the social class of the children. Robinson and Robinson (1971) found that economically disadvantaged black children did impressively better on standardized tests given periodically for the 2½ years that they were in day care, when compared to a group of children raised at home. Middle-class white children in day care also performed better than a home-reared control group, but the increases in their scores over time were less dramatic than the disadvantaged children's.

In a later study neither significantly good nor bad effects on children from middle-class families attending day care programs meeting government standards were found by Golden et al. (1978). These researchers concluded that economically disadvantaged children are the group most likely to show the greatest increases in test scores and in this sense experience positive effects in day care. There were fewer declines in their scores over time than in those of similar children cared for at home.

Tizard et al. (1972) studied 2- to 5-year-olds' language development in a different group care setting—residential nurseries in England. The researchers found, first, that the language of the 85 children in 13 nurseries studied was developing normally. In other words, being in an institution by itself had no general retarding effect. It was also found that the way the nurseries were organized affected the quality of language used by staff and children. The greater the autonomy—or number of administrative and instructional decisions that staff could make on their own—the higher were scores on measures of both language comprehension and production. Further, the more often the staff's talk to children was informative and the more often children answered staff in conversation, the higher were children's language comprehension scores. The staff-child ratio also made a difference. One adult with three to six children would attend much more to the children than two adults with a larger number, since adults together tended to talk to each other, instead of to the children. The organization and structure of child care, including ways of making everyday decisions, can have important effects on children's language growth.

A more recent study that includes a section on the effects of early day care on language is by Rubenstein, Howes, and Boyle (1981), who pointed out that most studies of the effects of day care have focused on university-based programs for the disadvantaged. In contrast Rubenstein et al. studied middle-class infants in community day care. Ten children who began attending day care at about age 1, and 13 home-reared children were compared at about 45 months of age. They were tested with a variety of social and emotional measures. Day care children were found to be more assertive and less compliant than the home-reared group. The investigators also used standard measures of language development, including the mean length of utterance (MLU), an index of syntactic development that tells the average length of a child's utterance, and the Peabody Picture Vocabulary Test, which tests comprehension of single words. On both measures the day care children had higher scores than the home-reared children. For the children studied, then, enrollment in infant day care did not lead to slower language development. The number of children in this study, as well as the total number of similar studies, is small, so that the results are not conclusive.

We know that the quality of care can vary from center to center, but studies of day care effects so far demonstrate that substitute care in itself is not damaging to children's development. Studies like that of Tizard and colleagues (1972) suggest that day care staff need to consider different organizational features of centers, as these may affect the quality of language development in significant ways. If day care can be a positive setting for facilitating language, how might individual caregivers accomplish this? In the next section we discuss the importance of caregivers' talk to children.

Caregiver Talk to Children

> *Example 4–1:* A caregiver in a day care center talks to three infants. She holds Chrissy on her lap, while Robert and Brian sit nearby.
>
> Adult: Bo-o-at. Puppy dog. What's a dog say, Robert? What's a dog say, huh?
>
> Child: (Babbles)
>
> Adult: Hey, Chrissy, what's a dog say? What's a dog say? Arf, arf, arf!
>
> Child: (Screams happily)
>
> Adult: No-o-se. No-o-se. Where's Chrissy's nose? Um hmmm. Bird. Bird. Can you flap your wings like a bird? Like this. That's what birds do. They fly. They go wheee!
>
> Child: (Noises)
>
> Adult: The birds. Whatcha got, Brian? Whatcha got? Uh boo! Uh boo!

Nonsensical, cute, repetitious, annoying—you might describe exchanges like this in all those ways. Whether or not you believe you sound like that when talking to children, researchers have found that adults do consistently change their speech for very young children (Snow & Ferguson, 1977). A written transcript fails to capture the quality of the adult's talk in our example. This woman caregiver in the infant room of a day care center used high pitch and a sing-song intonation pattern to talk about animals. (She was showing a picture book about animals to the group.) She also used other features that parents and other adults typically use in such situations: a slower rate of speaking, vowel lengthening (as in *bo-o-at* and *no-o-se*), repetition, and frequent questions. Since the child was not yet a speaker, the adult provided not only questions but also the answers. Researchers have called this special set of features "baby talk" and "motherese" and more recently—and more accurately—talk-to-young-children (Schachter & Strage, 1982).

Adults spontaneously and unconsciously use a number of strategies when they address children that are perceived as unable to speak, just learning to speak, or simply childlike, vulnerable, and small. They may also address other loved ones or pets in this way. Schachter and Strage (1982, p. 10) summarize these strategies:

1. Attracting and maintaining the child's attention, as when the adult speaks in a high-pitched voice or addresses questions to the child.

2. Simplifying one's speech with regard to sounds, meanings, grammar, and conversational patterns.

3. Repeating and rephrasing one's [own] speech. . . .

4. Repeating or rephrasing the child's speech, as when the caregiver expands the child's short utterances.

5. Mapping words onto the child's experiences as when the adult speaks in the present, and describes the child's desires or ongoing activities.

6. Speaking *for* the child, as when caregivers assume the child's role in the conversation, as well as their own role (for instance, when they answer their own questions).

7. Speaking responsively *with* the child, as when caregivers continue the topic of conversation initiated by the child rather than introducing a new topic of their own.

In Example 4–1 the caregiver used all of these strategies, except (4) and (7), which she could use only with a speaking child.

There are two questions that our students and workshop participants ask us before any others. The first is, "Is it bad to use 'baby talk' with children?" and the second, "Should we correct 'bad grammar'?" We address the second question in a later section on dialect differences. Our answer to the first is a qualified "no." First, the researcher's definition of *baby talk* differs from the layperson's since it includes features like shorter utterances and repetition. Adults can use short, repetitious utterances without the added features of high pitch and exaggerated intonation that most people associate with baby talk. Since short, clear utterances should help children understand us, they are not harmful to development. Even features like high pitch or simplification (changing *sleepy* to *seepy*, for example) may have no negative effect on children's speech. The best evidence for this statement comes from children themselves; they do not use unnaturally high pitch or simplified sounds in response to adults. If children do use simplified sounds, which adults appear to imitate, they generally drop them as their phonological and articulatory abilities improve.

There is a possible hazard in using the features of talk-to-young children that has as much to do with what is said as with the way it is said. Adults want to avoid oversimplifying. Instead they want to simplify—just enough—the form and content of their speech, at the same time that they present children with new linguistic structures, information, and challenges. Investigators have found that adults and older children continue to tailor their talk for children even after they begin to speak, but they use fewer simplification techniques as children get older and thus put more of the conversational burden on the child (Cross, 1977).

Our examples reflect this shift over time:

Example 4–2. Mark, the 11-year-old son of a male caregiver in a family day care home, talks to a 2½-year-old girl, Leah, about the puzzle she is assembling:

Leah: I'm put—

Mark: I don't think it goes there.

Leah: Goes there?

Mark: Try to put it there and see. No. It doesn't go there, Leah.

Leah: Right there?

Mark: No, put it in a little farther.

Leah: Like this?

Mark: No, put it in more.

Leah: This way?

Mark: Yeah!! That's where it goes.

The 11-year-old is providing the guidance in this exchange, but the child also contributes to the conversation. The pattern of interaction is more reciprocal than that in Example 4–1; the boy says and repeats less than the caregiver of the younger children.

Example 4–3: Here Bob, the adult caregiver, talks with Louise, a four-year-old, in the same family day care home.

Bob: We don't have a sink, Louise. We're going to have to fix one up, aren't we?

Louise: Yeah, where we gonna fix it?

Bob: I don't know. I was looking for a box or something we could use as a sink.

Louise: It doesn't have to be a good one.

Bob: Well, something that we could use that would look kind of like a sink would be nice, though, wouldn't it?

Louise: To wash dishes in.

In this example, Bob asks questions while Louise responds in reciprocal fashion. There is little in the adult's speech forms that indicates his listener is a young child.

Children Interact with Children

Although conversations with adults are crucial, a picture of the young child in day care is incomplete without a presentation of his interactions with other children. For years children younger than 7 or 8 years were routinely called *egocentric,* a term Piaget (1959) used to describe the child's inability to consider his listener's viewpoint. Being incapable of true communication, the child talks to himself without addressing a specific listener and takes no interest in the listener's response. Young children's play was often described as either solitary or parallel; they play either alone or physically close to each other, but do not interact (Parten, 1932). In the last 10 years this view of the child has been challenged by many researchers who believe that even infants are better described as *sociocentric* (Garvey & Hogan, 1973). That is, they seek social interaction and are capable of focusing on others at an early age.

We mentioned in Chapter 2, for example, that studies of infant-caregiver interaction show that the fundamentals of communication, including eye contact and turn-taking, are established within the infant's first 6 months of life. Within the first 2 years there are a variety of behaviors that indicate that infants are also interested in their peers (Vandell & Mueller, 1980). At 2 months of age infants look at each others' faces. By 1 year infants engage in reciprocal activities such as giving and receiving toys. They also laugh and smile at each other and imitate one another's behavior. When friendship is defined by mutual preference and positive interaction, 22-month-old children can be said to be friends. In general, research suggests that the more experience the young child has with peers, the more likely he will be to exhibit friendly behavior and initiate contacts with others. In this regard, then, early day care experiences provide a setting for a kind of social practice that home-reared children may lack.

The following anecdote shows how prelinguistic children, acting essentially independent of each other, do spend part of their time in parallel play:

Example 4–4:
Josh, 21 months old, and Winna, 13 months old, are in the toddler room and have finished their snacks. They are both standing next to the storage cabinets. Josh opens one set of doors and takes out four cardboard blocks, which he stacks one on top of the other. Without making a sound, he then knocks them down. Winna, not attending to Josh, opens another set of doors and starts taking toys out. She takes out a plastic fireman's hat and puts it on her head. Josh approaches her and looks at her briefly. He turns away and continues to empty the cabinet, independent of Winna, who soon gets down on all fours and crawls away.

In contrast these two 1-year-old boys, in the same toddler room as Winna and Josh, communicate with each other because they want the same toy:

Example 4–5:
Michael is playing with a puppet while leaning against a child-sized table. Norman has been watching Michael and comes up to him, grabs the puppet, and walks away. Michael then starts to follow Norman and says, "Mine!"

These 1-year-olds have enacted a scene familiar to parents and care-givers who are well aware that conflicts over possession of objects are common among toddlers and preschoolers. A few minutes after Michael and Norman's conflict, however, the following interaction occurred in a different part of the room:

Example 4–6:
Three 1-year-olds are seated on the floor next to a plastic toy, consisting mainly of a series of five jack-in-the-boxes. The lid of each box is numbered. The toy is in Michael's lap. Esther and Jay sit facing him, and Michael pushes a button to make the jack-in-the-boxes open. As he makes the boxes open, Esther and Jay push the lids down so that the boxes close. The three children's actions are clearly coordinated and self-initiated. None of the teachers are supervising them. After about two minutes, Esther and Jay leave the area and Michael is left with the toy.

This toy-centered interaction is not sustained for long, but it too shows that depictions of toddlers as unsociable and solitary are overdrawn and often inaccurate.

Turning our attention from early peer interaction to language development, we find a complicated network of effects that children may have on their peers' speech. Basic research in language acquisition in homes favors adults as the interlocutors who encourage rapid language development. Nelson (1973), for example, found that the more time a child spent with other children, the less likely he was to be an early developer of language. A similar result was reported by Bates (1975), who concluded that children's utterances were longer when talking to adults than to children. These findings make sense since we know adults can be better interpreters of unclear speech than young children. They are also likely to extend conversations and encourage the child to verbalize whereas other children may not perform these functions. No matter how willing a child is to socialize, he still is less apt as a conversational partner than an adult.

In contrast there is research that indicates that children who attend day care in infancy and toddlerhood do as well or better on language measures as home-reared children (for example, Rubenstein et al., 1981). We cannot tell whether adults' or other children's language is benefiting individuals' development, but in group settings for infants, it is clear that the adults are the ones to provide linguistic input. The interactive network becomes much more complicated when children of different ages are cared for in the same space. Hamilton and Stewart (1977) looked at three day care settings of different sizes and found varied patterns of verbal interaction, depending on the size of the center and the adult-child ratio. They found that children's imitative responses (responses repeating all or part of another's utterance) were made more often after an adult than after a child utterance. In an experimental study, on the other hand, the same researchers found that 21-month-old children could readily learn foreign vocabulary words from their peers. Further, there is anecdotal evidence that children's language production increases noticeably when a child advances from one age group to the next, for example, leaving the toddler room to join the 3-year-old group. The data from these few studies do little to assemble the puzzle of exactly who affects children's language and how. Children apparently learn more language in general from adults, but peers may advance specific aspects of language production in certain kinds of settings.

One feature of day care settings that promotes increased interaction, including verbal interaction, is multiaged grouping. As we said, and as parents sometimes note, some children's language production increases noticeably when they join a group of slightly older children. Similarly, Ross and Goldman (1976) found 18-month-olds had more frequent and more complex interactions with 2-year-olds than with 1-year-old playmates. The caregiver in a family day care home in Texas said that older (4-year-old) children have had different effects on their younger peers. Louise, a child currently attending the home, tended to "bring the other children up" to her level of speaking, whereas last year a 4-year-old regressed to the younger children's level. Factors such as children's experiences at home with parents and siblings and children's personalities would affect their ways of interacting and speaking in day care. And over time an individual child may have different effects on others, as well as different styles of interacting.

Such varied findings suggest some implications for day care teachers. The major one is that your decisions about grouping children could have important consequences (Freedman, 1982). In this country, as in others, we arrange children in single age groups. Many nursery schools, for example, have separate 3-year-old and 4-year-old groups. There are theoretical reasons for this practice; many adults believe that children of the same age are able to engage in similar activities and ready to learn similar things. With respect to early day care, single age groups are also a convenience. Children who are not yet walking require different spatial arrangements than those who walk. Infants require special supplies and furnishings that in part determine room arrangement. What day care directors and teachers must decide, then, is to what extent such arrangements are necessary and beneficial for children's development. As children become ambulatory and verbal, there may be good reasons to have multiaged groups, with children whose age range spans more than 12 or 14 months. From the point of view of language use, children may then have the benefit of both adult input and input from older children. Benefits may ultimately be not only linguistic, but also social since interactions depend on linguistic and social skills.

How adults converse with children and the ages and maturity of the other children in day care affect the ways an individual child communicates and speaks. Another factor that contributes to the social and linguistic context is dialect. Because day care settings often house adults and children from different races, ethnic groups, social classes, and sometimes different regions or countries, dialect differences, our next topic, are of concern to caregivers and parents.

Dialect Differences

Parent: My first language, as I learned it, was slave language, 'cause it was not by choice.

Parent: What we gonna stop is "not by choice." We want proper English taught.

Parent: Right! Get rid of it. Throw it away. Tell the kids. "Hey, don't speak that junk. Forget it!"

Parent: I really don't feel it's junk, because, sometimes, trying to express themselves, especially around the house, to show that this 3-, 4-, or 5-year-old is grown up and fits in with the family, he will use slang expression.

Parent: Why is street English, or whatever it is, why is that important at all? Or why should it be important? Like the way my mother speak—she's always spoken all broken up, and she's never cared one way or the other—for the same reason that she's never voted. So what? But why is it important to speak, uh, wrong—uh, not wrong—it's a different language. Why is it important to speak a slave language?

Parent: Well, I think most of us have two faces anyway. I think we speak one way at home and to our children and another way when we're in the street and when we're associating with other people. But I think that as long as you get the message—some people can put the message across most emphatically in their language.

(Cazden, Bryant, & Tillman, 1981, p. 74)

These black parents are debating whether it is important for their children to speak the dialect that many refer to as black English. The parents show an awareness that dialects convey as much social as linguistic information about a speaker. One who speaks "proper English" may be treated differently from those who "speak that junk." The popular notion of the term *dialect* is that, like dread diseases and misfortunes, it is something that other people have, especially people from another part of the country. From the language specialist's point of view dialect happens to everyone, commentators on the nightly television news and classroom teachers alike; everyone knows and uses one. Dialect is a neutral term that refers to the particular ways a group of speakers, usually identified with a region of the state or country or with a social class, talk. People recognize someone as a dialect user when he sounds "different"; he pronounces words differently. For example, those who have a "southern accent" are said to drawl, to modify vowel sounds so that a word like *yes* may sound like *ye-yes*. Linguists define a dialect, not just in terms of differences in pronunciations or phonology, but also in syntax and semantics.

The difference between ''Carrie's not here any more'' and ''Carrie ain't here no more'' is a syntactic one. Both sentences have essentially the same meaning, but the second sentence contains what standard English speakers might call a double negative. When listeners recognize such differences in syntactic rules, they show sensitivity to particular dialect differences. In other words, these differences convey to listeners social information about the speaker. People may judge one who makes ''mistakes'' in speaking as a member of a lower social class than they. Based on whether he sounds middle-, working-, or lower-class, some people make further judgments about his intelligence, trustworthiness, educational background, or educational potential. These judgments are made even though the use of one dialect or another has *no* necessary effect on other individual characteristics.

The most general—and significant—distinction that exists within any region is between standard and nonstandard dialects. In areas where there is a black community, the nonstandard dialect is often referred to as black English. It is clear, however, that black speakers are not the only ones to use the forms of that dialect, so that we prefer the term *nonstandard English*. Much has been written about the linguistic features of this dialect (Labov, 1972), and much has been written about people's opinions for and against its use (Whiteman, 1980).

Those who support the use of nonstandard English argue that one's language forms are a part of one's personal and ethnic identity and that to discourage their use is to denigrate the values of the ethnic group. And as the parent in the dialogue said, ''some people can put the message across most emphatically in their language [or dialect].'' The strongest proponents of nonstandard dialect believe that the use (usually temporary) of teaching materials containing nonstandard forms will improve children's academic performance. Those who oppose the use of nonstandard English either in conversation or in teaching materials believe that its continued use ensures the status quo. The poor will remain poor and thus continue to fail in school. According to this view, children need to learn standard English quickly, so that they can do well in school and have access not just to their own community but also to mainstream society. This second view is the prevalent one and is certainly difficult to counter. Speakers of standard English do have more personal, social, and employment options than nonstandard speakers.

How can the staff of a day care center deal with the issue of dialect differences? The staff, in consultation with parents, may want to determine a. ''language policy,'' which suggests how adults are expected to speak and encourage children to speak. The policy would probably include guidelines for hiring those who speak one dialect or another. In reality most centers cannot select staff solely on the basis of dialect use, so that they are likely to have both children and adults who speak standard and nonstandard English, as well as standard and nonstandard dialects of other languages.[2] Caregivers may themselves use nonstandard forms.

Our own position is that children should have the option of learning standard English. But we believe that the early childhood years are not the appropriate time to teach it formally and that the use of nonstandard English in the child's environment is not harmful to either linguistic or cognitive development. The reasons for our views rest on findings from research related to language acquisition and dialect questions and on our conception of what the goals of education—and language education— are. With respect to the process of first language acquisition, we know that the child's use of forms changes, especially in the preschool years. What he has internalized in his own grammar is difficult to change until he has unconsciously worked out the relevant rules for himself, as the child in this example demonstrates:

Example 4–7:
She said, "My teacher holded the baby rabbits and we patted them."

I asked, "Did you say your teacher held the baby rabbits?"

She answered, "Yes."

I then asked, "What did you say she did?"

She answered, again. "She holded the baby rabbits and we patted them."

"Did you say she held them tightly?" I asked.

"No," she answered, "she holded them loosely."

(Gleason, 1967, p. 1411)

While language is still developing, as it is in this 4-year-old, there is little point in focusing on "correct," adult-like forms.

Results of research also suggest that language thrives when those around children have an accepting style of interacting. What the child says is treated as meaningful, and what the adult says is responsive to

---

[2]Although we address dialect differences here, the issues for bilinguals and non-English speakers in American educational settings are similar to those for nonstandard English speakers. Many people believe education in two languages is a luxury and that non-English speakers are best off learning English as soon as possible. Further discussion of acquiring English as a second language is included in Chapter 5.

the child's utterances (Nelson, 1973; Wells, 1981). In the early child-hood classroom setting, a teaching style that is accepting, responsive, and task-oriented has been associated with academic achievement (Piestrup, 1973).

Personal conceptions of the goals of education are personal, and like most goals they depend on values. We value education, and language education, that has as a primary goal a thoughtful person who can use language as a tool for learning and a means for reflection. Education of this kind is based on the exchange of ideas, information, expressions of feeling, which occur in settings where there is talk and opportunities to express oneself in a variety of ways, through art, language, movement, music, and so on. Varied activities provide adults and children with something to talk about. And "something to talk about" is what we consider crucial in day care and early educational settings. How people talk, whether they use nonstandard English, British English, or a com-bination of nonstandard English and Spanish, is not as important as *that they talk.* As one day care center director recently said, "I know I'd rather have a teacher who says to the kids, 'We gonna pick up this book and have us a good old time' than someone who speaks perfect English but won't talk to them at all." Real communication occurs when people want to say things to each other and when they pay more attention to the meaning of what is said than to the correctness of forms.

In the first few years of a child's life, interaction is particularly important. Even if you do not agree with our views on education or dialect use, you may agree that you're very busy attending to a group of young children. The most practical approach may be to talk whenever possible and stop worrying about whether you and your children are using standard or nonstandard forms. For children and adults language is useful not as a set of correct forms but as a set of forms that are put to use for a variety of functions. Next we consider the kinds of functions caregivers might promote when children use language.

Functions of Language to Look for and Foster

Hand in glove, yin and yang, body and soul are couplings that come to mind when we seek a metaphor that captures the interdependence between form and function in language. You can't have one without the other whenever you speak. All speakers know both forms and functions of language without needing to be aware of them or how they blend form and function every time they speak. We have acknowledged that different groups of speakers use different forms and have judged that preoccupation with correct form is counterproductive. We want to encourage children's use of a broad range of functions that reflect their communicative competence, whether or not their forms are always standard. We introduce Halliday's seven functions (1973, 1975) here because they represent this range and are appropriate for analyzing the communication of both prelinguistic and language-using children. (For examples of other categories, see Tough [1977]. Her categories are based on Halliday's but are more refined and also useful for studying the language of teachers and school-aged children.)

According to Halliday, there are seven general functions that children use in interacting with others. Examples and explanations of these functions follow. The word *language* is used in some explanations, although children may be using cries or other sounds and actions to convey their meanings before the onset of speech:

1. Instrumental: What Halliday calls the "I want" function. The child expresses a desire for material or biological needs, such as food or a toy.

Example 4–8: A 5-month-old boy with his father:

Child: (Fusses, making cooing sounds.)

Father: That's a necklace, darlin'. You want to know what it is? You want to put it in your mouth? Is that what your deal is? Are you hungry? Huh? Are you hungry? Oh hohoho. You're hungry. I see. That is a finger. Oh, you want to try the knuckle now. OK, well let me go get the bottle ready, and we can do that. Let me get the bottle.

Child: (Fussing, still, begins to cry.)

This infant, combining sucking and biting behaviors with little more than cooing sounds and crying, gets his meanings across easily to an attentive father. The instrumental function is seen at the very beginning of the infant's life, and continues throughout.

2. Regulatory: The "do as I tell you" function. The child attempts to influence another's behavior. It is related to the instrumental function but has its focus on controlling another's actions, rather than on obtaining goods or services.

Example 4–9: 3- and 4-year-old children, Mary, Trisha, and Chad:

Mary: I don't like that, Russell!

Trisha: Hey, go tell Peter about that—

Mary: Go tell Peter about me.

Chad: No.

Mary: Russell, those are my bandaids. Leave them alone. Russell, Russell, use the ones I gave to you.

Language used to regulate can take various forms. Like adults, children might use questions, statements, or commands. In this short segment, Mary starts out making a statement that can be interpreted as regulatory; she could as easily have said "Stop that, Russell." After that both Trisha and Mary issue a series of commands.

3. Interaction: The "me and you" function. Language is used to maintain social interaction. Ritualized greetings or adults' small talk are examples. What is said or vocalized matters less than that something is said to sustain the pleasure of interacting.

Example 4–10: 20-month-old Kitty and adult:

Adult: What'd you say, Kitty?

Kitty: What?

Adult: What'd *you* say?

Kitty: What?

Adult: You know what I said.

Kitty: What?

Kitty has made a game of responding with, "What?" and seems to be doing so for the pleasure of maintaining a playful interaction. She finally stops saying "What?" and turns her attention to a nearby toy.

4. Personal: the "here I come" function. Here the child is asserting his own importance and uniqueness, including expressions of feeling:

Example 4–11: A teacher-directed lesson, with Jenny and 5-year-old Will participating:

Teacher: Does anyone remember what we talked about? What's inside of us, under our skin?

Jenny: Bones.

Teacher: Bones. Right. And we have places where our bones come together, and they bend. Those are called joints. Can everybody say *joints?*

Children: Joints!

Teacher: Right. Well, today I brought some paper and I want you to try to use it like your bones are used. . . . And when we get through, we'll have pictures that will move around on the paper.

Child: That's okay.

Teacher: You can put them on top of each other or however you wanna do it. Just, we can bend them and just glue. . . . I'll do a couple of glues here to show you how to do it. . . . And they'll be bent, which is just like our bodies will bend.

Will: Look what I can do. I can bend.

Teacher: You sure can. Look at his back bend just like that skeleton.

Will: I can bend!

Teacher: Right. Let me see your legs bend. How do your legs bend?

Will: This way.

Teacher: Wow. They bend up and down and back and forth, too.

Will: (giggle)

Although his contribution is not extensive, Will uses language that illustrates the personal function, to assert his own presence and importance.

5. Heuristic: The "tell me why" function. Language is used to explore the nature of the environment. Asking for names of things is an early manifestation. Later "curiosity" questions that reflect what children want to know are typical examples.

Example 4–12: Two children, 3½-year-old Dave and 5-year-old Jenny, playing together:

Dave: Tweetie bird. That's a tweetie bird. That's a puppet.

Jenny: How does it work?

Dave: It doesn't work anyhow. It doesn't work. See, see, see, it's, now, it's broken. See it's broken. Look. Look. Look. Watch. Look. It's broken. It broke.

Jenny: A train. What's this?

Dave: Look (He blows the whistle on the train, then gives it to Jenny.)

Jenny: Here?

Dave: No, that's not right. No. I'll show you (Jenny meanwhile is successful at blowing.)

Jenny asks for information about how something works, what something is, and where it is. The difficult "why" questions such as, "Why does the moon move?" are also good examples of the heuristic function.

6. Imaginative: The "let's pretend" function. The child uses language here to create his own world. When he is very young playing with the sounds of language as he coos or babbles may be imaginative. Later the language of dramatic play, story telling, and creative writing pieces are good examples.

Example 4–13: A 4-year-old, Esther, and a 5-year-old, Tina, are playing hospital:

Esther: Pretend that she's real, real sick. And this is the hospital.

 Tina: A *shot*-pital.

Esther: And this is another kind of shot.

 Tina: Pretend like it's over here.

Esther: I know.

 Tina: I want the real stethoscope.

Esther: I can't even get it out (of a bag).

 (Later the same morning:)

 Tina: We're gonna give her some medicine now. OK. Now, *examinate* her.

Esther: Tina, Tina.

 Tina: Examinate her.

Esther: Examinate her?

 Tina: Yeah.

These children are creating a fantasy world of their own. Tina also plays with language, making up words like *shot-pital* and *examinate*. As they use language imaginatively, they also use other functions, such as regulatory and informative. They create play through language, so that the telling of what happens is at least as important as the doing.

7. Informative: The "I've got something to tell you" function. Here language is used to convey information to someone who lacks that information. Halliday sets this apart because it is not present as early as the other functions. Although adults may believe this is the primary function of language, it is not one that occurs in infancy since it depends on certain linguistic concepts and skills.

Example 4–14: Five-year-old Missy tells her adult friend about the death of a young friend's mother. Their topics vary, from sick relatives to the burial of the friend's mother:

Missy: Well, see, um, Gammy, um, my mom's, um, my grandmommy lives up in Waco. She had cancer, and she didn't even die, and she's very, very old. Her food went down the wrong way, and she's in the hos—, the nursing home. She might die soon. She's very old.

Adult: Well, some people die before other people. Everybody has a certain amount of time to live, and she just got well and—.

Missy: Some babies die.

Adult: Uh huh, they do.

 (Later:)

Missy: And then, the graveyard was up in Smithville, so we went up there and had lunch, and then we, we, they, they didn't. She didn't get buried yet because her, um, where her name's gonna be in the stone, it's not ready yet.

Adult: I see.

Missy: So um ( ). I don't know when she'll be buried.

Any set of functions or categories will be limited in some ways when we apply them to real speech. Functions may overlap or may not capture everything the child is able to communicate. However, these seven functions have been useful in our own analyses of both children's and adults' talk in classrooms and centers. Because they do not all depend on the use of language, they are also useful in looking at infant and toddler interactions. And they remind us that in an ideal situation children have opportunities to use all of these functions. Since few situations are ideal, we need to encourage children to use as many as possible.

Observing Communicative Functions

In this section we describe basic ways of observing and document-ing oral language as young children use it, as they combine form and function in order to communicate with those around them. Three basic means of observing children's language are *checklists, anecdotal re-cords,* and *audiotaped recordings.* (For a range of general ways of observing, see Almy & Genishi, 1979; Boehm & Weinberg, 1977; and Irwin & Bushnell, 1980.)

Checklists

For day care teachers checklists may be the most practical means for documenting children's language use. Using them and interpreting what you've observed take little time. Figure 4–1 is an example of one that might be used in a bilingual setting where teachers and parents are curious about the frequency of language use and what language children choose to speak. Note that children's choice of activities can also be recorded. The checklist can be varied in a number of ways to suit your needs. For example, a form with no "Spanish-English" columns could be used to observe monolingual children's or teachers' interactions. The list should remain simple to use, at the same time that it provides the

East Valley Day Care Center

Observer _____   Date _____   Time _____

Child's Name	Talking?	Spanish	English	With Whom			Where				
				Child	Children	Adult	Art	Housekeeping	Juice	Blocks	Outside
Ruben A.											
Judy C.											
Alice C.											
Kiko D.											
Ruby E.											
. . .											

Figure 4–1 Language Use Checklist

information you seek. Especially in day care centers with large numbers of children, checklists can give teachers a general notion of how much children are verbalizing and whether some children talk so little that special attention or help might be appropriate.

Anecdotal Records

Keeping anecdotal records is more time-consuming than the use of checklists, but they can provide richer, more detailed information about individual children. They are a direct means of documenting what you observe and require no special equipment. All that is needed is paper and pencil (or index card and pen) and an incident or impression you've experienced. (In a preschool where the first author taught, we used index cards and filed them in a small metal box for 3-by-5-inch cards.) The format of the cards will vary depending on the amount of time you have and the amount of detail needed to reconstruct what you observed. Some teachers might observe interaction between two toddlers and document it in this way:

2/12/82 Observation in toddler room: interaction between two 1½-year-olds:

David sitting on floor with pacifier in mouth, next to Andy who has a basket in his lap. They grab opposite ends of it. Andy "wins." David takes a push toy and plastic flower, then holds flower above his head and throws it down. Then takes pacifier out of mouth and throws it on floor. Andy picks it up and gives it to David.

This anecdote is a straightforward record of behavior that one adult observed. She might add a comment or interpretation before filing it away, or she might wait to present it at a staff meeting for others to interpret with her.

A contrasting anecdote is one that records behavior, including speech, of other children and includes the observer's comments and impressions:

9/16/82 Observation on playground of Ryan, 4-year-old. (I decided to watch Ryan who's often disruptive indoors, on the playground to see if he's different when he's able to move around more.) Ms. T. is pulling 2 kids in wagon. Ryan with Adam, running and chasing. Betty tells Ryan and Adam to get down from side of tree house that they are climbing. Ryan gestures at Betty (as if he's about to hit her?).

Ryan: "Spiderman! Did y'all hear me? Spiderman!"

Ryan runs to barrel, gets in and rolls in it a couple of times. Adam runs off. Betty has become monster, chasing Ryan while she's on toy truck.

Ryan: "Nu nu nu nu nu nu," taunting Adam and Charlie in tree house.

"Hurry!" to girl on truck. Adds, "Hiya, Black Monster!" "Look at me, I'm holdin' on." (to Ms. T.)

Ms. T.: "Well, hold on real good, OK?"

Ryan: "Bee beep. Bee beep." Goes up to Lynn on tricycle, saying, "Bee beep."

(Ryan moves as fast outdoors as inside, but the outdoor space seems to give him more energy outlets.)

This teacher has put parentheses around her comments and interpretations. She records her motivation for making the observation as well as a summary impression of what she observed. When she reread the anecodote before a staff meeting, she noticed that Ryan verbalized frequently while playing and recalled that he also enjoyed making sound effects. It occurred to her then that she had no clear idea of how Ryan communicated in the classroom. This led her to ask at the staff meeting whether anyone knew how Ryan spoke indoors. She also made a mental note to herself to listen to Ryan in the classroom the next time she had a chance.

A little more than two weeks later, the same teacher took these notes:

10/4/82 Observation indoors of Ryan, 4-year-old. (I meant to do this earlier, but haven't had a chance.) Ms. Soto [the other teacher for the group] is singing with the whole class. Some of the songs are in Spanish. Ryan participates, with more enthusiasm than most of the other kids. Looks attentively at Ms. Soto. Ms. Soto then reads a story called *A Boy and His Robot*. She asks if everyone knows what a robot is.

Ryan: "I saw one on Star Wars."

In a few minutes he gently pushes Hank, sitting next to him, trying to get him to sit down, and says, "Sit down." Ms. Soto then dismisses children from circle so that they can choose next activity. Ryan chooses the block area, along with Thomas.

Ryan: "Look what I got here. Look a helicopter."

He's got the wooden helicopter and keeps spinning the propeller around.

Ryan: "Please can I see it? Please can I see it?"

He wants to see the toy car that Thomas has been playing with. Thomas gives it to him.

Ryan: "Thank you."

Takes car and makes it move fast enough so it hits a wall.

Ryan: "I crashed it. Slammed it."

(Ryan's language seems pretty far along to me. Must admit to surprise at his "pleases" and "thank you." Will mention to staff that Ryan's disruptiveness might not be the problem I thought it was.)

Tape Recordings

Teachers whose schools provide cassette tape-recorders or who have their own may supplement or replace anecdotes with records based on audiotapes. The audiotape has several advantages. First, taping preserves actual speech. If a teacher has no time to take handwritten notes, he can tape an activity or lesson for review later. Second, to document the growth of language over time, tapes can be saved and compared to each other. This might be especially informative for teachers with children acquiring a second language. Third, because memories are imperfect, records based on tapes may lead to more accurate judgments of children's language abilities than handwritten anecdotes. Careful listening to or transcriptions of talk can guard against overestimating or underestimating the quality of communicative performance.

If you are a novice at using audiotape recorders, these guidelines may help:

1. Locate a portable cassette tape recorder. (If you are planning to purchase a basic model, they range in price from about $25 to $150.) One that can be battery-operated might be the most practical. Since you probably won't record long interactions, a 60-minute audiotape cassette (30 minutes on each side) is suitable and sturdy.

2. Choose the activity or setting that interests you. Depending on the age of the children you teach, you may want to be present throughout the taping. You might choose the part of your classroom that is most free of background noise.

3. Do a trial recording with children present as soon as possible. If the equipment is a novelty to them, you may need a few desensitization sessions so that children have a chance to ask questions, perform, and learn what the tape-recorder does. Before you record, test to see that the equipment is working. Also, check occasionally while recording to make sure that the microphone is working or that you have not run out of tape. Generally, the sound quality is better with an attached microphone than with the built-in microphone that most recorders have.

4. Listen to your recording as soon as possible. If at first you get unintelligible samples of speech, try again, next time perhaps with the tape-recorder, or microphone, in a different place.

5. Once you have recorded some talk that is clear and that will tell you about an aspect of the children's communication, you might

Date _____				
Observer's Name _____				
Children Participating	Who Speaks to	Whom	Speech Fragment	Nonverbal Behaviors
Tina, Carl Lynn, Ellen	Ellen	Carl	Don't you wanna...	Picks up leg-os; shows to Carl
	Carl	Ellen	Yeah, I'm gonna put...	Starts building with leg-os.
				. . .

A coding sheet of this type may help with later transcription or interpretation by identifying speakers and concurrent behaviors.

Figure 4–2 Classroom Observation

choose typical segments to transcribe verbatim. Selecting what is typical or valuable for your purposes can be time-consuming; doing the transcription is more so. Both selecting and transcribing involve listening many times to the tape. The written record, however, may provide you with the richest documentation of your children's communicative performance.

6. For the ambitious or for those of you with aides or student trainees, there are additional bits of data that might be useful when a group of children are talking. A coding sheet could help make your observation more complete and systematic (see Figure 4–2).

The essence of communicative competence and performance is variation of language form and function from setting to setting. Recording, even for brief periods of time, in different settings or activities can contribute to a fuller and fairer assessment of children's performance in the classroom.

Mean Length of Utterance

For those with a special interest in language development or research, we include this section about the *mean (average) length of utterance*—a more technical way of assessing children's language. The measure, usually referred to as MLU, is an index of the typical length of a child's utterances, and, more importantly, of his syntactic development. What one counts to calculate a MLU is morphemes, the smallest meaningful units in the syntax of a language. Brown (1973) established the MLU as a measure for describing early stages of acquisition of English syntax, based on an indepth analysis of thousands of utterances of three young children. He divided these stages in the following ways:

Stage	Typical Values in Morphemes	Upper Bound in Morphemes
I	1.75	5
II	2.25	7
III	2.75	9
IV	3.50	11
V	4.00	13

(Based on R. Brown, 1973, p. 56)

A typical MLU for Stage II, for example, is 2.25 morphemes. The upper bound is the expected number of morphemes in the child's longest utterance for that stage. The range of morphemes per utterance for that stage, then, would be one to seven. Brown suggests calculating a MLU and upper bound, based on at least 100 consecutive child utterances, according to these guidelines:

1. Start with the second page of the transcription unless that page involves a recitation of some kind [such as a nursery rhyme or song]. In this latter case start with the first recitation-free stretch. Count the first 100 utterances satisfying the following rules.

2. Only fully transcribed utterances are used; none with blanks. Portions of utterances, entered in parentheses to indicate doubtful transcription, are used.

3. Include all exact utterance repetitions (marked with a plus sign in records). Stuttering is marked as repeated efforts at a single word; count the word once in the most complete form produced. In the few cases where a word is produced for emphasis or the like (*no, no, no*) count each occurrence.

4. Do not count such fillers as *mm* or *oh,* but do count *no, yeah,* and *hi.*

5. All compound words (two or more free morphemes), proper names, and ritualized reduplications count as single words. Examples: *birthday, rackety-boom, choo-choo, quack-quack,*

night-night, pocketbook, see saw. Justification is that [there is] no evidence that the constituent morphemes function as such for these children.

6. Count as one morpheme all irregular pasts of the verb (*got, did, went, saw*). Justification is that there is no evidence that the child relates these to present forms.

7. Count as one morpheme all diminutives (*doggie, mommie*) because these children at least do not seem to use the suffix productively. Diminutives are the standard forms used by the child.

8. Count as separate morphemes all auxiliaries (*is, have, will, can, must, would*). Also all catenatives: *gonna, wanna, hafta*. These latter counted as single morphemes rather than as *going to* or *want to* because evidence is that they function so for the children. Count as separate morphemes all inflections, for example, possessive (s), plural (s), third person singular (s), regular past (d), progressive (ing).

9. The range count [the shortest and longest utterance used by the child] follows the above rules but is always calculated for the total transcription rather than for 100 utterances.

(R. Brown, 1973, p. 54)

It is not practical to compute a MLU here for 100 utterances, but we use some hypothetical utterances to demonstrate the process. Here are five utterances, made up of varying numbers of morphemes, which are shown on the right. Inflections are special kinds of morphemes that are "bound" to another morpheme. In our examples, these are separated from their stems by means of dashes (*-s, -ing*). The stems are "free" morphemes that we recognize as words (*shoe, go*).

Mommy pickle.	2
Tracy shoe-s.	3
Allgone cookie.	2
Tracy wanna see.	3
Bubba go-ing there?	4
Total	14 morphemes

We then divide the total number of morphemes by the number of utterances, here 5, to compute the MLU, or 2.8. Since 2.8 is closest in value to the typical value of Stage III, or 2.75, we would estimate this child to be in Stage III of syntactic development.

As a child's MLU increases, we make certain assumptions about his growing cognitive and linguistic abilities. Not only is he able to remember more words so that he produces longer utterances, he is also able to express more concepts according to the syntax of his language. The appearance of inflections, such as the -s to indicate plural or the -ing to indicate an ongoing process, shows that words for the child are becoming "bundles" of concepts. He understands what a *shoe* is, as well as the concept of "more than one," expressed by the addition of -s. In this sense, syntactic development roughly mirrors conceptual development. What the child can think about he can begin to express through small but meaningful units of language.

Since the MLU at Brown's last stage is 4 morphemes, the measure is useful only for analyzing early syntax. Beyond Stage V, researchers have found that children begin to use ellipsis, shortening their utterances as adults do. Instead of saying, "Yes, I want more," the child can now say simply "Yes," even though he is able to construct a longer utterance. In addition, as children get older their speech is affected increasingly by the situations in which they interact. While interacting with strangers, their MLU may look deceptively low. Examples of utterances from contrasting familiar situations are needed to get a more valid measure of their language. As children's utterances increase far beyond four morphemes per utterance, a mean length is sometimes measured in words, rather than morphemes.

Summary

The institution called day care reflects the complexities of raising children in contemporary society. Questions about the effects of long-term out-of-family care, accommodating to children and staff from different ethnic groups, whether day care teachers should focus on academic preparation—these are a few general issues that teachers and directors confront. How day care might affect children's language development and the dialects that they might encounter in day care were initial themes of this chapter. Day care settings vary enormously in nature and quality, but with respect to language, two things seemed indispensable for children who are beginning to use language: (a) attentive caregivers who talk frequently and responsively and (b) opportunities for children to communicate nonverbally and verbally, expressing a variety of functions. As you foster multipurposed language, you can also notice and assess development by using a range of methods, from brief checklists to the mean length of utterance, typically a researcher's tool. These techniques for documenting and assessing are recommended for teachers in day care, as well as preschool and primary grade teachers. Our focus shifts next to the preschool and to the importance of varied activities in facilitating language.

Suggested Readings

Cazden, C. B. (Ed.). *Language in early childhood education* (Rev. ed.). Washington, DC: National Association for the Education of Young Children, 1981. A readable and relevant collection of articles about language acquisition and curricula for early childhood. Matters of dialect, curriculum selection and evaluation, English as a second language, and early literacy are all included.

Clarke-Stewart, A. *Daycare*. Cambridge, MA: Harvard University Press, 1982. An excellent, readable, and compact overview and analysis of important issues in day care. The author points out the difficulties of evaluating effects of day care and provides a checklist for identifying high quality care. Other topics include the history, kinds, and alternatives to day care, along with language-related topics.

Willis, A., & Ricciuti, H. *A good beginning for babies: Guidelines for group care*. Washington, DC: National Association for the Education of Young Children, 1975. This is a practical guide for working with infants in groups. Activities for infants are suggested, although the emphasis is appropriately on the importance of caregiver-child interaction.

CHAPTER 5

Children's Language in Preschool Settings

Introduction

Example 5–1: Two-year-olds, Tom, Sissy, Marcy, and Christopher, sit at the art table, applying finger paint to individual sheets of paper:

Tom: Red (sounds like *wed*).

Sissy: I have white.

Marcy: I have white.

Christopher: I have green (sounds like *gween*).

. . .

Christopher: I see Christmas store.

Teacher: Did you see the pretty lights?

Christopher: I saw pretty lights.

Example 5–2: Five-year-old Will, 4-year-old Jenny, 4-year-old Tessa, and 3-year-old Russell are playing. The scenario includes dinosaurs, Godzilla, and ordinary people:

Will: I'm gonna call the temperature (using a toy telephone). Sixty-nine degrees! Temperature, 80 degrees. Right!

Jenny (to Russell): Godzilla, are you cold?

Tessa: Be quiet so the baby can sleep.

Will: Temperature 20 degrees.

Russell: Hey, y'all—.

Jenny: Russell and I are fixin' to play with the Lite Brite.®

Will: I'm gonna call the temperature.

These examples reflect striking differences in the two groups' abilities to speak. The 2-year-olds' utterances are short and simple compared to the 3- to 5-year-olds, who can create an imaginary world of dinosaurs, monsters, and telephones. They move in and out of a fantasy world as they use linguistic structures that closely resemble those that adults around them use.

We can observe .other developmental differences between toddlers and preschoolers, for example, in their degree of mobility, as they engage in activities typical of their classrooms. Toddlers may move from one area of the room to another by crawling or walking; it wouldn't surprise us if one tripped along the way. The preschooler may confidently walk or run to reach her chosen activity. The contrasting images of a toddler and a preschooler in our mind's eye become richer and more informative as we describe the physical settings where they move about and learn. The toddler room has reminders of the home setting; boxes of paper diapers fill one counter; changes of clothing fill the children's cubbies. The floor of the room is relatively clear of furniture, except for child-sized tables and chairs, where children have snacks and meals. Several toys of varying sizes are on the floor, which is one large undifferentiated space for crawling, sitting, or walking. A room for 3- to 5-year-olds looks more cluttered because the space is divided into different areas: the housekeeping corner, an art table near easels, a library area with a number of children's books, a science area with the beginnings of a terrarium, and so on. These areas are characteristic of some preschool classrooms, particularly traditional nursery schools for 3- and 4-year-olds.

The variety in preschool settings is almost as great as the variety in day care. Some have several rooms with clearly defined activity areas; others have less space but are well equipped with learning toys that serve academic purposes; and others resemble primary grade classrooms, with few toys or activity centers in view. These have child-sized tables at which children work, and teachers distribute worksheets for children to color or complete. Work gets done with a minimum of talk among children. The preschools that we describe as desirable places for young children are of the first category: classrooms with a range of activities that encourage a range of language uses.

For our purposes *preschool setting* refers to a group of children in the age range of about 3 to 5 years and with productive language that enables dialogues—however elementary—with peers and adults. By this definition day care homes and centers as well as traditional nursery schools and government-funded Head Start programs and preschools are included. We do not exclude settings for the handicapped, but most of what we present relates to normally developing children. In this chapter we begin by emphasizing the important effects of settings on children's language. We then deal with language and play, the role of teacher talk, and the process of second language acquisition.

The Importance of Situations and Activity

So far we have discussed two major settings for interaction and language use, the home and day care. We have said that within those settings different people create different situations for children's early dialogues; adults and peers are contrasting kinds of interlocutors. Here we look again at adult and peer talk, as well as other features of the communicative situation, such as the amount of space available, amount of equipment, and type of activity. These features make up the child's physical environment and affect far more than the quality of children's language.

Different arrangements and amounts of space per child may be associated with different child behaviors. Day-to-day decisions about furniture placement, for example, may make a difference. A large table placed very close to a housekeeping corner may prevent children from easily entering the area; or once inside the area, children may play in a constrained way because of the lack of space. A room without free-standing bookcases or other dividers may be the scene of few spontaneous small group interactions and may offer little privacy for children to be alone or to talk in pairs.

The first author remembers the vivid contrast between the spatial arrangement of a preschool where she taught and another where she did research. The first had ample indoor and outdoor space and several center-like areas, including a housekeeping area with small upstairs and downstairs living spaces, carpentry table, wet sandbox, and swing area, all at a distance from each other. The other preschool had within one compact room, a housekeeping corner, block area, listening center, kitchen space, rug for circle time, library corner, and science center. The children in the first setting were normally noisy and frequently in motion, walking or running to change activities. In contrast, children at the second school seemed extraordinarily noisy and not very mobile. In one-to-one conversations the children's abilities to use language seemed similar. Yet, the available space in each setting made appreciation and assessment of what was said easy in the first and difficult in the second school. To make their program workable the teachers in the second setting were forced to be imaginative about aspects of the environment that they could control, such as arrangement of furniture and activity. To encourage block play among children, for example, they closed the adjacent science center on certain days, so that enough space was cleared for extensive block construction.

Two closely related aspects of preschool programs are activity and type and quantity of equipment and materials. Toddlers have been observed to pay more attention to each other when they play with equipment that is stationary. Doke and Risley (1972) found that children focus most intensively on play materials, and not each other, when they can choose among activities and have many materials available to them for individual use. Classrooms with Montessori materials, many for individual use, come to mind as ideal settings for deep involvement with materials. Providing a large number of toys and materials, then, has both positive and negative effects. There may be greater attention paid to objects and fewer conflicts among children when supplies are plentiful, but there may also be fewer opportunities for talk and for cooperative play.

Since the ways that teachers plan and structure activities influence children's language use, many researchers have studied the relationship between activity and children's behavior. Shure (1963), for example, found that 4-year-old nursery school children had the highest number of interactions in the doll corner and block area. Berk (1973) noted a variety of relationships in her study of nursery school programs that we have also seen in preschools and primary grades: there was more child-to-child communication in pairs than other group sizes, in activities requiring cooperation and coordination such as dramatic play, and in child-initiated activities. There was more teacher-to-child communication in large group and whole class activities, coordinated group activities such as singing, and in teacher-initiated activities. Finally, there was more child-to-teacher communication during activities not requiring coordinated action and those in which the teacher and children performed the same actions, as they might while cooking. We will refer to these varied kinds of communication as we portray preschoolers' activity-based language.

Another researcher who views activity as crucial is Ervin-Tripp (1982) who has written about "activity structure as scaffolding" for young second language learners. Across a variety of play situations, she described how 5- through 12-year-old children's knowledge of the predictable structure of a game or role play helped them communicate using a minimum of language. The activity itself, a telephone conversation, simulated soccer, board or card game, jump rope, or fantasy play, was the scaffolding, as in this exchange between Anne, a French speaker, and Karla, who is learning French:

> *Example 5–3:* Predictable board game activities provide routines that can be labeled, and the second language learner can repeat the labels or steps, as Karla does below:
>
> Anne: On change de jeu, eh. [Let's change games huh.]
>
> Karla: Je suis..[I'm. .]
>
> Anne: Non, on change. [No, we'll change.]
>
> Karla: Ah, oui. [Oh, yes.]
>
> Anne: On range. [We'll put things away.] (begins to)
>
> Karla: On range. [We'll put things away.]
>
> (Ervin-Tripp, 1982, p. 17)

Once children become more proficient with spoken language, they depend less on the presence and structure of the activity, or the scaffolding. That is, they eventually are better able to talk about things not present in the speech situation.

Whether the child is a first or second language learner, what she does or acts upon supports attempts to communicate. Anyone who speaks needs something to speak about, and for young children the "something" is often what they are doing at the moment, the here-and-now. This is a principle to keep in mind while planning activities that contribute to growth in language and thinking and when assessing children's language. In your classroom, then, you might take notes on or tape-record samples of children's interactions and activities to see whether an activity promotes language and how language varies with activity. In other words, you will assess the activity at the same time you assess children's language. Here is a sampling of two 3-year-olds' interactions, revolving around diverse activities, of the kind you might observe and record:

> *Example 5–4:*
>
> Three-year-old (3 years; 8 months) Allie is in the 3-year-olds' room of a preschool and chooses different activities during "center time." Her first activity is to make a construction paper collage. After she pastes the last piece of paper on her sheet, she matter-of-factly eats some paste and says, "I'm finished! I'm finished!" She then spends about 2 minutes trying to use a plastic socket wrench on a toy car. While she does this, she chants, "Dub, dub, dub, dub, dub, dub." She next turns away from the car and picks up a small plastic doll, lying on the floor near the car. She talks to the doll, "I told you to shut up, son! No way, this is no way!"

Example 5–4 shows Allie in three different activities, using language to inform ("I'm finished"), accompany action ("Dub, dub . . ."), and imagine she is a doll's mother ("I told you to shut up, son!"). Later in the same morning Allie sits at the art table "writing" with paper and pencil and takes part in this exchange:

Example 5–5:

 Allie: Are you my friend, Libby? (another 3-year-old)

 Libby: No.

 Allie: Teacher, Libby's not anyone's friend.

Teacher: Well, you just sit and write and in a minute everyone'll be happy.

  Jill: Allie, you can come to my house.

Teacher: Allie, Jill's talking to you. Say, "What?"

  Jill: You can come to my house.

 Allie: I'll give her my Pot Belly (her teddy bear, which she brought to school that day).

 Joey: Allie needs a diaper.

Teacher: Allie doesn't wear diapers.

 Allie: You know what I said? I wear panties, not diapers! *Babies* wear diapers!

Allie's and Jill's efforts in this example to become friends or maintain friendly interactions illustrate Halliday's interactional function of conversation. At the end of the excerpt, Allie uses what is called the personal function ("I wear panties, not diapers!" and so on) in response to Joey. Both children seem to be asserting their own importance, something preschoolers often do.

A younger 3-year-old (3 years; 0 months), Houston, also uses language for different functions at another preschool. In the following example he participates with his class in creative movement:

Example 5–6: The teacher tells a story about being in a rowboat, fleeing a monster. Children rock back and forth as if they're rowing.

Houston: Rock, rock, rock, rock.

 Doug: I see a snake.

 Tina: I see a bear.

Houston: The animal goin' to the zoo. Open the door.

In addition to using language imaginatively, Houston uses the instrumental function when he needs help:

Example 5-7: Houston works on a jigsaw puzzle of an airplane.

> Houston: No. I can't do it. (He sees that one of the pieces doesn't fit in the space he's chosen for it.)
>
> Houston (to teacher): Help me.
>
> Teacher: Do you need help? I'll put this piece in the front (of the airplane) and you do the back.
>
> Crane: Want me to help you?
>
> Houston: No, I want the teacher.

In Example 5-7 Houston refuses the help of an older child, whom he later joins on the playground:

Example 5-8:

> Crane (to all): Watch me go up the slide. (Personal)
>
> Houston: Hey, Crane, wanna get in? (He asks if Crane wants to get on the swinging tire with him and sees Jesse standing nearby.) (Interactional)
>
> Houston (to Jesse): Jesse, stop it, I wanna get on. (Jesse stops the swinging tire and Houston gets on without Crane.) (Regulatory or instrumental)
>
> Houston (to teacher): Please push me. (He gets a push and starts shrieking happily.) (Instrumental)

Example 5-8 shows two children using several functions of language in a short time. It also shows that functions may overlap in one turn of talk. "Jesse, stop it, I wanna get on," is Houston's attempt to regulate Jesse's behavior, followed immediately by an expression of his desire to be on the tire. In looking at similar conversations, teachers may transcribe short segments and label the various functions, as we have done above.

An alternative to labeling functions, as in Example 5-8, is use of a more formal observation record like the one in Figure 5-1, which shows two 5-year-olds with their teacher. Kate—who just became 5—and Jerry are at the older end of the preschool age range. We focus next on Kate, a generally active and talkative child, as she participates in a number of activities. She is in a preschool where the teacher has planned a unit for Thanksgiving. Two centers, one for grinding Indian corn with a stone mortar and pestle and another for stringing large bead necklaces, reflect the theme. Kate, Jerry, Ms. Miller, and Marvin sit at the table for grinding corn. Ms. Miller and Marvin talk primarily about

	Example 5-9		
Observer **S. Miller**	Date **11-18-82**	Activity	**Grinding corn - center time**
Speaker	What's said:	Functions	Forms
Kate	Jerry, should I do a little bit--should I put a little bit more in? I'll put in a couple more (kernels of corn). Maybe I could (). I'll hold it, and you hit it. (She'll hold the mortar while he grinds.)	Heuristic, informative, interactional, regulatory	Lots of questions Statements Some commands No problems
Jerry	It's going around. These things are falling around. These things are popping out!	Informative	
Ms. Miller	Yeah, they do when you grind them too hard.	Informative	
	(Jerry persistently grinds the corn, which is partly ground meal and partly whole kernels. A little later:)		
Jerry	Don't drop that much.	Regulatory	
Kate	Could I do a little bit?	Heuristic	
Jerry	A little.	Informative	
Kate	Is this all you're gonna do?	Heuristic,	
Kate (to Ms. Miller)	Are y'all doing this one? (another ear of corn) Are y'all doing this one?	regulatory?	
Ms. Miller	We've got a lot of (). We don't wanna take any more off. ()	Informative	
Kate	Come on, Jerry.	Regulatory	
	(Time passes with grinding noise.)		
Kate (to Ms. Miller)	Look at Jerry, he's done.	Regulatory, informative	
Ms. Miller	Oh, Jerry, look how much you've done!	Informative	

Comments:

I was zeroing in on Kate today. She and Jerry really cooperated to get the corn ground, even though a lot of it didn't grind easily. Another thing I noticed was the way she kept asking questions to make sure that Jerry was finishing up and she would get her turn at grinding.

Figure 5—1 Observation Record, Bluebonnet Learning Center

photographs in a book about Indians while Kate and Jerry grind corn. Jerry grinds while Kate helps in the excerpt in Figure 5-1.

Example 5–9 demonstrates that children easily talk about what they do. The observer noted the language functions of all three participants' talk and made brief observations about forms as well. Summary comments at the bottom of the sheet, which focus on Kate's purposes for communicating, will be helpful in reviewing Kate's progress with other teachers or Kate's parents. Depending on your preferences and teaching schedule, you may want to be more or less specific than this observer in keeping such a record. For example, instead of noting a function for each turn of talk, you might determine one or two functions that capture the whole interaction. In Example 5–9 the two dominant functions would be regulatory and informative. Like other records, this one is most useful as part of a series of observations and may be added to an ongoing collection of the child's products, including her art and dictated stories.

Kate and Jerry have used language to question, inform, and regulate each other's behavior. The two cooperate to get the task done ("I'll hold it; you hit it"), and the information they exchange is about the activity itself ("It's going around"). Although there are periods of silence as they watch what happens to the corn, Kate and Jerry show that working in pairs can be productive in terms of oral language and cooperative behavior, as the observer noted in her comments. Following this excerpt Kate gets her turn, and Jerry holds the mortar while she grinds. Their conversation continues to be focused on what they see happening.

After her turn at grinding, Kate spends a short time in the house-keeping corner. She puts on a "headdress" made of a few feathers and cardboard, takes it off, and decides to join Jerry, Tracy, Christiana, and the teacher at the art table. The children chat and draw with felt markers:

Example 5–10:

Christiana (to Ms. Miller): What do you think that says? What do you think that says?

Ms. Miller: Looks like you're writing your name, Christiana. What is it?

Christiana: I don't know what it says.

Ms. Miller: C-H-R-I (reading). No, that's not—

Christiana: That's nothing; that's not a letter.

Ms. Miller: It's not *I*? That's just a mark?

Christiana: Yeah, just a mark.

Ms. Miller: R-P-R.( )

Christiana: What's it say?

Ms. Miller: It says *Chrip*.

Christiana: Chrip?

Jerry: Teacher, make me a tent.

Ms. Miller: You can make a tent.

(A short time passes.)

Christiana: C-H-R-R-P-R, if you're gonna spell that. . . . My name's C-H-R-I, I don't know what else.

Kate: That's OK.

(Kate seems to be writing Christiana's name on her piece of paper.)

Christiana: That doesn't say Christiana.

(Kate walks over to the bulletin board to look at Christiana's name. Each child's name is written on a paper hand, and the hand is placed next to the picture of a task. A hand next to a picture of a glass means the child whose name is on the hand distributes glasses at snack and mealtime.)

Kate: Christiana, are you the cups? (Meaning, is your name next to the picture of a glass?)

Christiana: I'm nothing. Charlie's the cups.

(Christiana does not have a task assigned to her. Ms. Miller suggests that Kate remembers how Ms. Miller previously pointed out the similarities between Christiana's and Charlie's names. Since they both begin with *C-H*, Kate is not sure which hand has Christiana's name on it. Apparently Kate figures out it is not the hand near the glass and goes back to the art table.)

Christiana (to ?): Want me to make a teepee for you?

(Kate draws and doesn't talk much.)

Christiana (to Ms. Miller): Here's my paper. Write it (her name) on both sides.

Ms. Miller: OK, do you want to tell me anything about it?

Christiana: That's a teepee and on the other side that's the better teepee. (See Figure 5–2 for one of her drawings.)

(A little later:)

Ms. Miller (to Kate): You want to tell me anything about it, Kate? You want to tell me anything about it?

Kate: No. (See Figure 5–3.)

At the art table Kate appears to be task-oriented and does little talking, except for remarks about Christiana's name. In general, Ms. Miller and the children use the heuristic, information-seeking function, and the informative function. The teacher has done some on-the-spot assessment for the observer (the first author) by inferring that Kate went to the bulletin board to try to distinguish *Charlie* from *Christiana*. With only informal and sporadic explanations about children's names, Kate and Christiana have begun to read and write their own names in the context of drawing. Kate is able to write her name on her drawing, whereas Christiana, with a harder task, knows the first four letters of hers. The teacher presses neither Christiana to write her full name correctly nor Kate to dictate a caption for her drawing.

In another situation Kate willingly contributes to a chart, on which

That's a teepee

Christiana

Figure 5–2 Christiana's drawing, labeled in the upper right by her teacher

100

Figure 5–3 Kate's drawing

her teacher records children's responses to the question, "What did you like about our trip to the bus barn?" These are the responses:

Example 5–11:

> Our trip to the bus barn

Marvin: I liked the door (of the bus).

Nina: I liked the doors because they open by themselves, when you pull the handle.

Lynne: You seat down. You closed them.

Gracie: I liked the gas.

Jerry: I liked the big ole bus.

Kate: When we went bumping up and down.

Didi: I liked the brakes. They make noise.

John: Going in the front seat.

In this situation, a more structured one than the earlier art activity, the children take turns and have the opportunity to inform the teacher about a past activity they shared. They can see that what they say can be written down. Preschool teachers often extend the benefits of a field trip by making such charts, as they value the children's forms of expression by writing exactly what is said, even if the forms are not like those in textbooks. Kate's contribution, "When we went bumping up and down," for example, is what some adults call a sentence fragment. Lynne's, "You seat down," is not adult-like. Still they are both appropriate answers to the question, and the teacher accurately records them. (For discussion of this "language experience" approach in the kindergarten, see Chapter 6.)

Another group situation for Kate is the 15- to 20-minute period that the teacher calls "study time." It is partly teacher-directed (or storytelling) and partly a sharing time when children contribute what they know. The teacher talks about teepees before telling a story:

Example 5–12:

Ms. Miller: They (the Indians) didn't have a fireplace, but they had a fire.

Kate: Yeah. Yeah, they get sticks, and they get some sticks and build and make a fireplace. And then they rub and make fire.

Ms. Miller: Right. They put a fire right in the middle. But what would happen to the smoke?

Kate: It would go out.

Ms. Miller: Right. It would go straight out the top (of the teepee) where those points are and go out that hole.

Kate: And it would tell, it would tell when the Indians are lost.

Ms. Miller: Sometimes they do, and Ms. Hanson (the teacher across the hall) has that picture in her room. Sometimes they did send smoke signals, but it wasn't in the teepees.

Here Kate uses the informative function and shows that she can verbally sequence the steps for making a fire by recalling information from earlier lessons. The teacher directs the interaction with her questions and comments; some of these correct Kate's misconceptions about smoke signals.

Two other examples of Kate's communicative performance take place during free play time, independent of teacher direction. This one samples her language use on the playground:

Example 5–13: Kate and Christiana chase each other for a few minutes, laughing and saying little. Kate then climbs up on a low concrete fence.

Kate: Let's sit right here, OK?

Christiana: OK. (Next they stand on the fence and start singing.)

Both: "Sitting on the patio—"

Kate: No, "I'm a little teapot, short and stout. Here's my handle, here's my spout." (Both sing and move their arms to become teapots, but look more like cheerleaders than teapots as they move their bodies along with their arms.)

For these girls songs provide a way to be playful and imaginative with the words of nursery rhymes or favorite jingles. Imaginative language also occurs during dramatic play, fantasy play in which children assign roles to be played. Here Kate, Didi, and John play with a dollhouse, set on a table in their classroom, and take roles as they manipulate and animate small wooden people and animals. Through her talk Kate directs the play:

Example 5–14:

Kate (to John's wooden puppy): OK, you sit with the little sister. We'll be back at nighttime. We're just going for a little hunting. Who wants to go hunting? (Kate's voice is high-pitched as she plays mother.)

Didi: Wait for me! I wanna go hunting.

Kate: This is where we're spending the night (as she
places her wooden person next to the dollhouse.)

John: I wanna go hunting.

Kate: This is where we're spending the—Hey, look
where we're spending the night, little sister and
puppy! You can stay up watching television.
(John, the puppy, appropriately doesn't speak.)

In this section we have demonstrated the importance of children's activity as a basis for talk, by focusing on the language of two 3-year-olds and a 5-year-old. A variety of activities—artwork, creative movement, outdoor play, grinding corn, informal writing, study time, dramatic play—provided the scaffolding for children to display many language functions, including Halliday's seven functions, from instrumental to informative. The teachers in the classrooms observed can be pleased that the activities they planned or participated in encouraged talk of different kinds.

Although we were documenting the unique language of three individuals, the differences among them reflect some basic differences between 3's and 5's. The 3-year-olds' utterances were generally shorter and their words were not always clearly pronounced (though this lack of clarity didn't show in the transcripts). Forms were sometimes less adultlike (as in Houston's, "The animal goin' to the zoo"). Language was often used for the social purposes of establishing and maintaining friendships or asserting one's own importance, and the children frequently asked the teacher for help in their interactions. Allie, for example, expressed concern to the teacher that Libby was not her friend. Similar concerns also appear in 5-year-olds' interactions, but with less frequency. In Kate's case, her spoken language served additional functions. There were more teacher-directed group activities in the 4- and 5-year-olds' classroom that prompted children and teacher to demonstrate Halliday's heuristic and informative functions.

The general differences between Houston and Allie and Kate and her classmates reflect the development that occurs in children's language and thinking between 3 and 5 years. Both 3's and 5's engaged in imaginative or dramatic play, but the older children could use more complex language and enact more extended scripts. For preschoolers this kind of play is associated with large amounts of child-initiated talk. The nature of that talk, and how play can provide a showcase for children's communicative competence, are discussed further in the next section.

Play and Language

> In play a child behaves beyond his average age, above his daily behavior; in play it is as though he were a head taller than himself. As in the focus of a magnifying glass, play contains all developmental tendencies in a condensed form and is itself a major source of development. (Vygotsky, 1978, p. 102)

When children use language in play, they do sound "a head taller" than themselves, using language that they use nowhere else. They often try to sound like adults, and in doing so they stretch both the forms and functions of their language.

Recent support of Vygotsky's view of play comes from several sources. Social or dramatic play is seen as a complicated interaction that two or more children build cooperatively. According to Garvey (1974), to take part in social play children must be able to:

1. *Distinguish between reality and play.* Players may change pitch, loudness, or rate of speech when they switch to an imaginary register or style; or they mark play verbally, "Pretend you're the sister," or "it's hot—play like it's hot."

2. *Abstract rules for structuring play.* These are general rules for conversation, such as turn-taking, as well as specific rules about how children's characters are supposed to sound. Players expect each other to maintain role identities throughout an interaction. They also apply rules about acceptable features of roles, "Don't laugh. Doctors do not laugh."

3. *Cooperatively construct, or share a common image of, a theme in play.* Through talk children share responsibility for developing a theme. Maintaining play themes depends on abilities to persuade, negotiate, and acquiesce.

As children play, they are controlling and manipulating their environment, primarily through language. Talk is often used as a tool to influence others' behavior as in this example of the dramatic play of two 4-year-olds in a nursery school:

Example 5–15:

    Gay: Hi.

Daniel: Hi.

    Gay: How are you?

Daniel: Fine.

Gay: Who am I speaking to?

Daniel: Daniel. This is your daddy. I need to speak to you.

Gay: All right.

Daniel: When I come home tonight, we're gonna have . . . peanut butter and jelly sandwich, uh, at dinner time.

Gay: Where're we going to dinner time?

Daniel: Nowhere. But we're just gonna have dinner at 11 o'clock.

Gay: Well, I made a plan of going out tonight.

Daniel: Well, that's what we're gonna do.

Gay: We're going out.

Daniel: The plan, it's gonna be, that's gonna be, we're going to McDonald's.

Gay: Yeah, we're going to McDonald's. And, ah, ah, ah, what they have for dinner tonight is hamburger.

Daniel: Hamburger is coming. OK, well, goodbye.

Gay: Bye.

(Nelson & Gruendel, 1979, p. 76)

This is a conversation about dinner plans that two children had on toy telephones. The conversation is cooperatively structured, and the content reflects the children's preferences and experiences. There are *hi's* and *goodbye's,* and indications of adult-like questions and complex sentences, including an adverbial clause, "When I come home tonight," and a noun complement, "What they have for dinner tonight," forms not always heard in 4-year-olds' speech.

In addition to their linguistic competence, the language in this dialogue reflects the children's social knowledge, their knowledge of routines such as dinner, making plans on the phone, and so on. This verbal presentation of social knowledge may also contribute to cognitive development. The two children who talked about dinner plans share a common conception or script for dinner. If they didn't, the communication would have broken down, and the conversation would have been much shorter. Playful conversation is the setting for sharing a script and for speaking in a way that takes into account the listener's point of view. In other words, dramatic play might provide the setting for speech that is less egocentric than we would expect from preschoolers. They seem to be working toward true conversations or dialogues, which are models of appreciation of others' viewpoints.

Other evidence that children's language in dramatic play can be unusually rich comes from studies by Black (1979) and Hutt (1979).

Black compared the speech of 12 kindergarten children in three situations to see whether standardized or informal measures of language provided more complete information about linguistic and social competencies. The informal measures, such as Halliday's categories, were applied to talk from the children's sociodramatic play. Black found that children's language during play showed more diverse vocabulary; greater correct use of irregular word endings; more functions of language; and greater knowledge of appropriate social rules than the language used for the standardized test situations.

Hutt (1979) analyzed the language of children in British day care centers whose children were almost all disadvantaged. Although two-word utterances were typical in most situations, during play their language became much more complex. Utterances were longer, and the number of adjectives and adverbs increased. Apparently the play situation allowed children to produce language that reflected their competence to the fullest. It was a setting that was not only pleasurable and free from anxiety, but also one that children themselves controlled.

Our own observations show how complex preschoolers' play can be. Three Spanish-speaking 5-year-olds enrolled in Head Start enacted a doctor script in this way:

Example 5-16:

Diana: No, yo soy el doctor. [No, I'm the doctor] Ding dong! Ding dong! Ding dong! Ding dong!

Mari: Eh ¿qué . . . ¿Qué pasó, hija? [Hey, what happened, daughter?] (Mari clearly rejects Diana's attempt to play doctor.)

Diana: No, no soy hija, ni nada. [No, I'm not a daughter, or anything.]

Mari: ¿Qué pasó, hija? [What happened, daughter?]

Diana: No, yo no soy . . . Yo no soy hija. . . Yo no te conozco. No más que tú me llamas,¿OK? [No, I'm not—I don't—I don't know you. You just call me, OK?]

Mari: ¿Quién es? [Who is it?]

Diana: Vd. me llamó, ¿ verdad? [You called me, is that right?]

Mari: Sí. [Yes.]

Diana: Entonces, ¿por qué me llamó? [Then, why did you call me?]

Mari: No, es que quería, que, que mañana viniera a cuidarme la niña porque voy al mandado. [No, it's that, that, that I wanted you to come tomorrow to take care of the baby because I'm going to the market.] (Mari again foils Diana's attempt to be doctor.)

Diana: ¡No! Yo no cuido nada. [I'm not taking care of anything.]

Example 5–17:

Diana: Ding dong! Ding dong! Ding dong! Ding dong! (Diana is the doctor "ringing" the doorbell.) Yo era—tú abrías la puerta, donde estaba. Ding dong. [I was—you were opening the door, where I was.] No, ésa no es. Allá donde está el papel y ( ). Ding dong. [No, not there. Where the paper is and ( ).] (The paper seems to be the doctor's pad.) Mira. Ahora venía el doctor. [Look. Now the doctor's come.] Mira. Ding dong! Ding dong! Ding dong!

Mari: ¿Qué—Qué quería Vd.? [What did you want?]

Diana: Vd. me llamó porque—¿verdad que Vd. me llamó? [You called me because—isn't it true that you called me?]

Mari: Uh huh. Oiga. Oiga, ¿qué es—( ) [Listen. Listen, what is—]

Diana: Ah, que Vd. me llamó, Srta. Para que le atendiera a su hija. ¿Y dónde está? [Ah, you called me, Miss, so that I could check on your daughter. And where is she?]

Mari: Allí está en el cuarto. [There in the room.] (Adelita is the sick daughter.) Mira. A ver, quítate—Le va a dar un beso. Es que si le da un beso, luego no va estar mala. [Look. Let's see, take off—Are you giving her a kiss? If you give her a kiss, then she won't be sick any more.]

Diana: OK, ahorita. ¡Bien mala! Sí, es, Sí, es. [OK, now. Very sick! Yes, she is. Yes, she is.]

Mari: Hazle mmmmmmm. [Make a noise like mmmmmmm.]

Diana: No, no. Este es mío. [This is mine.] ¡Ya! [OK!]

Diana and Mari show themselves to be both linguistically and socially competent. The Spanish language has a complicated system of verb tenses, and these 5-year-olds use forms of the present (*soy*), imperfect (*abrías*), preterite (*llamó*), and past subjunctive (*viniera*) tenses in their short exchanges. Equally impressive is their ability to verbally manipulate the action. In Example 5–16, Mari wards off Diana's claim to being the doctor by talking to her as if she is Mari's babysitter. But Diana persists in establishing the roles as she would like them to be, and in Example 5–17 she and Mari carry out the doctor's visit to Mari's sick daughter.

In contrast one of the children, Diana, seems to be quite a different kind of speaker in this interview with the first author, who is asking her about languages:

Example 5–18:

Genishi: ¿Y en tu casa, qué lengua hablan? [And in your house, what language do you speak?]

Diana: Ummmm.

Genishi: ¿En tu casa? ¿Tu mamá habla inglés? [At your house? Does your mom speak English?]

Diana: Uh huh.

. . .

Genishi: ¿Cuándo te gustaría aprender el inglés? [When would you like to learn English?]

Diana: Cuando esté en la otra escuela. [When I'm in the other school.]

Genishi: ¿Y qué vas a hablar después de ir a la otra escuela? [And what are you going to speak after you go to the other school?]

Diana: Uh—los dos. [Both.]

Genishi: Los dos. [Both.] OK.

Although Diana had seen the first author many times and talked animatedly before and after her play sessions, she spoke haltingly and softly and displayed very little of her communicative competence in this question-answer situation. The nature of her talk reemphasizes the principle that aspects of the social situation strongly affect the kind of language children produce. The contrasting situation of dramatic play, however, was truly a showcase for her and Mari's competence.

We know that all children are not like Diana and Mari, and we know that children's play is not restricted to the housekeeping area. Some children are more comfortable creating situations in the block center or on the playground. These areas also lend themselves to negotiation and cooperation, for example, a child in the block center might say, "This is our fort. Look out! Uh-uh-uh-uh! (gun fire);" or on the playground, "Let's play witch. I'm the witch," and "I'll chase you." Other children may seldom use language to invent imaginary situations. The teacher may plan more structured dramatic activities to engage these children in play. They may be willing to enact a scene from a favorite story, particularly if they can use puppets or flannel board characters as props. Teachers enter into such activities to involve children and to encourage and assess the language they use.

Play and Emerging Literacy

Another kind of play involves talk that may occur in dramatic play, but may also occur when the child is alone. This is *play with language,* usually repetitious and rhythmic play with the sounds of language. It can begin as soon as the child begins to vocalize and may be noticeable when she starts to babble. Later as she is just beginning to use words, she may demonstrate awareness of sounds by imitating in a deliberate way intonations she hears adults use, for example: Adult: "Want to go outside?" Child: (An approximation of) "Outsíde?" The child's pronunciation may be inexact, but she successfully reproduces the adult's rising intonation and stress when saying *outside*.

Here is an example of a child-initiated exercise on adjective formation between older children, 5-year-olds:

Example 5–19:

Boy: Teddy bear's mine.

Girl: The fishy fishy is mine.

Boy: No, the snakey snakey is yours. 'Cause it's fishy too. 'Cause it has fishes.

Girl: And it's snakey too 'cause it has snakes and it's beary too because it has bears.

Boy: And it's and it's hatty 'cause it has hats.

(Garvey, 1977, pp. 69–70)

Examples of language play are charming, but they may also influence other dimensions of language and thinking. Play with language may lead to metalinguistic awareness, an awareness of language as an entity—something we can talk and think about—with specific characteristics. There are different levels of awareness that are observed even in preschoolers. When a child corrects herself and says, "He goed—I mean went," she is showing an elementary awareness of language forms. Or she might correct other speakers. Spanish-speaking children, for example, have corrected the first author for her mistakes in gender endings. If she refers to a girl, she should say *chula* [cute], not *chulo*. Children who can tell you if an utterance sounds "OK" or "funny" show another kind of awareness as they begin to be critics of language. Finally, there is the kind of metalanguage, or talk about language, that we ask children to use in school. Asking, "What's a long word?", "Is that a consonant or a vowel?", or "Did what you read make sense?" are all questions that depend on an understanding of metalanguage.

As children play with language, they unconsciously make it an object that can be analyzed. It can be broken down and described in terms of sounds, syllables, words, pitch, intonation, and so on. As they become literate, they learn that some of the elements of language are represented in specific ways in print. Garvey (1977) believes that dramatic play is a "reframing of activity" in which child players are able to tease apart and dramatize elements of their prior experience. We think language play is a "reframing of language" that may ultimately help the child become not only literate but also reflective about the nature of language.

Valuing language play because it might lead to language awareness leads to a dilemma: whether or not we can help children to engage in it. Many people believe that play of any kind is not play unless it is initiated by the child. For them, real play with language consists of children's spontaneous utterances. Children like the 5-year-olds in Example 5–19 need no help in attending to certain aspects of language, but to acquire the vocabulary to talk about those aspects, other children might benefit from mild and well-timed intervention from a teacher. For example, 4-year-old Robert said:

Example 5–20:

"Can you read my shirt? It says, 'Thick or thin at Pizza Inn,' inn, min, pin, pin, kin, kee, kee, bee, bee," and then he giggled. The teacher said, "Those words rhymed with *inn*." Robert was silent a moment, then said, "Oh, yeah, they sound like it, right? Yum, yum, mum, tum, tummy!" and he chuckled a little at his understanding of it and patted his stomach.

(Almy & Genishi, 1979, p. 132)

Many children are different from Robert and cannot spontaneously produce rhyming words, or they may be unable to think of an example of a word when the teacher asks for their favorite words. For children who do not play with language on their own, you can provide lots of exposure to print, riddles, recitation of rhymes, hearing and saying tongue-twisters, songs, chanting together. All of these activities are standard fare in preschool settings that contribute to the development of language awareness and literacy.

A setting full of interactions that promoted awareness of language and informally prepared 3- to 5-year-olds for literacy and the more formal instruction of the public school looked like this: a small brightly painted room contained seven children and a teacher. One child is standing, playing teacher, and the others are sitting or lying on the floor. Two small blackboards are also on the floor, inviting children to write on them. Several children make marks on them and go on to other activities. At least two conversations are going on simultaneously. Kai Kai, the "teacher," is in charge:

Example 5–21:

Kai Kai: I get an A.

Child: Look what I did.

Kai Kai: Uh huh. And who else gets an A? Terry gets an A.

Terry: I already got an A. Johnny gets an A.

Johnny: I already got an A.

Kai Kai: Who gets an X? Anita gets an X!

DJ: You make your own name (talking to someone who wants to sign a "ticket" to Florida).

Kai Kai: Who else gets an X? And who else gets an X? Annie, Annie gets an A. Raise your hand if you want an A+.

DJ: Come write your name (still carrying on a side conversation). Johnny, stay here again. Here, sign your name again.

Children in this room were playing at being students receiving grades—although no grades were given by their teachers—and pretending in some cases to be literate. The talk reveals knowledge of letter names and of the importance of signatures to make purchases. This language-related knowledge was embedded in dramatic play and supported by teachers who allowed time for play, provided props like blackboards and chalk, periodically and informally talked about letters and numbers with children, and made approving comments about attempts at writing or reading.

Teacher Talk

Since our main interest is children's language, we have dwelled on characteristics of children's speech across different activities. We know, however, that regardless of the activity that children engage in, there is always the possibility for important teacher-child interaction. In this section we direct our attention toward the role of teacher talk in the fostering and assessment of oral language. Like anyone engaging in conversation, teachers can have a facilitative or stifling effect on what is said. Consider what happens on a preschool playground, near the block area, when the teacher enters this scene:

Example 5–22:

Brandon: I'm Billy Good-Guy!

Tray: I'm Billy Good-Guy!

Jack: Me too!

Tray: We're trapped in the jail.

Brandon: Here comes Terry!

(Terry uses a broom handle to lift up two of the large wooden blocks.)

Tray: What's he doing?

Terry: I'm gonna save you guys.

(Teacher appears, removes broom from Terry's hand, then gives it back to him, saying:)

Teacher: Terry, take this broom to the tree house (then to other children): Boys, we're going to clean up in a minute.

(Teacher walks away with Terry. The three other boys run over to the swings.)

In this example the teacher, who is concerned with cleaning up, abruptly ends the imaginative talk that preceded. Had the school schedule allowed, she might have intervened differently, for example, by joining the conversation and asking how the broom was helping Terry rescue his friends.

Teacher talk, including questioning, is perhaps the most direct means of both facilitating language and informally assessing it. If we want to gauge what a child knows, we can ask her questions. In asking and telling, teacher and children use language in focused and goal-oriented ways, although the activity that serves as the context for talk need not be a lesson. This teacher's participation in preschoolers' play promotes language and thinking, rather than stifling it:

Example 5–23:

Teacher: I like the look of this railway, Tim, what's going on here?

Robert: I made this bit and he did that bit.

Teacher: Um, it looks great, doesn't it, Tim?

Tim: We need another coach to put on there.

Teacher: I'm afraid there aren't any more. Can you tell me about your trains? What's happening?

Tim: Mine goes round here, then Robert goes, then I go back again.

Robert: Then sometimes we smash, look! (crashes trains together)

Teacher: That looks rather dangerous. Couldn't we find a way so the trains don't crash?

Robert: Look! They've crashed again!

Tim: (appropriate noises)

Teacher: Um, well, look, Tim, how about your train going to the station?

Tim: We haven't got a station.

Teacher: Oh dear.

Robert: Come on, let's make a station.

Teacher: That's a good idea. I'll come and see it when you've done it. (The teacher returned when the station had been built.)

Tim: Get on people, get on the train, we're leaving.

Teacher: What about the signals? Is it safe for the train to leave?

Robert: Don't crash mine, Tim, I want to come to the station.

Teacher: I wonder where we could put Robert's train, while Timmy's comes along here.

Tim: You'll have to take it off.

Teacher: Well, you can't really just lift a train off the rails.

Tim: With a crane you could.

Teacher: What does a real train do, I wonder?

Tim: It goes on another line and it has one that goes like this (he points obliquely).

Robert: There's lots in the box—look! We'll make another line.

Teacher: Come on then, where can you put it?

Tim: Where? Oh, we can make a bit on here—like this, so it can run back and get off.

Robert: Look, use this bit—it'll join that one, then it can go off on that—and come back on the other one.

(Tough, 1977, pp. 162–163)

Tough presents these dialogues as illustrations of teacher intervention during constructive play that leads the children to go beyond what they have habitually done. The teacher had observed Robert and Tim over a period of time assembling the railroad and then staging a crash. She decided that some questions from her might push the boys beyond the stalemate in their play. The questions ("Couldn't we find a way so the trains don't crash?", "What about the signals?") led them to new constructions and to consider the consequences of some of their actions in expanded and realistic situations.

Tough refers to this as an "orienting strategy," one that urges the child to think about something in a particular way. In these examples the teacher asks Robert and Tim to predict and imagine what might happen to their trains. In the process the children use language to solve hypothetical problems. Tim, for example, says that a crane could lift the train off the rails, in response to a comment from the teacher. Her intervention in this activity-based interaction has changed a repetitive play sequence into a more complex one, richer in children's thinking and language. She has been able to stimulate language to solve hypothetical problems about how trains operate. Writing an anecdote to document the kinds of things Tim and Robert said in response to her intervention could be this teacher's next step.

Not all dialogues centering on children's play are as developed and orderly as Example 5–23. Casual questions from the teacher can also orient children to specific topics and activities. In this example 3-year-old Marvin is building a fence around a toy farm when Ms. Miller sits down to chat. She has just heard Marvin say that there is a picture of Animal on someone's clothing:

Example 5–24:

Ms. Miller: What does Animal play, do you know?

Marvin: He plays a Muppet (refers to "The Muppets," a television show).

Ms. Miller: Yeah, he's the drummer. He plays on the drums in the band when the Muppets play.

Marvin: Yeah.

Ms. Miller: You gonna finish your fence?

Marvin: Yeah.

. . .

Marvin: What is this called?

Ms. Miller: It's called the plow.

Marvin: A plow cuts. A plow cuts. A plow. I know what a plow do.

Ms. Miller: You're right. What does a plow cut?

Marvin: It cuts food.

Ms. Miller: Well, sometimes they have an attachment that cuts food, but this one just cuts the ground. It rolls; it cuts the ground. When it rolls, it cuts the ground all up so they can plant the seeds.

Marvin: OK.

Ms. Miller: Let me think for a minute. You go ahead and build your fence and I'll be back, OK?

Ms. Miller responds to Marvin's interest in the television Muppets and to his question about plows. She both informs and orients the child to complete his task of building a fence.

In Example 5–24 Ms. Miller asked straightforward questions of Marvin ("What does a plow cut?") that required short responses. At other times she asks more demanding questions like those of the teacher in Example 5–23 ("Couldn't we find a way so the trains won't crash?''). There are many ways of classifying teachers' questions (Bloom, 1956; Sanders, 1966) that remind us to ask a range of them. Questions can prompt single, correct answers based on recalled facts, or they can lead to a number of acceptable answers that require an evaluation or judgment from the child. Classification systems for questions are useful and important, but most teachers may lack the time to record and analyze their questions according to six or more types (for example, Bloom's Knowledge, Comprehension, Application, Analysis, Synthesis, and Evaluation categories). Instead teachers might consider asking two broad kinds of questions as they teach: high-level, so that children talk about *how* things happen or work, *why* they happen, and *what their opinion is* about them, as well as the lower level—*who* did *what* to *whom*.[1]

Toward the There-and-Then

In Examples 5–23 and 5–24, the children's activity provided the basis, or scaffolding, for talk. The teacher's talk encouraged extensions or continuation of the constructive activities. Another major role the teacher performs is orienting the topic of children's language and thinking away from the here-and-now of concrete activity and toward the there-and-then of things or events that are not present. Although curricula for the preschool and primary grade child are often based on things she can see and manipulate, we know that an eventual goal of schooling is a child who can think and talk about the present, past, and future. Therefore, we enable children to use language in contextualized ways, in situations that are present and natural, with things to perceive and act upon, at the same time that we prepare them to reflect on and talk about past experiences and hypothesize about the future. The teacher in Example 5–23 helped Tim and Robert hypothesize when she asked them, for instance, to imagine what real trains would do to avoid accidents. In this section, we discuss two other activities that can orient children toward the there-and-then—story time and interviews.

Story time

Story time can serve as a bridge to the there-and-then, since it often leads to questions and responses that refer to past events in stories or in

---

[1]We are grateful to Dr. Alberta M. Castaneda of the Department of Curriculum and Instruction, The University of Texas at Austin, for reminding us of this practical distinction.

the children's lives. In the next example Ms. Miller has read a story about an Indian boy and is now talking about it with her 4- and 5-year-olds:

Example 5–25:

Ms. Miller: And his mother and his baby sister and his grandmother. ( ) bows and shield made of buffalo skin.

Didi: Where's his grandfather?

Ms. Miller: Maybe his grandfather has gone to hunt the buffalo.

Didi: Maybe his grandfather died.

Ms. Miller: It could be his grandfather died. When they get old, they do. Everybody dies when they get old.

Didi: But not me! I'm never gonna die!

Bart: Yes, you are—sometime.

(Ms. Miller returns to talking about the story. Linda and Didi have a conversation of their own.)

. . .

(A little later):

Linda: Teacher, Didi says she's never gonna die, and she is when she gets old.

Bart (to Didi): You're gonna die.

Ms. Miller: Linda, Didi and her mother have talked about that a lot at home. We'll let them talk about it.

The content of a story has prompted Didi to ask about an absent character, the grandfather. Her comment about the grandfather's possible death initiates a short argument among the children. Ms. Miller later explained to the first author, who had been observing, that Didi's grandfather had in fact died and that Didi and her mother talked about that at home. The children demonstrate that they can make connections between story content and past experiences in their own lives and that they can, in their own way, talk about an unknown phenomenon like death in terms of the future (''when she gets old'').

Many preschool and primary grade teachers plan additional time for children to tell stories about their own artwork. Ms. Garza, for example, wrote 5-year-old Everett's and 5½-year-old Lacey's narrations on their pictures:

Example 5–26: Everett has just drawn with crayons six leggy dinosaurs, a red, black, and purple man, and a time machine.

The dinosaur was chasing him. That dinosaur ate him. They were fighting. See them two, they were fighting again. That dinosaur wanted to be the strongest dinosaur. The man was in the quicksand. The dinosaur smashed the time machine.

Everett's story closely matches and refers to the content of his drawing (''See them two''). Yet the here-and-now that he has drawn is based on stories Everett either remembers from the past or that he is himself inventing; the there-and-then he narrates may dwell in his imagination.

Lacey's story is probably an account of real events from her past:

Example 5–27: With felt markers Lacey has drawn pink and purple flowers, a many-legged purple bug, grass, and rain.

My garden has those kind of flowers. This is when the storm came down yesterday. This little bug was inside my grass and I didn't know until my daddy was digging up some weeds. Then I put it in a jar and let it stay home and get cozy in a jar with a blanket from my dolls that was very dirty.

Lacey too refers to elements of her drawing (''those kind of flowers,'' ''This little bug . . .''). She conveys a greater sense of how events are sequenced through language than Everett when she says, ''when the storm came down yesterday,'' ''I didn't know until my daddy was digging up some weeds,'' and ''Then I put it in a jar. . . .'' For a way of systematically documenting such aspects of children's stories, see Figure 5–4.

When teachers write down children's sketchy or elaborate descriptions and narrations, as Ms. Garza did, they establish sequences permanently. The written record shows children that what they do in the here-and-now can be talked and read about in the there-and-then. Story or study times prompt sequenced language from children not only about fantasies and past events, but also about how things are done. Earlier, Kate—in Example 5–12—told how to make a fire (''they get some sticks and build and make a fireplace . . .''), in response to Ms. Miller's question. Teachers might write these responses on large, easy-to-see charts, much as they record recipes for cooking or children's reactions to field trips. A more structured way of asking children what they know, the interview, is considered next.

Interviews

A context that allows the teacher to assess what children can say about the past, the future, or how things are done is the one-to-one conversation or interview. Much has been written about how young children are at a disadvantage in such interview situations. Children

Teacher	L. Garza					
		Language		Structure		
Date	Child	Fluent	Varied Vocabulary	Detailed	Sequenced	Comments
11/9/82	Lacey S.	✓	✓ suddenly	+	–	L's pictures may not always be detailed, but her stories are.
12/5/82	"	+	✓ (Here the teacher may want to write examples: dinosaur, elevator, etc., or the child's utterances, as in examples 5-26 and 5-27.)	+	+	Another example of L's interest in bugs.

+ = very or most
✓ = moderately
– = seldom or never

Figure 5—4 Story/Interview Record and Checklist, Prairie Preschool who are unfamiliar with either the testing situation or the interviewer in fact may show very little of their linguistic competence. The teacher's advantage is that she is not a stranger to the child and, although she is in the position of authority, she is a familiar figure. What can the teacher learn in interviews that she cannot learn through spontaneous talk or eavesdropping? First, one can learn about things that are typically not talked about in spontaneous conversation or in lessons. Second, one can briefly evaluate what an individual has learned about a particular subject, whether it was learned on a field trip or in a social studies lesson. Third, the interview—often unplanned and casual—allows teachers to talk with normally quiet children, who may be willing to talk to the teacher individually but is withdrawn in groups.

French and Nelson (1982) suggest that interviews can also reveal specific aspects of young children's language. They found that 3- to 10-year-olds readily answer questions about routine events (technically termed scripts) in their lives, for example, having a fire drill, having lunch at day care, having a birthday party, and going grocery shopping. As they respond to questions like, "What happens at a birthday party?" children distinguish between the article *a,* and the article *the.* (The use of *the* shows that they view certain roles as general; many individuals might fill the role of *the* waiter or *the* teacher. *A* waiter, in contrast, suggests a specific person or event.) Another syntactic feature that appeared in many children's responses was the use of the "timeless" present, which need not actually refer to present, past, or future. The use of *walk, make, put,* and so on, in the following example illustrates this timelessness:

Example 5–28:

> Interviewer: Can you tell me what you do when you have a fire drill at school?
>
> Child (4 years; 2 months): You walk fast but you can't put your coats on 'cause you need to hurry.
>
> . . .
>
> Interviewer: (Asking about how to make cookies.)
>
> Child (5 years; 5 months): When you make cookies, well ya, um, make the dough, and you, cut 'em and put decorations on. And then put 'em in the oven, and then when they come out, you could eat 'em.

> (French & Nelson, 1982, p. 2)

French and Nelson also noted that older subjects' responses were much more elaborate than younger ones'. Teachers may, therefore, want to interview their children at different times of the year to assess growth in the ability to remember, sequence, and verbalize routines.

Interviews can, of course, be about things other than routines and may begin casually, sometimes because a child initiates a conversation. In the following exchange, 5-year-old Paul asks his teacher about her family:

Example 5–29:

> Paul: Do you have a husband?
>
> Ms. Tano: No, I don't.
>
> Paul: Do you have a daddy?
>
> Ms. Tano: Yes, and I have a mother, too.
>
> Paul: Where do you live?
>
> Ms. Tano: Well, I don't live with my mother and father. I live close to this school. Where do you live?
>
> Paul: Seca Street.

Ms. Tano guessed that Paul had seen her talking with a male teacher from another classroom and wondered if he were her husband. She continued to ask Paul about his family and learned that he had two older brothers. By building on this child-initiated interview, Ms. Tano discovered something about Paul's idea that people must be members of families and about his own family. What struck her too was the interest in her that he was able to express by means of his questions. She noted this interest later when she wrote down the content of the interview.

Whatever the topic of an interview, you may want to document short segments of it as in Examples 5–28 and 5–29, to keep a systematic record of what is learned. You can then compare length and complexity of utterances and the completeness of responses from one interview to the next. Or you may choose to use a form like that in Figure 5–4 when children's talk becomes story-like or elaborate.

Children talk about things not present well before they become story-tellers. A 2-year-old, for example, might say, "Allgone doggie." During the preschool years, however, their abilities to talk about the past and future increase noticeably. As children reach their fifth birthday, we view them as speakers who are beginning to communicate at times without the scaffolding of objects or activities. Before moving to the kindergarten context, where the teacher more formally orients children toward the there-and-then, we consider second language learners.

These are people who may be able to talk about past, present, and future in one language but are just learning how to refer to the here-and-now in a second language.

Second Language Acquisition: Activity and People as Scaffolding

Example 5–30:

Mari: Hablamos en inglés. Hablamos en inglés. [Let's speak in English. Let's speak in English.]

Diana: (A little later) I'm gonna call you—I'm gonna friends is you—(talking to toy telephone).

Adelita: I'm friends.

Diana: I already told you. I'm gonna call you at H.E.B. (a supermarket). One, two, eight, nine (dialing the toy telephone).

Adelita: I'm gonna sit me down, OK?

Diana: OK. Don't cry. You promise to me.

Diana (later to Adelita): Ouch, ouch, ouch, ouch. Ouch. Dije que te salieras, Adelita. ¿ Sabes qué quiere decir *ouch*? Que te salgas. [Ouch. I told you to get out, Adelita. Do you know what *ouch* means? To get out.]

Five-year-old Spanish speakers, Diana and Adelita, readily follow the suggestion of their friend Mari and begin to speak English as they engage in dramatic play. After Diana's last turn in the example, Adelita loudly and confidently uses gibberish, perhaps a playful version of English or her notion of a foreign language. The initiator Mari never follows her own suggestion. This fascinating example provided the first evidence for the first author-observer that Adelita and Diana could speak English. It is clearly playful practice—but with possible serious, positive consequences. The children demonstrate behaviors that reflect the general processes of first and second language acquisition in naturalistic, nonlesson settings. Like first and second language learners Diana depends on a familiar activity as the scaffolding for her attempts at English. The telephone provides opportunities to recite numbers, and the structure of a pretend phone conversation allows her to speak authoritatively, take her turn, pause, and suffer no bad consequences if the "listener" fails to understand her.

Also like beginning language learners Diana and Adelita make the most of whatever they know (Fillmore, 1976). Although the dialogue is not always coherent, there are clear messages conveyed, sometimes in adult-like English (as in "I already told you"). Both girls seem to be tapping their memories for whatever phrases or sentences they can verbalize to keep up the flow of talk. Even Diana's "ouch," which she nicely translates into Spanish, serves to prolong the interaction.

Episodes of these girls' speaking English occurred twice in a period of several weeks. These children, then, will not soon learn English through their play alone. If children have competence in their first language by the time they are preschoolers, how can their teachers foster the acquisition of a second language and adequately assess it? In this section we suggest the use of procedures and checklists presented earlier to help in the fostering and assessing of what children say and do as novices in the complex processes of second language acquisition.

As we use the term, *second language acquisition* refers to learning a language other than the one a child has learned or begun to learn at home. Since English is used in most public schools in the United States, second language acquisition in the school context usually means learning English as a second language. An exceptional context is that of bilingual programs. Bilingual programs for non-English speakers vary with respect to when children begin to learn English. In some cases, children experience a transition period, during which there is use of the home language in the classroom before English is introduced. In addition to these transitional programs, there are maintenance programs, whose goal is to maintain the child's use of the home language, at least for a few years; at the same time lessons are taught in English as well. Such programs are often difficult to staff with bilingual teachers, possibly costly, and not popular. Many parents, like parents whose children use nonstandard dialects, expect schools to educate their children in standard English and are willing to forego what is viewed as the luxury of maintaining the home language in school.

With this prevailing attitude and policy in mind, in the suggestions that follow we address readers in a situation typical of most sections of this country: a monolingual English-speaking teacher or teachers with a classroom that is not officially called "bilingual." The teachers may have no formal training in teaching English as a second language. (Depending on where you live, this may or may not be typical.)

Fostering a second language

Fostering language in these typical classrooms depends primarily on the teacher's ongoing program, ideally one with varied activities—like the classrooms introduced earlier in this chapter. What may be helpful when non-English speakers enter the classroom is a consideration of these assumptions and guidelines regarding the second language learner:

1. If the child is of preschool age, she is most likely a beginning speaker of one language. The child, then, is becoming a bilingual; she does not come to the classroom an "alingual," with no language.

2. Regardless of age, a child may not use her first language in the classroom, and she may spend a long time being silent (in rare cases, months). She should not be judged as unintelligent or "learning disabled" because of her silence. A teacher's concern about disability might be justified if the child's parents express concern about an inability to speak her first language.

3. In many ways second language learners are like first language learners. Both need to have activities available that interest and engage them. Perhaps what teachers become most aware of is the importance of visible scaffolding, that is, objects that are easily labelled and talked about. Like the first language learner, the child becoming bilingual uses what she already knows about the world, as well as clues from the observable context to learn new words and concepts. For the second language learner the context becomes more crucial, for she needs clues that the monolingual no longer needs.

4. Both first and second language learners need not only the scaffolding of objects and activities but also that of people to learn from. The teacher will want to treat the second language learner "like everyone else" but will probably—unconsciously—converse with her more often than with other preschoolers. The teacher will also watch for developing friendships. If the child is at ease or communicates well with particular children, small group activities might be organized accordingly.[2]

5. At times the second language learner is in a classroom with others who speak her first language. Speakers of that same language can ease or slow the transition to English. Forbidding the use of the first language is indefensible, but teachers might structure small groups so that whenever possible the second language

---

[2]For a brief overview of research on bilingualism and second language learning and guidelines for teaching English as a second language in early childhood, see Saville-Troike (1982).

learner needs to use English to communicate. Like adults, a child is most apt to use a second language when her listeners understand and use only that language. Monolingual speakers of the second language, then, provide extremely valuable scaffolding for the second language learner.

6. Also in classrooms with several children who speak the same home language, children may alternate, or code-switch, between the first and second languages. This is likely to occur in states like California, New York, and Texas, which have large Spanish-speaking populations. (Nonstandard dialect speakers may also code-switch into standard English.) In some cases code-switching acts as a bridge to the use of English. In other cases language specialists view it as a long-standing practice that serves important social purposes (Durán, 1981). As such, teachers will not want to discourage code-switching when bilingual children speak to each other.

Individual second language learners will respond differently to teachers' attempts to encourage interaction and talk. As Fillmore and Ervin-Tripp (1979) have suggested, in second language acquisition the child's social style and personality can have complex effects on how quickly the child learns the language. Assessing the progress of two individuals with their unique styles of acquiring English is our next topic.

Assessing progress in the second language

Hiroshi is a Japanese child with a buoyant and outgoing personality. His preschool teacher Ms. Ranger recalls that, speaking almost no English, he could happily play with anyone in his class within 3 weeks of joining the group. His parents speak Japanese at home though he hears English when his father reads to him occasionally and when the family watch television. Hiroshi's 6-year-old brother attends kindergarten, where he too may be learning English as a second language. Ms. Ranger knows no Japanese but takes a special interest in Hiroshi's language and documents many of his utterances for the year that he is in her class of 4-year-olds. After Hiroshi has been in school for 6 weeks, Ms. Ranger and he have this brief exchange:

Example 5–31: Children are sitting at the snack table, eating peanuts.

Ms. Ranger: Before—

Hiroshi: *Be-fore* (stresses both syllables)

(*Later:*)

Hiroshi: Thank yuh! (Said to parent, giving him a snack.) Peanut! Peanut![3]

Since his first day at school, Hiroshi has used politeness routines like "thank you" and "bye." Though he says little, he seems attentive to what others say and enthusiastically labels things that he sees and handles.

After 6 months in the nursery school, Hiroshi has begun to count. He demonstrates this as he works with play-dough, which he has put on two plastic lids at the art table:

Example 5–32:

Hiroshi: Teacher! One! Two! See?

Ms. Ranger: What?

Hiroshi: One, two.

Ms. Ranger: One.

Hiroshi: Two.

Ms. Ranger: Two. Two things of play-dough.

Again Hiroshi refers to what he can manipulate and see and, in this instance, count. The teacher, like an adult with a beginning first language learner, appropriately elaborates his utterances.

After almost 7 months in the classroom Hiroshi and his friend, Travis, play a card game in which children match the card showing an animal with the card showing the food that animal eats.

Example 5–33:

Hiroshi: Banana. (Holds up gorilla and banana cards.)

Travis: Who eats cheese?

Hiroshi: Cheese?

Travis: Doggies eat dog food.

Hiroshi: Carrot? (Shows picture)

Travis: Who eats carrots? (Finds rabbit)

Hiroshi: This—and this? (Shows two cards)

Travis: Yeah.

---

[3]We are grateful to Barbara Anderson for these examples, based on data from her dissertation.

Hiroshi: Yeah. Yeah.

Travis: Put it right here. A rabbit eats carrots. A rabbit eats carrots.

Hiroshi: Orange?

Travis: Rabbits eat carrots. I'll show you. Put it like this.

Hiroshi: A rabbit? (Holds up two pictures)

Travis: (Nods)

Hiroshi: What's this?

Travis: Where is the animal for this? (Holds up corn.) Here's the doggie.

Hiroshi: Here's the doggie. Doggie!

Travis: Yeah, the doggie takes this one.

Hiroshi: Teacher (to teacher as she passes center).

Ms. Ranger: What you doin'? Putting them together? What's that?

Travis: Pussy cat.

Hiroshi: Pussy cat.

Ms. Ranger: And the pussy cat eats what?

Hiroshi: Milk.

Ms. Ranger: Milk. All right. And the monkey eats?

Hiroshi: Banana.

This is an excellent example of how the structure of an activity, here a card game, provides a scaffolding (Ervin-Tripp, 1982) for an orderly dialogue between a second language and a native speaker. The question-answer format allows Hiroshi to ask short questions ("A rabbit?", "What is this?") and make short replies ("Here's the doggie," "Pussy cat"). In an anecdote, the teacher notes later that Hiroshi is using more advanced forms (*what's, here's*) and that Hiroshi is quick to answer his friend's questions. The lesson-like quality of the dialogue also impresses her, and she writes a reminder on the anecdote to make more card games available to the children.

As months go by Hiroshi has become a more able speaker of English though he still formulates only short utterances. The kind of activity that he engages in also prompts him to be more or less verbal. Note the minimal responses he makes in this conversation about a wordless book:

Example 5–34:

Adult: Let's see what she does in the next picture. What's she doing? In that picture?

Hiroshi: Jo is (?) Down.

Adult: The cat is down?

Hiroshi: Yeah.

Adult: Where did the cat go?

Hiroshi: (He points)

Adult: Uh, huh. Where is that? By the (pause). What is that? Remember what that's called?

Hiroshi: Tree.

Adult: Uh, huh. He's by the tree. (She turns page.) What's that lady doing?

Hiroshi: St-pop (?)

Adult: Huh?

Hiroshi: Stop.

Adult: They've stopped.

Hiroshi: Yeah, he stop.

Adult: The policeman is telling the boy to uh, stop.

Although this exchange occurs a month after Example 5–33, Hiroshi's speech does not reflect the development that his teacher knows has occurred during that time. She guesses that the situation was one that might have led Hiroshi to be less verbal than usual. The adult talking about the book with him is a visitor to the classroom and is, therefore, unfamiliar to Hiroshi. The book provides some scaffolding or predictable structure for Hiroshi to respond to, but a more familiar person may have fostered more talk.

The support a second language learner receives from activities is considerable, but like the language of all speakers, his language will vary from setting to setting. The teacher is an additional valuable source of support, just as she is for beginning first language learners. Hugo, the other second language learner we consider, demonstrates the importance of activities and receptive people as effectively as Hiroshi did.

Hugo was 3 years, 4 months old at the time the first author began to observe him in the half-day parent cooperative nursery school that he attended. According to his father, Hugo began to speak Spanish in his native country of Honduras at the age of 2 and is talkative at home, where he speaks Spanish with both parents. His father would like Hugo to speak more English but doesn't want to force him; his progress in English seems to him to be satisfactory. Hugo's nursery school teacher, Maureen, recalled that for about 3 months at the beginning of the school year, he said virtually nothing, but seemed to understand whatever was said in English. Ellen, his teacher when he was a 2-year-old in the same school, said he was responsive and comprehended English though when he spoke, he spoke Spanish. At the end of his time in Ellen's room, Hugo was beginning to use routine phrases like "Oh, gee." The nature of his progress in a 3-month span in Maureen's classroom is reflected in a number of examples.

Hugo was observed on his first day back at school, following a 3-week break. During that time his parents had Spanish-speaking visitors. His interactions could be summarized in an anecdote, as follows:

Example 5–35:

January 27: Hugo came back today after 3 weeks' absence. He spent a lot of time with 4-year-old bilingual Ana, who spoke to him in Spanish. They sat at the art table and seemed to be talking about the magic markers and puzzles they were using. When he wasn't with Ana, he didn't say anything. Mostly he watched what was going on and was especially watchful of Maureen. Once he took her hand but said nothing. (She seemed interested in encouraging him to be independent.)

About 4 weeks later, Hugo still spends much of his time watching others, but he is more vocal.

Example 5–36:

Hugo (to girl): This? (Sounds like "Dis.") This? Is this? Is this? (Girl is oblivious to Hugo.)

(and later the same morning:)

Hugo: Eight, eight, eight, eight. (Pointing to a picture of an elephant in a book for counting from one to ten.)

Parent helper: That's *one* elephant, isn't it? (There's one elephant in the picture.)

Parent helper: (to Hugo and two other children) OK, let's make something out of the blocks. Let's put two blocks together like this. Let's put two like this. Let's put two like this, OK? OK, put one down here. Look what we made—a little house.

Hugo: See? (Points to blocks and repeats "See?" about ten times.) Boop boop. (Pushes one block along the floor; makes the noise of a train?)

In this example both adult—a father volunteering at the parent co-op—and Hugo use much repetition as they sit in the block area. Hugo first focuses on a book, then engages in block play with the father, his son, and a Chinese-speaking boy. (The teacher had asked the father to spend some time with these three children.)

The importance of concrete activity and well-defined goals for maintaining conversation is also shown in this exchange between an English-speaking substitute teacher and Hugo as they work on a puzzle together:

Example 5–37:

Hugo: What color that is? (Sounds like "wha' color tha' is.")

Teacher: Oh, where are they going to fit? How would it fit around this corner here?

Hugo: Blue. ("Bu.")

Teacher: Blue. Right!

Hugo: This. (Puts another piece in the puzzle and finishes it. He then watches the teacher talking with a girl who's also working on a puzzle.)

Hugo (to teacher): This. This. (Takes another puzzle off the shelf.) This here. This here. This? (All said as he tries to complete the puzzle.)

Teacher: Carrot.

Hugo: This?

Teacher: Bunny, a rabbit.

Hugo: This is here. This is this. (Continues working on puzzle.)

This conversation reminds us of Hiroshi's exchange with his friend Travis as they played a card game. Hugo, like Hiroshi, depends on his partner to provide information, and the nature of the activity provides the scaffolding for a question-answer sequence. We are also reminded of interactions between parents and children as they learn their first language during book-reading and other routines.

Three months after the observer's first visit, she recorded in long-hand the information in Figure 5–5, an observation sheet like the one introduced in Figure 4–2. The constant reference to what Hugo is doing recurs, as does the one-to-one (Hugo-to-adult) pattern of interaction. Some of his utterances, however, are longer and more sophisticated than earlier ones ("I want do this one," "I want some paper," "I finished with that.") A week later during Genishi's final observation, she audiotaped some talk; a segment is transcribed on an Observation Record sheet shown in Figure 5–6. The tape-recorder was useful because Hugo's language was becoming more frequent and complex. There were details to listen for, as noted in the "Forms" column, which had been absent before. In a 3-month period Hugo has expanded his utterances from one- and two-word utterances to four or more words per utterance, including grammatical endings such as *-ed* and *-s*.

Date 4-27-83			
Observer's name Genishi			
Children Participating	Who Speaks to | Whom	Example 5-38 Speech Fragment	Nonverbal Behaviors
Hugo with aide	Hugo (H) | Aide (A)	Here.	H. brings puzzle over to aide.
"	" | "	I want it.	Refers to puzzle?
	A | H	What's this?	Points to puzzle piece.
	H | A	The sun.	
	A | H	Sun.	
	H | A	Another one.	Goes over to get something else from shelf
	" | "	I want do this one.	Aide has started to walk away, but comes back.
	" | "	See, I put it! I put it here. " " " "	Put sounds like "pu."
	" | "	I put it. I do it . . .	(Few minutes pass.)
	H | A	I want some paper. There. (There sounds like "dere.")	Takes piece of paper. Uses glue and makes ellipse. Goes around again
	H | Maureen (M)	See? Do round.	
	M | H	Go around and around and around.	Said as H. puts glue on paper.
	" | "	Look, Huguito, there's glitter inside if that glue. See the glitter?	
	H | M	Yeah.	
	" | "	I finished with that.	
	M | H	Oh, you're finished with that one?	
	H | M	What happened? . . .	(a little later)
	H | A	Go round and round. See? Go round and round.	

Figure 5–5 Classroom Observation

Both 4-year-old Hiroshi and 3-year-old Hugo have had the advantage of teachers who believe, first, that second language learners cannot be pushed to speak and, second, that language develops best in conversations about interesting activities. Both boys initially spoke very little English for several months in their preschools. But when they began to

```
                        OBSERVATION RECORD              Page  4  of  7
                        University Parent Co-op

Observer   Genishi        Date    5-5-83        Activity  Book "reading"
                                                          Playing store.

                   Example 5-39
Speaker            What's said                   Functions      Forms

Hugo (to     Here's your book.  Here is your book.  Informative   Is contracted
Mary)        You have two books.                     Regulatory?   Is used in
                                                                   full
                                                                   Plural ending

Hugo (to     Dinosaur.  Dinosaur.                    Informative
self)

Hugo (to     What's that book?  (Refers to book      Heuristic      Is contracted
teacher)     in her hand.)

                 (Later:)
Hugo (to     Two dollars.  (Plays with toy cash      Informative   Plural ending
boy)         register.)  Here.  (As if to say,       Regulatory
             "Take this.")

Teacher      I don't have any money.                 Informative
(to H.)

Hugo (to     I have dollars.                         Informative   Plural ending
T.)          Three dollars!  (says two more times.)      "             "

Teacher      Thank you.                               Interactional

Hugo         Thank you.  (Sounds like "sank you.")       "          S sound
                                                                     substitutes
                                                                     for TH.

Comments:
    The last couple of visits, I've noticed more adult-like forms.  Where S
    sounds used to be left out, Hugo now uses them ("Here's your book.").
```

Figure 5–6 Observation Record, University Parent Co-op

speak, what the boys saw and did indeed provided the scaffolding for learning the second language. Both were resourceful and confident enough to capitalize on monolingual English speakers' abilities to maintain conversations with them. In Hiroshi's case peers were often his partners; Hugo appeared to rely more on the support of adults. With two different styles of interacting and learning language, without formal instruction they are becoming young bilinguals.

Summary

The language of the active, speaking child in the context of the preschool was the subject of this chapter. The sociolinguistic premise that the social situation strongly affects communicative behavior was supported by examples of children engaging in a range of activities. We used anecdotes, transcribed segments of audiotapes, a chart for recording language functions and forms, and a checklist for stories and interviews to show in how many ways children from 3 to 5 years demonstrate their communicative competence. Activities, the physical factors of thoughtful classroom arrangement and varied materials, and the human support of adults and peers all provided the scaffolding for children's thinking and talk. Dramatic play was highlighted as a showcase for especially rich communication.

Through the selection of activities presented, we favored the preschool program that allows for children to participate in many activities, from swinging on a tire on the playground to contributing to a language experience chart. Opportunities for children to choose what they did and direct their play during an extended "center time" were characteristic of programs that encouraged much child-to-child and teacher-to-child talk. Teacher-led times were focused and at times highly goal-oriented but did not dominate the curriculum. We referred to the foundations of reading and writing as they were routinely included in daily activities, reflecting our support for an informal—not academic or highly structured—approach to literacy.

Since language entered naturally into most activities, the curriculum was integrated, like the child's use of language in which function and form were unified. By the age of 4 or 5, forms were developing well, so that adults focused on offering opportunities for expressing many functions. When children used language in settings that engaged them, forms usually took care of themselves. Both cognitive and social aspects of language were reflected in the functions; children sought and presented information while they maintained friendships and established their own importance. We saw the fusing of these aspects in looking at the functions and forms of 3- and 5-year-olds, as we followed them, across many activity settings, on one or two days in their preschools. We also observed a 3- and 4-year-old over a period of months as they began to learn English as a second language. We saw, then, language develop through activity and social interaction in children whose linguistic energies were directed primarily toward oral expression.

Some of the children that we introduced began to get meaning from print as they recognized friends' names or wrote their own. In the next chapter we continue the themes of diverse activities and integrated curriculum, at the same time that our emphasis shifts to the child in transition from being an oral language specialist to becoming an explorer of print. The teacher begins to guide the child more directly toward the there-and-then, toward using language in settings with less activity-based and human support. The broader area of language arts, which includes spoken and written forms and functions, becomes more prominent as we focus on children in kindergarten.

Suggested Readings

Cazden, C. B. Evaluation of learning in preschool education: Early language development. In B. S. Bloom, J. T. Hastings, & G. F. Madaus (Eds.), *Handbook on formative and summative evaluation of student learning*. New York: McGraw-Hill, 1971. A classic reference to consult for a comprehensive and balanced discussion of evaluating preschoolers' language. In considering well-known early childhood programs of the 1960s the author groups programs according to their goals and the degree to which teachers set the structure of children's activities. She includes informal (gamelike), experimental, and standardized means of program assessment.

Chukovsky, K. *From two to five*. (Trans. and ed. by M. Morton). Berkeley: University of California Press, 1968. A unique collection of children's speech and poetry and an effective ''short course'' in language appreciation. The book, written by a Russian poet, also appealingly presents insights into preschoolers' thinking and language.

Fleming, B. M., Hamilton, D. S., & Hicks, J. A. D. *Resources for creative teaching in early childhood education*. New York: Harcourt, Brace, Jovanovich, 1977. A comprehensive and useful collection of activities, many of which foster preschool children's language.

Goodwin, W. L., & Driscoll, L. A. *Handbook for measurement and evaluation in early childhood education*. San Francisco: Jossey-Bass, 1980. Chapter 6, called ''Cognitive measures: Developmental and handicapped screening surveys, language and bilingual tests, and creativity tests,'' presents a critical review of recent assessment measures, with general information about such characteristics as scoring, reliability, and validity.

Tough, J. *Talking and learning: A guide to fostering communication skills in nursery and infant schools*. London: Ward Lock Educational, 1977. This book, not widely available in the United States, is based on an extensive study of English nursery and primary schools, involving researchers and 1500 teachers. It provides a comprehensive framework and guidance for assessing and fostering children's language through careful analysis of examples of teachers' and children's classroom talk. Teacher strategies in dialogue, learning a second language, foundations of literacy and mathematics, and the teacher's role in children's play are major topics.

Appendix A

Because we emphasize assessing language in informal ways, we have said little about tests. A nonstandardized test that can be both revealing of what children know and interesting for child and tester is one created by Berko (1958), mentioned in Chapter 2. It can be administered in 15 to 30 minutes to individual children between 4 and 8 years to discover what they know about forming certain kinds of English words (for example, plural, past tense, possessive). From our perspective, the point of the test is to see *how* the children respond, that is, what their own rules are, and not just to see how many items they answer in adult-like ways. (A list of adults' responses follows the test.) Since children are expected to respond by adding appropriate endings to nonsense, or made-up words, we know that they are not imitating what others have said before. We can infer that they know the rules for such things as plural or past formation. By giving the test, you can supplement what you learn about children's language through informal observation and documentation. You are both assessing and appreciating what children can do.

Students in our classes have made their own materials (cards with pictures of things mentioned in the test items), so that they could give the test as part of a class project. They have noted that the test is enjoyable for themselves and the children they test. Remember that this is a test of *spoken,* not written, language. If children seem unsure of how to respond, you might give them one or two practice items, using real words, such as *cat,* instead of *wug,* in item 1 below. As in any testing situation, you should stop if the child is uncomfortable or clearly unable to respond to the questions. If you use this test to assess children for instructional purposes, please refer to the full article by Berko for further information and guidance about interpreting your results.

1. Plural. One bird-like animal, then two. "This is a wug. Now there is another one. There are two of them. There are two _____."

(Adult says:
  This is a wug.)

(Adult says:
Now there is another one.
There are two of them.
There are two ____ .)

2. Plural. One bird, then two. "This is a gutch. Now there is another one. There are two of them. There are two _____."

3. Past tense. Man with a steaming pitcher on his head. "This man is a man who knows how to spow. He is spowing. He did

the same thing yesterday. What did he do yesterday? Yesterday
he _____."

4. Plural. One animal, then two. "This is a kazh. Now there is
another one. There are two of them. There are two _____."

5. Past tense. Man swinging an object. "This is a man who knows
how to rick. He is ricking. He did the same thing yesterday.
What did he do yesterday? Yesterday he _____."

6. Diminutive and compounded or derived word. One animal,
then a miniscule animal. "This is a wug. This is a very tiny
wug. [a.] What would you call a very tiny wug? This wug lives
in a house. [b.] What would you call a house that a wug lives
in?"

7. Plural. One animal, then two. "This is a tor. Now there is
another one. There are two of them. There are two _____."

8. Derived adjective. Dog covered with irregular green spots.
"This is a dog with quirks on him. He is all covered with
quirks. What kind of dog is he? He is a _____ dog."

9. Plural. One flower, then two. "This is a lun. Now there is
another one. There are two of them. There are two _____."

10. Plural. One animal, then two. "This is a niz. Now there is
another one. There are two of them. There are two _____."

11. Past tense. Man doing calisthenics. "This is a man who knows
how to mot. He is motting. He did the same thing yesterday.
What did he do yesterday? Yesterday he _____."

12. Plural. One bird, then two. "This is a cra. Now there is another
one. There are two of them. There are two _____."

13. Plural. One animal, then two. "This is a tass. Now there is
another one. There are two of them. There are two _____."

14. Past tense. Man dangling an object on a string. "This is a man
who knows how to bod. He is bodding. He did the same thing
yesterday. What did he do yesterday? Yesterday he _____."

15. Third person singular. Man shaking an object. "This is a man
who knows how to naz. He is nazzing. He does it every day.
Every day he _____."

16. Plural. One insect, then two. "This is a heaf. Now there is
another one. There are two of them. There are two _____."

17. Plural. One glass, then two. "This is a glass. Now there is
another one. There are two of them. There are two _____."

18. Past tense. Man exercising. "This is a man who knows how to gling. He is glinging. He did the same thing yesterday. What did he do yesterday? Yesterday he _____."

19. Third person singular. Man holding an object. "This is a man who knows how to loodge. He is loodging. He does it every day. Every day he _____."

20. Past tense. Man standing on the ceiling. "This is a man who knows how to bing. He is binging. He did the same thing yesterday. What did he do yesterday? Yesterday he _____."

21. Singular and plural possessive. One animal wearing a hat, then two wearing hats. "This is a niz who owns a hat. Whose hat is it? It is the _____ hat. Now there are two nizzes. They both own hats. Whose hats are they? They are the _____ hats."

22. Past tense. A bell. "This is a bell that can ring. It is ringing. It did the same thing yesterday. What did it do yesterday? Yesterday it _____."

23. Singular and plural possessive. One animal wearing a hat, then two. "This is a wug who owns a hat. Whose hat is it? [a.] It is the _____ hat. Now there are two wugs. They both own hats. Whose hats are they? [b.] They are the _____ hats."

24. Comparative and superlative of the adjective. A dog with a few spots, one with several, and one with a great number. "This dog has quirks on him. This dog has more quirks on him. And this dog has even more quirks on him. This dog is quirky. [a.] This dog is _____. [b.] And this dog is the _____."

25. Progressive and derived agentive or compound. Man balancing a ball on his nose. "This is a man who knows how to zib. What is he doing? [a.] He is _____. [b.] What would you call a man whose job is to zib?"

26. Past tense. An ice cube, then a puddle of water. "This is an ice cube. Ice melts. It is melting. Now it is all gone. What happened to it? It _____."

27. Singular and plural possessive. One animal wearing a hat, then two. "This is a bik who owns a hat. Whose hat is it? [a.] It is the _____ hat. Now there are two biks. They both own hats. Whose hats are they? [b.] They are the _____ hats."

28. Compound words. The child was asked why he thought the following were so named. (No pictures were used for these items.)

a. afternoon
b. airplane
c. birthday
d. breakfast
e. blackboard
f. fireplace
g. football

h. handkerchief
i. holiday
j. merry-go-round
k. newspaper
l. sunshine
m. Thanksgiving
n. Friday
(Berko, 1958, pp. 156–157)

Adult responses:

1. wugs
2. gutches
3. spowed
4. kazhes
5. ricked
6. (a) wuglet, little wug, wuggie
   wuggette, wugling
   (b) wughouse, wuggery,
   wugshouse, wughut.
7. tors
8. quirky
9. luns
10. nizzes
11. motted
12. cras
13. tasses
14. bodded

15. nazzes
16. heaf, heaves
17. glasses
18. glinged, glang
19. loodges
20. binged, bang
21. nizzes'
22. rang
23. (a) wug's; (b) wugs'
24. (a) quirkier; (b) quirkiest
25. (a)zibbing; (b) zibber
26. melted
27. (a) bik's; (b) biks'
28. varied responses
(Berko, 1958, pp.
159–163)

Appendix B

A modified and translated version of the Berko test has been created in Spanish (Kernan & Blount, 1966) and tested in Mexico. The authors found a few practice items, using real Spanish words, helpful for each child. Adult responses to the questions follow the test. Again, we suggest that the test is most useful for discovering children's internalized rules for specific word formations. If you use the test for instructional purposes with bilingual children and second language learners, it should be used in conjunction with your informal observations and you should consult Kernan and Blount's article for further information.

The following is the complete test, in the order in which the items were presented, with the omission of the examples. Pronunciation is indicated by regular Spanish orthography. A statement of the grammatical rule being tested precedes each item. Each item is given in Spanish, as it was presented, and it is followed in parentheses by an English translation.

1. (Plural) Esta es una tifa*. Ahora hay otra. Hay dos de ellas. Hay dos _____. (This is a tifa*. Now there is another one. There are two of them. There are two _____).

2. (Plural) Esta es una fepa*. Ahora hay otra. Hay dos de ellas. Hay dos _____. (This is a fepa*. Now there is another one. There are two of them. There are two _____).

3. (Plural) Este es un fetor*. Ahora hay otro. Hay dos de ellos. Hay dos _____. (This is a fetor*. Now there is another one. There are two of them. There are two _____).

4. (Diminutive) Este es un fetor* pequeño. ¿Cómo se llama un fetor* pequeño? (This is a small fetor*. What do you call a small fetor*?)

5. (Diminutive) Este es un tifo* pequeño. ¿Cómo se llama un tifo* pequeño? (This is a small tifo*. What do you call a small tifo*?)

6. (Agentive-active) Este es un hombre que sabe ticar*. Está ticando*. ¿Cómo se llama un hombre que tica*? (This is a man who knows how to tica*. He is tica*-ing. What do you call a man who tica*-s?)

7. (Place of business) Esta es una tienda que vende pretas*. ¿Cómo se llama una tienda que vende pretas*? (This is a store that sells pretas*. What do you call a store that sells pretas*?)

8. (Agentive-occupation) Este es un hombre que vende pretas*. ¿Cómo se llama un hombre que vende pretas*? (This is a man who sells pretas*. What do you call a man who sells pretas*?)

9. (Future Tense) El hombre tica*. Mañana lo hará. Mañana, él _____. (The man tica*-s. Tomorrow, he will do it. Tomorrow, he _____.)

10. (Present Perfect Tense) El hombre tica*. Lo ha hecho muchas veces. Muchas veces, él ha _____. (The man tica*-s. He has done it many times. Many times, he has _____.)

11. (Past Tense-Imperfect) El hombre tica*. Lo hace todos los días.

Todo el año pasado, lo hacĭa. Todo el año pasado, él _____.
(The man tica*-s. He does it every day. All the past year he did
it. All the past year, he _____.)

12. (Past Tense-Preterite) El hombre soste*. Lo hace hoy. Ayer, lo
    hizo. Ayer, él _____. (The man soste*-s. He does it today.
    Yesterday, he did it. Yesterday, he _____.)

13. (Present Perfect Tense) El hombre soste*. Lo ha hecho muchas
    veces. Muchas veces, él ha _____. (The man soste*-s. He has
    done it many times. Many times he has _____.)

14. (Future Tense) El hombre soste*. Mañana, lo hará. Mañana, él
    _____. (The man soste*-s. Tomorrow, he will do it. Tomor-
    row, he _____.)

15. (Past Tense-Imperfect) El hombre tote*. Lo hace todos los
    días. Todo el año pasado, lo hacía. Todo el año, él _____.
    (The man tote*-s. He does it every day. All the past year, he
    did it. All the past year, he _____.)

16. (Future Tense) El hombre tote*. Mañana, lo hará. Mañana, él
    _____. (The man tote*-s. Tomorrow he will do it. Tomorrow,
    he _____.)

17. (Past Tense-Preterite) El hombre tote*. Lo hace hoy. Ayer, lo
    hizo. Ayer él _____. (The man tote*-s. He does it today.
    Yesterday he did it. Yesterday, he _____.)

18. (Present Perfect Tense) El hombre suecha*. Lo ha hecho mu-
    chas veces. Muchas veces, él ha _____. (The man suecha*-s.
    He has done it many times. Many times, he has _____.)

19. (Past Tense-Preterite) El hombre suecha*. Lo hace hoy. Ayer
    lo hizo. Ayer él _____. (The man suecha*-s. Today he does it.
    Yesterday he did it. Yesterday, he _____.)

20. (Past Tense-Imperfect) El hombre suecha*. Lo hace todos los
    días. Todo el año pasado, lo hacía. Todo el año pasado, él
    _____. (The man suecha*-s. He does it every day. All the past
    year, he did it. All the past year, he _____.)

21. (Possessive-singular) Esta es una tifa* quien tiene una botella.
    ¿De quién es la botella? (This is a tifa* who has a bottle. Whose
    bottle is it?)

22. (Possessive-plural) Hay dos tifos*. Los dos tienen sombreros.
    ¿De quién son estos sombreros? (There are two tifos*. They
    both have hats. Whose hats are they?)

(Kernan & Blount, pp. 3–5)

Adult responses

1. tifas
2. fepas
3. fetores
4. fetorcito; fetorito; fetorocito
5. tifito; tifocito; tifonito
6. ticador
7. pretería
8. pretero
9. ticará
10. ticado
11. ticaba
12. sostió
13. sosteado; sostido
14. losteará
15. totiaba
16. totiará; totirá
17. totió
18. suechado
19. suechó
20. suechaba
21. de la tifa; de ella
22. de los tifos; de ellos

(Kernan & Blount, p. 6)

CHAPTER 6

Fives and Sixes: Starting School

Introduction

Barbara: I wish for strawberries. I like strawberries to eat.

Teacher: Do you get to eat a lot of strawberries?

Barbara: I do got a strawberry patch, but I never get nobody's strawberries out of it.

Teacher: I wonder why.

Barbara: Probably there is not enough rain to make 'em grow. (Barbara turns to the front cover of her homemade book and tells her teacher:) I want you to put "My Wish Book" up here on it.

Teacher: OK. *My . . . Wish . . .* (writing)

Barbara: *My, Wish, Book.*

Teacher: Do you know what *book* starts with?

Barbara: *B.*

Teacher: Hm mmmmm. What else do you think belongs in *book*?

Barbara: *K.*

Teacher: Yeah. And there's two *o*'s in there too.

Barbara: I love strawberries.

Teacher: Do you want to write anything else in your book?

Barbara: *I wish I could eat a big round strawberry.*

Teacher: Want to write the first part?

Barbara: I (writes *I*) . . . that's all.

Teacher: (writes the rest of the sentence) Now, what does this say?

Barbara: (pointing accurately to each word); *I wish I could eat a big, round strawberry.*

Five-year-old Barbara has just entered the world of elementary-school children, a world of expanding contexts—and a world where written language will assume an increasingly important role. During center time, she had been thumbing through magazines, looking for a picture to paste in her "Wish Book." She spotted a huge red strawberry and promptly cut it out. As she was pasting it into her book, Barbara's teacher came by and talked to her about her book, helping her put her ideas into print.

Which aspect of the four language arts was Barbara involved with here? Reading? Writing? Listening? Speaking? Clearly she was purposefully engaged in all four language-based processes. From noting such interactions with Barbara over time, her teacher can learn about Barbara's growing control over both oral and written language.

In this chapter, then, we observe kindergarteners talking, listening, reading, and writing for a variety of purposes in a variety of situations. Although the focus is initially on oral language, then on written language, the shift is one of emphasis only. As Barbara demonstrated, oral and written language growth are intertwined.

Continuing Growth in Oral Communicative Competence

The kindergarten classroom presents a wide variety of settings for interaction. Children converse informally with teachers and peers. They participate in group discussions. They collaborate with others in varied small group activities, from imaginative play to scientific investigations. Further, kindergarteners, more often than children in any other public school grade, have occasion to use language for diverse purposes as teachers organize activity centers lending themselves to different language functions. We will consider the opportunities which the kindergarten classroom presents for fostering and assessing language growth. We focus on observing children's ability both to interact effectively in varied settings and to use a range of language functions (see Chapter 4 for a discussion of types of language functions). Although most of the examples are from the classroom, many of the activities discussed are typical also of the home and center.

Spontaneous conversation

Freddy was a "know-whatter." He actively sought his teacher's attention so that he could share stories about his mother, father, and older sister Monique. Yet, he seldom spoke in groups of four or more. During center or free-choice time, he would seek out the company of one or two friends. In contrast, Tracy seldom approached her teacher. She answered the teacher's questions with a shrug or a few words. Yet, at a center with a small group of peers, Tracy would share stories on such topics as birthdays and holidays:

> You know what? My grandma has a present for me in the bathroom. I can't look at it 'cause it's a—I want to be surprised.

Eager to share her experiences, Tracy elaborated and clarified her ideas for her friends. Her talk in such situations was more fluent, framed in more complex sentences, and composed of a more diverse vocabulary than any interaction with her teacher.

As we have seen with the younger children, then, many factors affect a child's talking and listening. It makes a difference whom the child is talking to. Is it a friend? A teacher? A stranger? The number of people talking together also matters. Is it a one-to-one interaction? A small group activity? A teacher-led, large group discussion? The topic and the place of conversation are other significant features. Such factors help explain the variations in children's talkativeness which often mystify parents attending parent-teacher conferences. For example, Vivi's mother felt that surely her daughter was a problem in school as "she'll talk from the time I get home . . . and I'll say, 'Oh, radio—I've got a radio.' And she'll say, 'Mom, I'm not a radio.' She talks, talks, talks." But in the school context, Vivi was attentive in teacher-led discussions and in conversations with her friends.

Anecdotal records on individual children's social behaviors can help teachers plan language-stimulating situations for children who appear reluctant to speak in school. The records may reveal particular children the child approaches or activities he or she shows an interest in. (A discussion, with examples, of anecdotal records is included in Chapter 4.)

All children benefit from diverse interaction experiences, including ample opportunities for talking with peers. Situations in which young children converse among themselves demand conversational skills which are often not needed in teacher-led discussions. Without a teacher indicating who may have the floor and when the floor should be yielded to another, the children assume responsibility for initiating, sustaining, and terminating talk. They jointly construct the interchange, at times reaching back to individual experiences in other contexts in other times which relate to a present, common theme. In addition, children can demand explicitness and clarity from each other to match or surpass the most demanding teacher. In the following scene, Rachel is drawing at the art table with several friends, including Courtney and Tracy:

> Rachel: I'm gonna make Courtney. She's gonna have her pony tail. . . See, she has her ponytail. See? That's Courtney.
>
> Courtney: That's not me.
>
> Tracy: Courtney, you can't even see it.
>
> Rachel: Uh huh [Yes, it's you.] You're pretty. You got your hair on one side.
>
> Courtney: I can see it, but it's [my hair's] in the back, dummy. (Note how Courtney is responding to both Tracy and Rachel.)
>
> Rachel: I didn't want it in the back.

In this discussion, which also occurred at the art table, not only do we see the demand for clarity and accuracy, we also see a budding negotiator:

> Tracy: I'm coloring the smoke orange.
>
> Courtney: Smoke is supposed to be white.
>
> Linda: Uh uh. Smoke is suppose' to be black.
>
> Tracy: Orange.
>
> Linda: Smoke is orange?
>
> Courtney: Fire's orange.
>
> Rachel: Uh uh. Fire's red.
>
> Linda: The colors are yellow and red and orange. Those are the three colors that are fine.

Teacher-led interactions

Kindergarten teachers plan regular large group discussions on a variety of topics. They expect children to listen and participate. But participating in such discussions is quite different from participating in spontaneous conversations. In fact, one of the teacher's primary problems is to keep the large group discussion from disintegrating into small patches of spontaneous conversation. In large group discussions, children are generally sitting on the classroom rug, reacting, for example, to a book the teacher has read, a demonstration she has given, or a large group activity in which everyone has had a turn. Children must attend simultaneously to the theme or activity, to the question posed by the teacher, and also to each other's reactions. In addition, as the discussion develops, they must bid for a turn by raising a hand, which leads to such frustrations as ''I never get a turn to say anything,'' or, ''I wanted to say that.'' In such discussions, each child may offer his or her own personal reaction to the teacher's comment or question without reacting to each other's ideas. At times a child's comment may not, as far as the teacher can tell, relate to the topic. Or, the child may repeat a comment made by another child or simply invent an experience to have something to contribute:

Child 1: I have 18 stars on my football helmet.

Child 2: Well, I have 28 stars.

Child 1: No, you don't.

Child 2: I have a hundred.

The teacher can help children to listen and to build on each other's comments, as Vivian Paley (1981) does in the following discussion with her 5-year-olds. The class is discussing their sprouting lettuce seeds. Ms. Paley responds in a conversational tone to her children's ideas— and her children respond in kind to each other. Through her comments, Ms. Paley seeks to help her children clarify and refine their thinking and hence their language:

Rose: It doesn't look like lettuce.

Paley: It takes time to grow taller. By the way, it's possible the lettuce won't be ready before school is over.

Lisa: You could bring it over to our houses.

Deanna: Why can't we come here and have a party in the summer?

Eddie: When people come to this school after the summer and they'll be in first grade, then you could bring it to them.

Wally: Just give it to us in the summer if you see us.

Paley: Would I have the lettuce with me if I happen to see you during the summer?

Wally: No. So we better all come back to school.

Tanya: We could have more school—extra school until the lettuce is ready.

Eddie: That's good.

Palcy: We can't do that. There's a summer program here, right in these classrooms. Could we share the lettuce with the summer school children? (p. 181–183)

In addition to class discussions, kindergarteners participate in formal "lessons," classroom events which will increasingly dominate the school day as children progress through the grades. In lessons, teachers have particular concepts, points, they are attempting to make. In the following small group lesson, Ms. Peters is introducing the concept of families, focusing on what defines a family and on the varied nature of the family unit:

Ms. Peters: Who knows what a family is?

Donald: Somebody who live with you and raise you.

Ms. Peters: Somebody who's raising their hand, nice and quiet. Matt.

Matt: Someone you care about.

Ms. Peters: Someone you care about. Very good. Does anyone else have an idea what a family is? Elizabeth?

Elizabeth: Someone who you live with,

Ms. Peters: Someone you live with.

Elizabeth: and you like very much,

Ms. Peters: Very nice.

Elizabeth: and love.

Ms. Peters: and love. That's very special. April.

April: Mmmmm

Ms. Peters: Did you forget? (April nods.) Kay. When you remember, raise your hand, and we'll come back to you. Donald.

Donald: It's somebody you love and live with you and raise you.

Ms. Peters: Someone who you love and you live with and who raises you.

Donald: Yes. And raises you when you was a baby.

Ms. Peters: Kay. And what kind of people are in your family?

Patrick: My brother, and my mommy.

Donald: Only my mama lives with me.

Ms. Peters: OK, let's raise our hand. Elizabeth.

Elizabeth: I got um a daddy, a mommy, and . . .

Patrick: a brother

Elizabeth: and a brother . . .

Patrick: and a sister

Ms. Peters: A sister.

Elizabeth: I don't have any sister.

> Patrick: Either do I.
>
> Ms. Peters: Some families do have brothers and sisters too.
>
> Donald: Only my mama ⎡lives with me.
>   ⎣And what about if you have a dog or a cat,
>
> Ms. Peters: are they part of your family too?

In the above lesson, Ms. Peters is both presenting information, and observing what her children know, about families. The pattern of interaction in her lesson is identical to that repeatedly observed in classroom lessons: she asks a question; a child answers; and she evaluates the answer.

We focus here on two of Ms. Peter's students, Elizabeth and Donald, in order to illustrate the skills required to participate effectively in lessons. Both children made relevant comments about the family. In particular Donald noted that a family raises children, while Elizabeth brought out the love associated with the family. They both noted the variability of families ("Only my mama lives with me," "I don't have any sister."). Yet, Elizabeth received the most positive feedback from Ms. Peters—not because her academic performance was stronger but because she followed the interactional rules of the lesson.

We are not suggesting that children do not need to meet the interactional demands of classroom settings. But, we do suggest that teachers acknowledge that their assessment of what individual children know academically is dependent upon children's ability to participate appropriately in classroom interactions. Teachers might also consider the types of settings in which particular rules are necessary; perhaps raising hands would not always be needed in small group situations. In any case, children like Donald may benefit from explicit statements of the teacher's interactional requirements ("Raise your hand if you have an idea about what a family is.") They also need opportunities to display their knowledge in other school contexts, in Donald's case, perhaps through less structured activities—drawing, dictation, dramatic play. We now turn to the classroom activity centers which give rise to child-organized interaction.

Dramatic play

"Let's play house" or "doctor" or "school"—opening lines for many an impromptu production in the dress-up or housekeeping center. Children negotiate and cooperate to create the scenes, characters, plots, and themes of their dramas. The themes often reflect the children's experiences in the home:

> Andrew wears an apron in the housekeeping center. He has two children and a horse. He didn't want a horse; he wanted a dog. But, in the interest of maintaining the peace, he acquired a horse:
>
> Marcie: I'll be the horse. (She crouches down on all fours.)
>
> Andrew: No, the dog.
>
> Marcie: Horse.
>
> Andrew: No.
>
> Marcie: Yes. (She bites him.)
>
> Andrew: OK.
>
> Marcie: I'm the horse.
>
> Andrew: (to the running horse) It's gonna upset the food if you don't be careful.
>
> (Andrew begins to feed the baby:)
>
> Andrew: (with a wide smile and a high voice) Open wide. It's good, good, good.
>
> (When the baby shoves the spoon away, Andrew cheerfully tries again:)
>
> Andrew: Open wide. I've got something good for you. Here it comes. ZZZZZZZZZZOOOOOOOOOOOOOmmmmm!
>
> (And into the baby's mouth goes the spoon.)

And so Andrew, with the skillful assistance of his friends, adopts the role of mother, fulfilling her familiar functions: regulating, loving, pleading, persuading.

In this next example, children again negotiate roles, here to enact an action-packed fight scene:

> Marco: Romero, I'm your friend, OK?
>
> Kiko: No, you in, you in that team.
>
> Romero: There's only two of us, against lots of them.
>
> Kiko: I know, but sometimes, sometimes, there's four.
>
> Esteban: Aquéllos no son amigos de Vds. [Those aren't your friends.] (sound effects of fighting)
>
> Esteban: Maté a Kiko. [I killed Kiko.] Me quité la flecha. [I took out the arrow.] Y maté a Romero. [And I killed Romero.]
>
> Romero: : Yo traigo casco, loco! [I've got a helmet on, stupid!] (to Esteban) No me muero porque traigo dos cascos. [I don't die because I've got two helmets.]

This particular example also displays the unique social and linguistic abilities of the bilingual child. Romero, who spoke English to Kiko, spoke Spanish to Esteban, a monolingual Spanish-speaking child. Like other bilingual children, Romero was sensitive to the linguistic ability of his listener.

As noted in Chapter 5, teachers may observe certain children who do not visit the dramatic play center and who thus may need more structured opportunities for play, for example, through a teacher-guided improvisation of a favorite story.

Art center

Danielle, a quiet child who did not participate in group discussions, was eager to share with her teacher or friends the stories that evolved during her drawing or painting:

> That's me and I'm at the store with my mommy and I'm a bit lost. I'm going to be walking through there 'cause my mommy's been there in the store. Oh, there's my mommy.

Like the drama and block building centers, the art center provides opportunities for children to interact with unstructured materials. Their organization of these materials reflects their interests and thinking to a greater degree than the completion of structured tasks, such as puzzles and games. Working with the materials can assist children in organizing their experiences and, in addition, can serve as a stimulus to talk. The child's organizing of experiences through drawing may be reflected in relatively more fluent, complexly organized talk than is the case in spontaneous conversation (Zepeda-de-Kane, 1980).

In addition to depicting home and family themes, children may spontaneously work through experiences being studied in class. During a unit on fire in a kindergarten classroom, the free drawing center was dominated by the fire theme, as children drew pictures of and discussed the concepts they had been studying. Noting their spontaneous interest in the topic assisted the teacher in assessing the children's involvement in, and comprehension of, the study unit.

As do the activities of painting and drawing, a diverse array of materials in the art center can also foster talk. Cooperation and negotiation are required as the children share supplies or cooperate on a common project. In addition, the variety of concrete sensory experiences provided allows opportunities to assess and foster vocabulary as children discuss and select among the various colors, sizes, patterns, and textures.

Science and mathematics activities

Science and math activities lend themselves particularly to language for describing, analyzing, and predicting. The young children in the following excerpt have been observing a bird's nest which, as luck would have it, was built under the school's roof. The children's descriptions and reasonings flow from the teacher's language; she focuses their attention on particular features of the situation, requests elaborations, and seeks clarifications. Yet, the children themselves have a role in structuring the evolving interaction:

Teacher: I've got something to tell you. Mr. Jackson found the shell of one broken egg on the ground the other day. (Cries of Ah! Oh!) And he thought, "There's one baby bird, because here's the shell that's broken now. The baby's come out of the shell." Mr. Jackson thought there was only one baby bird, but really there are. . . ?"

Paul: Three.

Teacher: Three babies. How do you know there are three?

Paul: Because I saw all their heads pop up.

Teacher: What did we see yesterday?

Paul: All their heads popped up. And they all made a noise. And they all went . . . and two went down. No. One went down and. . . They both they stayed up. . . And for a little while they both popped down again.

Teacher: And when they popped their heads up, what did they do? Can you tell us about it, Gary?

Gary: When I was at home, I saw this egg. And it was broken. And there was a little baby bird laying there dead.

Teacher: Yes. Sometimes they fall out of the nest, don't they?

Paul: What?

Gary: The egg was broken.

Paul: What happened?

Gary: The egg was broken. It must have been the bird was out. And he fell on the ground and was dead.

Rachel: It must have been cracking open. It must have rolled over and he must have fell.

Sance: I know. A cat must have had it.

(Rosen & Rosen, 1974, p. 46)

Careful description and thoughtful reasoning do not, of course, occur only in science and math; nor are science and math confined to activities so named. For example, in the art center, Ms. Bloom's children were making Christmas chains. They were to construct chains from eight green paper strips and eight red ones, 16 links to stand for the 16 days left until Christmas. This seemingly "simple" art activity led not only to describing and reasoning, but also to ample use of such academic concepts as ordinal and cardinal number and comparatives:

> Let's see whose is the longest.
>
> I've only got 6 more to go.
>
> I need it longer.
>
> I'm on my seventh one.
>
> I'm fixing to be on my eighth.

Most children kept track of which number they were on by continually recounting how many red or green strips they had already used, then deciding if they needed "more." Others counted on their fingers in order to determine exactly "how many more": "1–2–3–4 red ones and [on fingers] 5–6–7–8. I need four more!"

As the children counted their chains, they used talk to monitor their actions. Certain children in the group took the role of teacher, using their talk to guide the actions of their peers:

> No, put a green one there, not a red.
>
> No, put this green strip up on this end. Yeah.

Styles of using language

As children create in the block building center, the housekeeping center, or the art center, language frequently accompanies their actions. By listening to their talk, we can learn about differences in interests and in styles of expression. Sance, for example, often played with the sounds of language. She would pick up on other children's words, playing with their form: "Bye-bye, Sie-sie, Bye-sie, Hi-bye, My-my." Sance's spontaneous conversation often displayed this sense of enjoyment of language: "I can see my mouse when I get home, my little ratty head, little bitty rat head. I have a Big Mama rat head." Even Sance's requests for words at the writing center reflected her characteristic style of expression:

(Sance wrote *Troy*, her brother's name. She then asked for *Toy*, and then *Roy*.)

Roy, he lives next door. . . . How do you spell *Shoy*?
Shoy lives next to us.

Croy lives by Shoy. How do you spell *Croy*? . . . Spell *Poy*.
Poy lives by Shoy.

Like Sance, Rachel displayed an enjoyment of talk. Rather than playing with the form of language, Rachel's most distinctive use of language was in narrating and dramatizing elaborate stories about moms, dads, and kids. These stories were told as she drew in the art center; they were acted out in her play in the housekeeping center. Here is an example of Rachel's narrative style; this story accompanied the drawing of Figure 6–1:

> He's pushing her mom because she wouldn't hurry up. And she couldn't find the door . . . the way to find that Christmas tree. She was trying to get to the other side to get her little baby. Here—see, that's her little baby. And she was trying to get her 'cause she might get hurt. She's just a little bitty girl.

Rachel's interest in drama and in the relationships between people was reflected in her writing as well. Unlike many kindergarteners, Rachel seldom attempted to write the alphabet or to copy print displayed in the environment. Rather, she attempted to write the dialogue of characters in her drawings or to write notes and letters to her friends.

Freddy, in contrast, seldom played with language or engaged in spontaneous dramatization or narration. He was a well-organized, neat child who enjoyed constructive activities, such as building with blocks or with leggoes and drawing at the art center. At each center, Freddy carefully made objects—especially forts, houses, cars, and planes—which he labeled (for example, "This is a plane.") At the writing center, Freddy wrote primarily his own name and was reluctant to ask questions or to attempt to write words he did not know.

Sance, Rachel, and Freddy are all proficient in language. But they have clearly different ways of functioning. Being sensitive to such differences between children may help teachers plan varied types of learning activities to match individual styles. For example, Sance might enjoy exploring word families, which the Dr. Seuss books would help her do, or hearing books which use forms of language play, such as rhythm, rhyme, alliteration, and onomatopoeia. Such "nonsensical" approaches to literacy would most probably be less appealing to Rachel.

Figure 6–1

Acquiring the cognitive code

As we have sampled the children's language at the classroom activity centers, we have noted the children's use of such concepts as color, shape, number, and relationships of quantity, space, and time (words such as *more/less, greater/fewer, same/different, before/after, between/behind/on top of, big/short, tall/small, wide/narrow, high/low*). These concepts are typically stressed by kindergarten and early primary grade teachers and are particularly useful in school learning situations, hence the term "the cognitive code." Note how concept-rich Linda's language is as she searches for exactly the right crayon at the art center:

> Which black was the goody goody goodest? Which was the lightest? This is not the lightest. I want the big fat one. Was this one the lightest? Let's see. . . No, it's not this one. Is this one the lightest as this one I just used? Yep. Gimme this one. This one was the lightest, the lightest, the lightest.

Children learn these words over time by gradually sorting out their meanings as they meet them in different situations, a learning process that begins well before the kindergarten year. At times children may appear to understand a *word* when they really understand the *situation*. In other words, they know what the adult would most likely want done in that situation. For example, a child may be able to place one picture after another in a sequence game where the pictures follow each other in a clear, orderly progression, but may be unable to follow directions in less contextualized situations, such as teacher directives which are not part of any ongoing activity: "Jenny, put the paper in the box *after* the red one for me" or "Jesse, could you bring me the *narrowest* ribbon on the shelf?" Knowing that children learn words through encountering them in a variety of situations, many teachers and parents are sensitive to opportunities to use these words in their daily interactions with their children.

Many children come to school already using these terms. Some teachers informally test the children's grasp of them by, for example, having the children pick up different colors or numbers of crayons, or different sizes or shapes of papers from a displayed set. Teachers may keep checklists or grids of the children's mastery of these terms. Figure 6–2 provides an example of such a checklist. It is far easier to accurately assess the child's understandings of color, number, and shape than it is to assess the words dealing with relationships. As we have discussed, the child's understanding of such words is dependent on the

Child's Name	Can orally label sets of objects:						Can orally label shapes:			
	0–5	6	7	8	9	10	△	◻	○	▭
Efren	+	✓	✓	✓	–	–	–	–	+	–
Ruth Ann	+	+	+	+	+	+	+	–	+	–
Melissa	+	+	+	+	+	+	+	✓	+	✓

+ – child knows

✓ – child sometimes knows

– – child does not know

Figure 6–2 Math vocabulary

situation. Whether or not one accurately assesses the child's mastery of the cognitive code, an awareness of the child's difficulty with these words sensitizes teachers to the child's potential puzzlements.

Emerging Written Language

Five-year-old Barbara settled comfortably on the rug, intent on reading a favorite book. Erica, a classmate, objected:

"Barbara, you don't know how to read."

"I'm gonna read anyhow," Barbara answered. And she did.

Long before children are formally taught to read and write, they begin experimenting with these processes and talking with the skilled writers and readers who surround them. In the following sections, we look at typical activities of the home, school, or center, where children's working knowledge of written language, as well as oral language, can be observed and fostered.

Listening to stories

"Read me a story" is a familiar request for both teachers and parents. Caregivers can gain insight into young children's interest in written language through such requests. They can note: How frequently does the child ask to be read to? Has being read to become a valued part of the daily routine? Are there particular types of books the child shows an interest in? Does the child ask to hear favorite stories again and again?

As they read to the child, caregivers can also note the child's attentiveness and apparent involvement. Young children may show their enjoyment of, and involvement in, literature through nonverbal responses. They may inch ever closer to the reader, laughing, gasping, or sighing in response to a new development. They may respond verbally to the book with a "Hey, that's a good one," or a "Read that again, teacher." Often they attempt to read along with the adult.

Books with repeated phrases or refrains invite the child to participate in the reading, allowing the child an opportunity to use the language of the book. The repeated line, "But he was still hungry," in Carle's (1969) *The Very Hungry Caterpillar* is irresistible to many children. Books with cumulative patterns in their plot also allow children to easily join in. In Tolstoy's (1968) *The Great Big Enormous Turnip,* for example, succeeding characters attempt to pull the enormous turnip out of the ground, allowing young listeners to easily predict the book's language. Familiar folk tales, rhymes, and songs, such as *The Three Bears, The Three Billy Goats Gruff,* and Mother Goose verses, also invite children to participate. Rhodes (1981) has suggested still other characteristics of predictable books, including (a) a use of familiar concepts, (b) a good match between the text and its illustrations, (c) rhythmical language, and (d) the use of familiar sequences, such as days of the week, the alphabet, or numbers. A list of suggested predictable books is included at the end of this chapter.

Retelling stories

As children have repeated experiences with books, they form their own sense of how stories flow. Children display this sense as they retell familiar tales. Children may retell these stories to each other in small groups, using puppets or the flannel board. Or, like Erica, a five-year-old in an after-school day care program, they may retell the story into a tape recorder so that it may be shared with friends later:

> The Three Bears: Papa Bear, Mama Bear, and Baby Bear. One day Mama cooked some porridge. Daddy said it was too hot. "Let's go take a walk in the woods." And then a little girl came. She knocked on the door. "Knock, knock." She knocked on the door again, "Knock, knock." Nobody answers so she opened the door and peeked in. She saw three bowls on the table with porridge in them. First she went to Daddy Bear's, and it was too hot. Then she went to Mama Bear's and it was too cold. Then she went to Baby Bear's and it was just right. So she ate it all up. Then she was tired so she went to the chairs. . .

and so on until Baby Bear, at the end of the tale, screams, "'Somebody's been laying in my bed.' She jumps up and never came back."

Erica began her story formally with *"One day* Mama cooked some porridge." She included all major characters and events of the story. She also attempted to logically link those events: "Nobody answers *so* she. . ."; *"Then* she was tired *so* she. . ."

Bess retold Cinderella, a story with a more complex plot:

> Cinderella wanted to go to the ball. Her sister did not let her go to the ball. She said, "How could you with those dirty clothes?" But her fairy godmother came. She said, "Go get a pumpkin." She turned it into a carriage. Cindrella went to the ball.

Although Bess did not retell all major events of the story nor did she include all major characters, her story does flow logically from a clear beginning to a satisfying ending.

From regular tape recordings of children's retellings, teachers can document not only children's growing sense of how stories flow, but also growth in vocabulary, fluency, and complexity of language. Although certainly these aspects of language vary greatly across situations, story retellings—in which children adopt the language of the book—may evidence relatively sophisticated use of language. King (1977) offers this sampling of change in a child's story retelling during the first month in school:

Three Billy Goats Gruff

> They went over the bridge. Trip trap, trip trap, to get so fat. The big troll said, "Who is going over my bridge?" In a little teeny voice, "I am." Trip, trap, trip, trap. "Wait for the next one—the third one." "Wait for the last one." "Come and eat me." The next one. All fall to pieces. Only his arms, his legs, everything fell to pieces.

The Gingerbread Boy (one mo. later)

> This is about the gingerbread boy. This woman and old man, them have no boy, no boy. "How about I make a gingerbread boy?" Then them make a gingerbread boy. The father walked in and the smoke and this little boy sitting on the bench and the paddle. "Run as fast as you can, you'll never catch me, I the gingerbread boy. Run as fast as you can, you can't catch me, I the gingerbread boy. I run from the old lady and old man. I run from little boy."

and on the latter story went until—

> The gingerbread boy run from everybody and then even one single time. The fox ate the gingerbread boy. He got so fat he didn't know what to do. The end.   (pp. 413–414)

This child's teacher might have made a written notation of changes evident in the second retelling. For example, she might have recorded them in this form:

STORY RETELLING

   Child: *Carl*   Date: *Oct. 6*
   Story: *The Gingerbread Boy*

  Language:

        Fluency—258 words [as compared to 67 words in first retelling]
             —few pauses or verbal fillers ('um," "uh")

      Complexity—greater number of complete sentences
             —in addition to coordination ("and"), uses complementation ("He got so fat he didn't know what to do.")

      Vocabulary—more precise; fewer pronouns with no referents [Compare "They went over the bridge" in first retelling to "This woman and old man, them have no boy" in second.]
             —included more of story's vocabulary

        Usage—his own, rather than story's, usage patterns evident ("throwed")

  Story Structure:

      Major events—recalled story's beginning and end; included or alluded to the majority of events; sequence confused at times

    Linking of events—some attempt made to link events ("Then them make. . .")

In addition, or as an alternative, to such written notation, Carl's teacher could have used a checklist to note the changing characteristics of Carl's retellings. An example of such a checklist is given in Figure 6–3.

Telling stories and singing songs

Children not only retell others' stories but also create their own. As with story retellings, their original creations offer opportunities to sample their growing command of story or narration.

When invited to tell a story into a tape recorder, Janie listed significant, recurring experiences in her life:

Child								
		Language					Story Structure	
Date	Story Title	Fluent		Complete sentences	A variety of sentence patterns to express ideas	Precise, descriptive words	All major events	Accurate sequence	Linked events
		Word count	Absence of verbal fillers						

+ — always or completely
√ — usually or most
− — seldom or few

Figure 6-3 Story retelling

I like to play outside and in my room. And I like to play with somebody. I like my new dress at home, and I like going to school and I like playing with people at school. And at Halloween it's scary.

In contrast, Maria attempted a narrative. Although her story has the rudiments of a plot, we, as listeners, are left with many puzzling questions, such as, how did Maria escape?

I went into a witch—a scary witch. She ate my brother for cake and saved me for a week. I was too scared. I was too scared because first I was too bony . . . in a neighborhood. I was scary.

To a greater degree than Janie and Maria, Amy was capable of telling a sophisticated story with characters, an action-packed plot, and a clear beginning and end:

It's called "A Monster That Ate Kids." One time there was a haunted house, and a monster lived in it. Kids didn't know that, but they came to it. That monster was mean. When they found out it was a monster in there they tried to get out, but the doors were locked. The monster knew they were in there. When he knew they were in there, he locked the doors before they got to it. They tried to get out, but they couldn't. Then they went upstairs and then they found the monster laying there dead.

Wordless picture books with straightforward plots can provide support for young storytellers. The children tell their "own" stories by interpreting the pictures. If the illustrations are sufficiently and explicitly detailed, children may be able not only to supply the basic plot line, but also to infer characters' emotions and motivations. With the aid of such books, many can tell sophisticated stories with clear beginnings, consistent characters, and logical actions leading to a climax, followed by a satisfying conclusion. A list of suggested wordless picture books is included at the end of this chapter.

A teacher with an appreciation of poetry and song may inspire children to make up songs, which demonstrate children's growing sense of another literary form. Here are a few 5-year-olds' songs, sung into a tape recorder on a rainy day. Note the developing sense of rhythm and pattern their work displays:

It's rainy
  and foggy.
It's rainy
  and foggy
    today.

It's rainy. It's rainy.

It's rainy. It's rainy.

It's rainy today.

I wish it was sunny.

The sun isn't out.

It's raining today.

I hoped it would be sunny today.

BUT

It's raining today.

It's raining today.

I hoped it would be sunny today.

Responding to print throughout the day

As parents and teachers of young children, we aim to foster children's appreciation and understanding of written language. Through observation and anecdotal record-keeping, we can document children using literature and other forms of print in a variety of daily activities to reflect upon or to add enjoyment to their lives.

With fives and sixes, the appeal of poetry's rhythms and patterns is especially notable. For example, Linda, drawing long green grass, commented to her friends at the art center, "Look at this. 'The green grass grows all round all round (beginning to sing). The green grass grows all around.'" The other children joined in and the song went on.

On another day, Vivi drew a black house and remarked, "This is a dark house." Ginny then added, in a shaky voice, "'In the dark, dark house. . .'" Soon two other children joined in "'there was a dark, dark room. In the dark, dark room, there was a dark, dark cupboard. . .'"

Characters and themes from literature may emerge in the children's talk, painting, or drama. Janet Hickman (1981), who has studied young children's spontaneous responses to literature, reports these responses by a group of fives and sixes to Maurice Sendak's *Where the Wild Things Are*:

October 4. Mel and Warren are making a mural. Their man-in-the-moon face is scowling, with sun rays around its head:

"Is it a daytime picture or a nightime one?" asks Mrs. H. Mel hesitates. Warren looks at the book lying nearby and says, "Night." He explains that it's a story about Max and the place where the wild things are.

October 5. Warren is holding up the Wild Things mural and chasing people with it. "It isn't finished yet," he says.

October 6. Warren and Mel's mural is on display, with writing:

> Warren and Mel by the picher of where The wild things are. One night Maxs rode in his boat. In the night maxs saw a ilind. He saw monsters. The king one said—I am the schogeit [strongest] He said. And maxs said I'am the schogeit! he said.   (p. 347)

In the corner bookshelves of homes, classrooms, and centers, children have opportunities for independently exploring books. In their use (or nonuse) of such book corners and small libraries, children reveal their attitudes and interests in literature. Teachers can observe which children visit the library regularly. Which type of book do individual children appear to prefer? How long does each child spend with any one book? How does the child go about "reading" a book?

Teachers can learn about young children's understandings about written language and books by using a test developed by Marie Clay, *Concepts about Print* (1979c). In this test, the adult reads a small paperback book called *Sand* to the child. As the teacher reads, she asks the child to "help" her by pointing out certain print and book features. The following questions to be asked of the child, and the complementary questions for the teacher to ask herself, are adapted from Clay's test:

Ask the child:
1. Show me the front of this book.
2. I'll read you this story. You help me. Show me where to start reading; where do I begin to read?
3. Show me where to start. Which way do I go? Where do I go after that?
4. Point to what I am reading. (Read slowly but fluently.)
5. Show me the first part of the story.
   Show me the last.
6. (On a page with print on a left and a right page): Where do I start reading?

Ask yourself:
1. Is the child familiar with the physical format of a book?
2. Does the child know that the print, rather than the pictures, tells the story? (i.e., Did the child point to the pictures or the print when you began to read?)
3. Is the child familiar with the directional orientation of a page?
   Does the child know that:
   a line of print goes left to right
   at the end of a line, the reader goes to the left end of the next line (i.e., there is a return sweep)?

4. Does the child understand "word-space-word" concept?
5. Is the child familiar with the correspondence between parts of a story and parts of a book?
6. Does the child know that the left page is read before the right page?

In addition to noting how individual children physically handle books, teachers can listen to children "read." Young children's reading reveals the strategies they use to find meaning in books. We stress *finding meaning* here, rather than accurately identifying words. Young children learn a great deal about print before they read in the conventional sense of the term. From her studies of what she calls emergent readers (young children not yet reading in the conventional manner), Clay (1979b) identified early knowledge about print which children acquire through interaction with adults about books and other sources of print. Clay points out that children must learn that:

Print can be turned into speech.

There is a message contained in the print.

The picture is a clue to that message.

Some language units are more likely to occur than others.

There is a particular message in a particular order of particular words.

Memory helps.

The following anecdotes illustrate children's varying competence at making such knowledge operational—at making sense of print.

Eric began at his book's back cover and moved, page by page, towards the "front." He read a message by using the book's pictures as a guide. But, the language of his read message was not distinguishable from his spontaneous speech; he did not yet "talk like a book":

There go the real Santa Claus. There go the mouse. The mouse gonna act like he Santa Claus.

Eric's teacher talked to him, helping him to connect the strands of his story: "Now what's happening to the mouse, Eric?" "Now he gets caught."

Lisa began reading her book by labeling the pictures; then she moved into more complex uses of language. But, like Eric's, her narrative lacks any consistency or logical flow:

A red horse. . . A dog in it. . . Brick. . . White horse. . . The horse is jumping. The horse is jumping. Black horse is trying to catch up with her. And he jumped over the gate. And the black horse got caught.

In contrast, Kristy creates a coherent story from a book which has no apparent thematic line in text or pictures. The book (*A Row of Crows* by Batherman, 1973) is a collection of rhymes. Kristy reads (each section represents one page):

Text	Kristy
A Row of Crows (cover, which has picture of crows on it)	This is called ''The Early Birds.''
What other words Do you know That rhyme with the last word In each row?	The Early Birds. One day the early birds went up, and they were very very sad.
Said the head crow To ten crows in a row When the horns blow We'll begin the show. (This is the only text which is accompanied by a picture with crows in it.)	And then one day the early birds tried a trick. They whooped and whooshed and flied and flied.
A green goat In a red coat Bought a boat That wouldn't float.	He saw a creepy monster through the sun.
A silly cat With a baseball bat Hit my hat And now it's flat.	And then something happened—very very strange happened, happened, happened: A cat had a bat.
A surprise for Fred Is under the bed, It's a sled. The sled is red.	He was a very unhappy bird.
I saw some mice Skating on ice Eating cookies of spice I saw them twice.	He was a very unhappy bird They was the early birds.
Minnie the snake Lived near the lake. She ate with a rake. She always ate cake. (The rake in the accompanying picture looks like a bird. The snake is coiled around, looking like a series of eggs.)	Then something happened. A egg caught open and snatched him.

At noon a raccoon And his friend a baboon [who looked like a tiger] Blew up a balloon And flew to the moon.	And then the early birds and the tiger went and had a very happy holiday.

In Kristy's story, we note a formal beginning consisting of literary language ("One day . . .) and a formal ending. Although the book did not do so, Kristy held the major characters constant, attempted to create a sequence of events, and tried to create a climax or pivotal problem ("and then something happened"). She read the story fluently and expressively.

All three children, Eric, Lisa, and Kristy, may have invented more coherent texts if they had been reading well-known stories. Rachel's mother explains the ease with which Rachel, like many children, reads favorite stories:

> Rachel likes for me to read stories to her. Last night I was studying, and she wanted me to read this story to her. I'd already read it to her three times . . . so, she went and read it to her dolls. . . . They [Rachel and her sister] already know the book 'cause I've read it, so they'll go and try to read it over to their dolls.

This ability to memorize text is seen by recent investigators of literacy acquisition as an important developmental step (Doake, 1979; Holdaway, 1979). Children initially strive to reproduce the text's meaning in syntactically-acceptable language (with no ability to match one oral word to one written one, referred to as "voice-print match"). More advanced children memorize text, particularly text with rhythm and pattern and, of course, favorite, often-heard stories. The "predictability" of the text supports children as they begin to match spoken with written words.

Thus, before formal school instruction begins, children may combine memories for words, recalled visual cues from text, picture clues, and their own ability to predict from the language of that text, and begin to read independently. In their increasing focus on the text itself, some readers may actually be assisted by nonreaders who are still dependent solely on pictures and their understanding of the language of books. As 5-year-old Doug, a proficient independent reader, read a book for the first time, he was assisted by Joe, a nonreader:

> (The huge whale in the illustration is comparing his size to that of the pictured ships.)
>
> Doug: "Two boats are not as big as I am. Three boats are not as big as I am. Four boats are not" . . . mmmmm

Joe: "just about"

Doug: "just about as big as I am." (Text reads "almost as big as I am.")

Of course, knowledge about written language does not come only from books but from a variety of experiences with print in the everyday environment. The mothers of Vivi, Tracy, and Freddy illustrate this concept in the following anecdotes.

Vivi's mother talked about Vivi's reading behaviors during their weekend shopping trips:

> We'll be at the mall and see something on a building, and she'll say, "What do that spell?" And I'll tell her and next time we go by it, she'll say the word and ask "Is that what that spells?" And she'll be right.

Vivi's mother also recounted her daughter's strong interest in the mail; sometimes Vivi's mother would mail her daughter a card just so Vivi would receive some mail. Vivi "would walk around with that card for days."

Tracy's mother recalled her daughter's interest in traffic signs:

> She's always been interested in signs. There's a sign at the end of the street here, *Stop Ahead*. She asked me what it said. Now everytime we go by it, she says, "Stop ahead."

And Freddy's mother recalled her son's interest in reading about sports heroes:

> He got the *People* magazine. He was just reading it, and he was telling me that it was Reggie Jackson. And I said, "That's not Reggie Jackson." And he said, "Yes it is." And I had to read it and, "Yeah, it *is* Reggie Jackson."

It is from such adult-child interactions in meaningful print situations—with books, street signs, product labels, commercial captions, billboards—that reading begins. The adult observes the child's interest, answers questions, and provides opportunities for interest to expand. Noting what parents say anecdotally about their children's home experiences with print is another means, then, of assessing children's interest in and use of written language.

In the classroom and center, teachers foster that interest in written language, not only by reading to their children, but also by providing for class "stores" stocked with cereal and other product boxes, classroom "post offices" filled regularly with letters from teachers to student as well as from student to student, traffic or direction signs, charts of class rules, wall calendars where significant events are recorded, and so on.

Dictated writing

Five-year-old Sara's mother credits Sara's early interest in writing to a desire to write to Grandma: "That's how we really started. I would write a message to Grandma, and she'd copy."

In many classrooms and centers, this technique of writing down the child's words is referred to as the "Language Experience" technique. The children dictate for a variety of purposes, including to label their drawings, report a personal experience, narrate a story, or record observations. By regularly filing samples of children's dictations, growth in written language skill can be assessed and documented.

In planning language experience activities, teachers may include both individual and group activities. Children may respond more readily in one or the other situation; in addition, each situation lends itself more readily to particular types of interactions. Both types of situations are illustrated in the following discussion.

Ms. Bruin made pudding with a small group of kindergarteners. She asked the child to recall the cooking steps for a class recipe book. Ginny offered, "You gotta stir it," and Walt added, "It's got milk in it." As the children offered ideas, Ms. Bruin wrote down their words exactly as they spoke them, without changing any nonstandard language forms: She put *their* talk into print. Then, she helped the children to organize and clarify their comments: "Which of these things did we do first? And then?"

Ms. Anderson's children have journals. At least twice a week, the children illustrate and then dictate a composition about a personal or class experience. As she moves from child to child taking dictation, Ms. Anderson notes the ease and fluency with which the children dictate, the adequacy of the children's vocabulary for expressing their ideas, the coherence of the dictation and accompanying illustration, and the dictation's clarity and organization. The following two dictations illustrate striking differences in ease and organization of dictation. For Jennifer, the dictation is simply a labeling of parts of her illustration:

This is a tree.

This is a house.

This is popcorn.

In contrast, Lucinne's is organized into a narrative:

> We went to the fair with our boy friends and it rained. We went home and played a game.

Ms. Anderson talks with Jennifer and Lucinne and their peers, helping them to elaborate and clarify their journal entries. For example, after Ms. Anderson had read Viorst's (1972) *Alexander and the Terrible, Horrible, No Good, Very Bad Day,* Jesse dictated:

> I don't know it was Saturday.

He then began to create a design of circles on his page. Ms. Anderson commented:

> "Wait now, Jesse. You didn't know it was Saturday and that made it a bad day?
>
> "Mm mmm [yes]"
>
> "Well, what happened because you didn't know it was Saturday?"
>
> "I got up and got ready for school and cartoons were on."
>
> "Oh no! You could've been watching cartoons but you were getting ready for school?"
>
> "Yeah."

By talking with Jesse, Ms. A. was able to clarify the ideas he wished to express in his journal. After writing down Jesse's additional comments, she asked, "Wonder what you could draw to help the other kids know about your bad day?"

"I could draw me in bed," offered Jesse, and he did. With Ms. Anderson's help, then, he clarified his dictation and, in addition, established a logical connection between his dictation and the illustration.

Certain children may find the whole concept of "dictating what you want to say" a puzzling task. Consider, for example, the language experience stories in Figures 6–4 and 6–5. Both Fredricka and Jeff drew pictures of Herschel Walker, a popular Georgia football player. Both also requested that the teacher write some things about the picture. Jeff dictated fluently "what the man who sits in the little box" was saying about Herschel (and even added the *et* himself). In contrast, Freddy asked the teacher to "write some stuff about him and me." Freddy did not appear to understand that his own words could be put on the paper. The teacher pressed, "Well, what do you want to say about Herschel?" Freddy appeared to interpret this as "What do you want to

HersheLWALKER

Hershal just got a touchdown.
Buck Belue threw the ball
to Hershel. That is how
he got the touchdown.
Lindsay had the ball
and dropped it and
that's how Buck got
it and threw et.

Figure 6–4

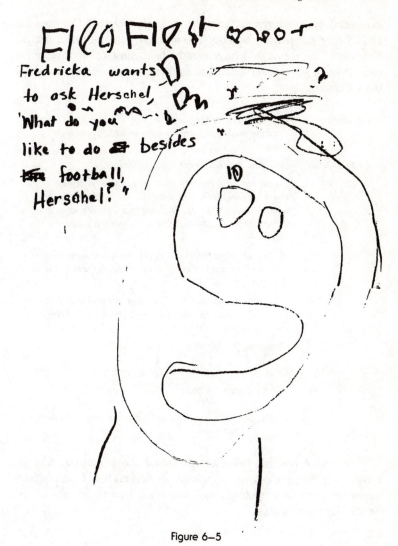

Fredricka wants to ask Herschel, 'What do you like to do besides football, Herschel?'

Figure 6–5

say *to* Herschel?'' as he answered, "I wanna ask, 'What do you like to do besides play football, Herschel?' ''

After writing the child's story, teachers often have children read back their dictation. The children's reading reveals additional information about their developing knowledge of written language. Teachers can ask themselves, Does the child look at the print or at the picture when reading? Does the child read back (or attempt to read back as evidenced by self-correction) the same words dictated? Or, does the child freely paraphrase, as though it were only the message, not the wording of the message, which must be held constant? By asking the child to point as he or she reads, the teacher can gain information about the following:

Directionality:	Does the child read left-to-right?
	Does the child read down the page in the conventional manner?
Voice/Print Match:	How does the child match voice and print?

    Less advanced children may, for example, sweep the finger back and forth over the entire line as they recite the written message. Or, the child may point to each segment of the text, repeating the entire message for each successive segment.

    More advanced children may point in a seemingly random fashion to segments of the text, but they begin and end at the appropriate places.

    Certain children may have an unconventional but systematic way of connecting voice and print, for example, through use of a syllable technique:

Text:	my	birthday		cake	
	↑	↑		↑	↑
Child:	my	birth		day	cake

Text:	Santa	Claus	
	↑	↑	↑
Child:	San	ta	Claus (Child comments that text is
		inaccurate.)	

    The varied possible behaviors described above illustrate that the relationship between talk and print is not an obvious one. Careful observation of children's reading can reveal their hypotheses about how written language works.

Independent writing

Fives and sixes not only dictate; they themselves write. But their writing is often not acceptable in schools, where conventional, adult-like writing may be the only writing of interest. As Freddy remarked, ''I used to write, but not anymore . . . I come to school now.'' Freddy reported that he stopped writing when he started kindergarten. Other children, like Danielle, ''write at home, but not in school.'' Writing, especially when the writer is aware of the discrepency between his or her own writing and that of adults, involves risking oneself. In an environment supportive of writing, children do write, and teachers can gain information about children's knowledge of our alphabetic writing system, the writing process, and the functions that writing can serve.

Let us begin by looking at young children writing at home. Five-year-old Sara's mother, whom we heard from earlier, recalled Sara's early interest in making a "word." Sara would manipulate the magnetic letters on the refrigerator, periodically asking her mother, "Is this a word?" From there, Sara began to ask for particular spellings for special words. Recently Sara had demonstrated an interest in a wide variety of functions, including letters to Grandma, creating balloon-type comics, and writing "joke stories" (funny stories). With growth in function came increased skill with the mechanics of writing. As Sara's mother explains:

> I may be cooking [as I call out to Sara]: "I–B–K–E–B [sic]. . ." She knows when to leave a space in "I love you." A lot of times I'll have to say, "That's the end of that word." Or she'll say, "Is this a period?" When she first started writing, she wanted to go Chinese style, right to left, bottom up [but not anymore].

Sara's mother also noted increasing coherence between the messages Sara wrote and the accompanying illustrations. At first, when Sara would make a picture to go with her letter to Grandma, the two would not be related. The thematic relationship between picture and message was recent.

Vivi's mother reported similar beginnings—an interest in trying to make a word ("Mama, read this for me") and the subsequent interest in writing real words. Vivi, who had a large extended family, was primarily interested in people's names. She had not yet begun to write messages as complex as Sara's or for as wide a range of purposes.

When given the opportunity to write, children will write in these same ways in school. They may make "how writing looks," using cursive-like script, letters, and letter-like forms. The children who write, as April did to produce Figure 6–6, demonstrate a knowledge of letter forms and of the linearity and directionality of text. April referred to her letters as "words" which she could not yet read. Thus, although she displayed her knowledge of the recursiveness of written language— that a finite set of letter forms is used and reused—she did not appear to be aware that "readable" text is not conveyed by repetitive rows of the same letter.

Figure 6–6

First readable messages are often names. In centers and schools, some 5-to-6-year-olds are still struggling to differentiate the letters of their names, as is Shay, who writes *Sbay*, while others can write the names of many family members and friends. For example, Ms. Marshall noticed Jeanne printing MOM on the side of her painting. Ms.

Marshall talked with Jeanne to find out the extensiveness of Jeanne's written language vocabulary:

Ms. Marshall: Do you know any other words?

      Jeanne: (Shrugs)

Ms. Marshall: What's your big sister's name?

      Jeanne: Reannie.

Ms. Marshall: Can you write *Reannie*?

      Jeanne: Yeah (writes *Reannie*)

Ms. Marshall: What about your little sister's name?

And so the conversation went until Jeanne had written the names of her father, mother, and two sisters. Ms. Marshall wrote out the names on 3″ × 5″ index cards. She put the cards on a ring and told Jeanne that they would add to it as Jeanne learned new words.

Children are not only interested in family members' names but also in peers' names. These names are an important reference point in learning about print. By eavesdropping on the children as they work in the writing center, the teacher can document the growing specificity of individual children's knowledge about written language. Here are sample comments by children on their own and each other's work:

Hey, that's part of Justin's name (in reference to a J).

That's me (Mark is referring to an M.)

This goes in Brian's name (in reference to a B).

From an interest in their own names and the names of family members and friends, children may develop an interest in the names of people and objects in their environment. Among Mark's first conventionally written words were *Star Wars* and *Sally* (Charlie Brown's sister). Among Tracy's were *Santa Claus* and *HBO* (*Home Box Office* television).

Young children may use writing for a variety of purposes beyond labeling. In centers and schools teachers may observe the child's growing awareness of writing purposes. Children may use these writing functions in their play as they make grocery lists, write prescriptions for a sick baby, dash off a quick note to their child's teacher. Children may also use writing for a real situation in their daily lives, although their products may not be in conventional form. For example, Rachel's letter to Vivi, in Figure 6–7, demonstrates an awareness of the positive social value of letters (the reaching out to another person), although the letter does not communicate a particular message.

No one writing sample can reveal all of a child's knowledge about writing, but—by collecting samples of children's work over time—the

Figure 6–7

teacher can learn about the children's purposes for writing as well as their growing command of the writing task. Children gain control over both *the message to be expressed* in writing (for example, teachers can note: Did the child freely formulate the message? Or, were all messages copied? Were all messages confined to the child's known words [words the child could easily spell]?) and *the system for expressing messages* (for example, the teacher can note: Did the child appear to be randomly making letters? Or, did the child use systematic procedures for deciding what letters to write? How conventional were the child's procedures? Can you read the child's message?)

Here are some examples of kindergarteners' writing behaviors. What can we learn about their control of the writing task?

Shawna copies print from books and from displayed charts, but she hasn't any idea what message she is conveying nor is she particularly interested in the message. "They're words; I don't know what they say," she says to an adult curious about her writing. Her writing appears conventional but she has little control over the expression of a personal message.

Terry makes patches of words on her paper. The words are the names of family members and peers. Terry knows what she's writing (her message) and she knows the conventional spelling for the message (the system)—but her writing is confined to this small set of known words.

Rachel, who can write her sister's and her friends' names, often writes sentence-length messages which no one but she herself can read. Although she appears to select the letters which will represent her message randomly, she clearly is assuming command of the message of writing.

Children may initially provide both the message and the system for expressing it; for example, a page full of letters and letter-like forms may be confidently "read." As children become aware of the gap between their own writing and that of adults, they may copy any displayed print or request help to convey a particular message. Over time, then, children may move back and forth between writing independently and seeking information from other, more skilled writers.

Encoding: Going from message to print

In their move towards independence in writing, children may experiment with their own systems for encoding messages. There are various possible strategies which children may use to invent spellings. For certain children, this inventing may involve simply putting down a number of letters or letter-like forms for each object to be represented. For an example, note the following exchange between Kevin and the second author:

Dyson: What are you writing, Kevin?

Kevin: I'm writing this flower. (See Figure 6–8; Kevin writes letters around flower.)

Dyson: And now?

Kevin: I'm gonna spell that little dot on it. (Kevin adds more letters for the "dot" in the middle of the flower. Note how Kevin appears to be using primarily letters from his own name.)

(Anecdote first reported in Dyson, 1982, pp. 373–374.)

Other children attempt to write visually-recalled patterns of words. For example, Damon recalled the conventional spelling of *cow* and then decided to write *moo: coow*.

When children begin to make a connection between talk and print, they may adopt a syllable-based strategy. Using this technique, children make a certain number of letters for each syllable or word segment, as Vivi did to produce:

HR	PB	HO	RB
↑	↑	↑	↑
Mama	isa	sin	ger.

Children may also use this technique to read or analyze their own writing. Pete Shelton often attempted to write his last name, which he never wrote exactly right. One day he wrote half of an attempt (*sell*) and remarked that it said "Shelt."

Certain 5-year-old children are able to invent their own spellings based on their growing knowledge of the relationships between sounds and letters. Children can invent spellings by relating the sound of the word they are attempting to spell to the sound of the letter name. They may initially write the name of one or two letters to represent the sounds they hear and then add other letters to "complete" the word. For example, Vivi wrote *H* ("aich") for the sound she heard in *chicken*, and then added other letters to produce *RDHO* ("chicken"). The same strategy led from *P O* to *RPOP OPOH* for *peopo* ("people").

Eventually, children begin to write only letters related to speech sounds they hear in the oral word. Children may initially omit vowels in their created spellings, as illustrated in the first of the following compositions by two five-year-olds; the compositions arose from a class project in which the children grew and then sold plants:

The PLT is GRLLK wh mT (The plant is growing. We measured [it].)

Figure 6–8

We MaLRD oar PLas min was 5enhs hi we pat popsecalsecs in sowe cad maLR THEm we pat morcs on the secs so we wad be abol to naw haw hi tha war the pepL how Got the paLas war me and sowsun marci cade MoLLe crste cende and tona.

(We measured our plants. Mine was five inches high. We put popsicle sticks in so we could measure them. We put marks on the sticks so we would be able to know how high they were. The people who got the plants were me, and Susan, Marci, Cedric, Mollie, Christie, _____?_____, and Tonya.)

To attempt spelling, especially when one is aware that the resulting products are not exactly right, involves risk-taking. Children who freely invent spellings can explore the nature of our spelling system and may also achieve an early fluency in written expression. If, as parents and

SOM MohSTers graool

(Some monsters growl.)

Figure 6—9

teachers, we react with interest and acceptance to their spelling attempts, they may reward us with delightful pieces of work. Consider, for example, Kelly's three compositions, arranged in chronological order, in Figures 6–9, 6–10, and 6–11. Although she was initially reluctant to spell independently, her teacher, sensitive to Kelly's sophisticated sound/symbol knowledge, encouraged her to try. Within only two weeks, Kelly became quite fluent.

In any group of 5- and 6-year old children, the teacher may observe a variety of strategies for making messages visible on the empty page. Strategies a child uses might be recorded as they appear by simply making notes on periodically collected writing samples. Or, the teacher might use a grid, such as that in Figure 6–12, for recording children's strategies.

The most helpful teacher response to these strategies would appear to be to accept whatever strategy the particular child uses, respond to the child's written message (if there is one), answer the child's emerging questions, and, through sensitive questioning, prompt the development of new strategies. Viewing only one encoding strategy as acceptable could cause a child to abandon his or her exploration of writing. For example, Sara, whom we met earlier, wrote at home with Mom's

The NIGhTMARe
ONdrMY BeD   Kelly
isOCe
The NiGhTMABe
WMY noW S iS
TerBL aNd

(The nightmare under my bed is ugly. The nightmare
in my house is terrible and [noisy].)

Figure 6–10

My SroTiS ILM riTN aBauT MY SiLF and WiT and SoMTiMS haSa rLNBo and IgaTriT MY eyes anT BLu MY NaMe iS Kelly vcriguD

(My shirt is white and has a rainbow and my eyes
are blue. I'm writing about myself and sometimes
I can't write very good. My name is Kelly.)

Figure 6–11

assistance, but was reluctant to write at school where the teacher was
interested primarily in conventional, independently-produced writing.
At home Sara could ask her mother for help or, in her words, "write
what it looks like . . . make up what it looks like." At school, Sara's
teacher followed a readiness curriculum which stressed "sound/ symbol" associations; she taught the children to "sound out" words, a
technique which Sara never used.

In contrast, Robin, another 5-year-old who wrote at home with
Mom, was allowed to use diverse encoding strategies at school. The
teacher worked with Robin and a small group of her peers who were
already writing in a conventional manner. The children "sounded out,"
recalled patterns, and requested spellings from each other or from the
teacher:

Child's Name	Appears to write letters randomly	Writes letters for syllables	Writes visually-recalled pattern	Requests spellings	Spelling Phonologically -based on letter names	Spelling Phonologically -based on consonant sounds
Rachel	10/8		10/14 Julie (her sister)	10/20 - peers' names		
Vivi	10/14	10/17	10/8 - family names		10/23 - combines this & syl. method	
Nate			10/14 - peers' names			10/8 - does w/ ease

Date entered when behavior first noted.

The behaviors listed are possible encoding strategies. No fixed developmental sequence is implied.

Figure 6–12 Grid for Recording Children's Encoding Strategies

Robin: (She has just completed a drawing.) Look at all the people in the window.

Teacher: OOOOOOOOOOHHHHHHHHH.

Robin: 'Cause they're gonna have a party. Now, I'm gonna write my words. . . The (writes *the*) . . . (to teacher) How do you spell *house*?

Teacher: How do you think it starts?

Robin: *H* . . .

Teacher: Mmmm mmmmm. . . Now what? . . . (Teacher writes *hou*) Can you tell what comes next? *House*? . . . (writes *se*)

Robin: *H-O-U-S-E*. . . The house is (writes *is*) too (writes *to*) little . . . (to teacher) How do you spell *little*?

Teacher: Why is the house too little?

Robin: Because there's going to be a 154 people!

Teacher: Oh my gosh!

We have discussed varied behaviors which teachers may observe in order to assess children's understandings of the purposes and processes of writing. Figure 6–13 summarizes these behaviors.

Summary

For young children, starting elementary school signals an expansion in the variety of situations available for meaningful use of both oral and written language. In this chapter, we discussed the varying opportunities for talk presented by classroom activities, many of which are also activities commonly found in the home and center. The children described were using language for a variety of purposes—to inform, direct, describe, analyze, persuade, question, imagine, and narrate in a variety of situations with a variety of conversational partners. Through observation of their children in differing contexts, teachers can gain information necessary for planning experiences which both build upon and extend individual children's interests, styles, and competence in language use.

Starting elementary school also marks the beginning of greater use of language in its literary forms; children grow in their appreciation of the literature of others and in their ability to create their own literature, both orally and in writing. We described what adults can learn from observing children's early attempts at reading and writing, considering children's interest in becoming literate, their awareness of written language's functions and forms, and their knowledge of the reading and

Figure 6–13 Guidelines for Observing Kindergarteners' Writing

When observing (watching, listening to, talking to children about) their writing, you might consider the following questions:

The Message

1. Does the child believe that he's written a message? If so,
2. Does the child know what the message is? That is, can he read it? If so,
3. Did the child freely formulate his own message? Or, did the child simply copy something? Or, was the message confined to a small set of words which the child could easily spell?
4. How long was the message?
   –one word or a list of unrelated words
   –a phrase
   –a sentence
5. How does the child's written message relate to other graphics on the page?

The Encoding System

1. Can you read the child's message? If not,
2. Does there seem to be any system to how the child went from the formulated message to the print? For example, the child may have
   –put down a certain number of letters per object
   –rearranged the letters in his name
   –written a certain number of letters per syllable
3. If you can read the child's message, can you tell how the child encoded it?[a] For example, the child may have:
   –recalled the visual pattern (e.g., *COOW,* child intended to write *moo*)
   –based spelling on letter names (e.g., *PT,* which is read *Petie*)
   –requested spellings from peer or adult
   –based spelling on phonological analysis (e.g., *APL,* which is read *apple*)

The Written Product

1. How conventional are the child's written symbols? (Do they look like letters?)
2. Did the child follow the left-to-right directionality convention?
3. Is there any order to the way letters or words are arranged on the page? Or, does it appear that the child simply put letters where there was empty space?

Message Decoding

1. Does the child appear to have written without any particular intended message? If so,
2. Did the child attempt to decode the written message?
3. If so, how did the child go from text to talk? The child may have:
   –engaged in apparent fantasy behavior
   –requested that an adult read the unknown message (e.g., "What does this say?")
   –based the decoding on the perceived text segments (i.e., matched a number of oral syllables to the perceived number of segments in text)
   –used a letter-name strategy (i.e., "read" a word containing the name of a written letter, as reading "Debbie" for *PARA NB*)
   –based decoding on visual recall of a word similar in appearance

Writing Purpose

1. *Why* did the child write? Possible reasons include:
   –simply to write; no clearly identifiable purpose exists beyond this (e.g., "I'm gonna' do it how my Mama does it.")

(continued)

Figure 6–13 (*Continued*)

–to create a message; the meaning of the message is unknown to the child (e.g., "Read this for me.")

–to produce or to practice conventional symbols (e.g., the *ABC*'s, displayed written language) without concern for a referent

–to detail or accurately represent a drawn object (e.g., the *S* on Superman's shirt)

–to label objects or people

–to make a particular type of written object (e.g., a book, a list, a letter) without concern for a particular referent

–to organize and record information (e.g., to write a list of friends)

–to investigate the relationship between oral and written language without concern for a particular referent (e.g., "If I do [add] this letter, what does it say?")

–to express directly feelings or experiences of oneself or others (i.e., direct quotations, as in writing the talk of a drawn character), and

–to communicate a particular message to a particular audience

---

[a]It may be that the child *is* using one of these methods, but you simply cannot read it. After asking the child to read the paper, you may be able to detect patterns in the child's encoding system.

writing processes. Like oral language, written language grows as children are actively involved—as they read and write to fulfill a variety of purposes in an environment that respects and responds to their efforts.

Suggested "Predictable" Books

Bonne, R. *I know an old lady.* New York: Scholastic Book Services, 1974.

Carle, E. *The very hungry caterpillar.* New York: World Publishing, 1969.

Charlip, R. & Burton, S. *Mother mother I feel sick.* New York: Parents Magazine Press, 1966.

de Regniers, B. S. *May I bring a friend?* New York: Atheneum, 1965.

Edelman, E. *Boom-de-boom.* Toronto: Pantheon Books, 1980.

Emberley, B. (adapter). *Drummer Hoff.* Englewood Cliffs, NJ: Prentice-Hall, 1968.

Emberley, B. (adapter). *One wide river to cross.* Englewood Cliffs, NJ: Prentice-Hall, 1967.

Galdone, P. *The old woman and her pig.* New York: McGraw-Hill Book Co., 1960.

Galdone, P. *The three little pigs.* New York: Seabury Press, 1970.

Galdone, P. *The gingerbread boy.* New York: Seabury Press, 1975.

Ginsburg, M. *Good morning, chick.* New York: Greenwillow Books, 1980.

Hogrogian, N. *One fine day.* London: Macmillan Co., 1971.

Jeffers, S. *All the pretty horses.* New York: MacMillan, 1974.

Jeffers, S. (adapter). *Three jovial huntsmen.* New York: Bradbury Press, 1973.

Keats, E. J. *Over in the meadow.* New York: Four Winds Press, 1971.

Kellogg, S. *Can I keep him?* New York: Dial Press, 1971.

Langstaff, J. *Over in the meadow.* New York: Harcourt, 1957.

Mosel, A. *Tikki Tikki Tembo*. New York: Holt, Rinehart and Winston, 1968.
Rockwell, A. *The monkey's whiskers*. New York: Parents Magazine Press, 1971.
Sawyer, Ruth. *Journey cake, ho!* New York: Viking Press, 1953.
Spier, P. *London Bridge is falling down!* New York: Doubleday, 1967.
Stobbs, W. *Henny Penny*. Chicago: Follett, 1968.
Tolstoy, A. *The great big enormous turnip*. New York: Franklin Watts, 1968.
Viorst, J. *Alexander and the terrible, horrible, no good, very bad day*. New York: Atheneum, 1977.

Suggested Wordless Pictures Books

Anno, M. *Anno's Italy*. New York: William Collins, 1980.
Anno, M. *Anno's journey*. New York: William Collins, 1979.
Baum, W. *Birds of a feather*. Reading, MA: Addisonian Press, 1969.
Briggs, R. *The snowman*. New York: Random House, 1978.
Carle, E. *Do you want to be my friend?* New York: Thomas Y. Crowell, 1971.
Carroll, R. *What Whiskers did*. New York: Macmillan, 1932.
Carroll, R. *The chimp and the clown*. New York: Henry Z. Walck, 1968.
Carroll, R. *Ruth and Latrobe*. New York: Henry Z. Walck, 1970.
dePaola, T. *The hunter and the animals*. New York: Holiday House, 1981.
Goodall, J. S. *The adventures of Paddy Pork*. New York: Harcourt, Brace, and World, 1968.
Goodall, J. S. *Shrewbettina's birthday*. New York: Harcourt, Brace Jovanovich, 1970.
Goodall, J. S. *Naughty Nancy*. New York: Atheneum, 1975.
Goodall, J. S. *The surprise picnic*. New York: Atheneum, 1977.
Heller, L. *Lily at the table*. New York: Macmillan, 1979.
Hogrogian, N. *Apples*. New York: Macmillan, 1972.
Hutchins, P. *Changes, changes*. New York: Macmillan, 1971.
Krahn, F. *A flying saucer full of spaghetti*. New York: Dutton, 1970.
Krahn, F. *Who's seen the scissors?* New York: Dutton, 1975.
Krahn, F. *A funny friend from heaven*. Philadelphia: Lippincott, 1977.
Krahn, F. *The biggest Christmas tree on earth*. Boston: Little, Brown, 1978.
Lisowski, G. *The invitation*. New York: Holt, Rinehart, and Winston, 1980.
Mari, I. *The magic balloon*. New York: S. G. Phillips, 1967.
Mayer, M. *Frog, where are you?* New York: Dial Press, 1969.
Mayer, M. *Bubble bubble*. New York: Parents Magazine Press, 1973.
Mayer, M. *Frog goes to dinner*. New York: Dial Press, 1974.
Mayer, M. & Mayer, M. *A boy, a dog, a frog and a friend*. New York: Dial Press, 1971.
Mayer, M. & Mayer, M. *One frog too many*. New York: Dial Press, 1975.
Schick, E. *Making friends*. Toronto: Collier, Macmillan Canada, Ltd., 1969.
Shimin, S. *A special birthday*. New York: McGraw-Hill, 1976.
Ward, L. *The silver pony: A story in pictures*. Boston: Houghton Mifflin, 1973.
Wezel, P. *The good bird*. New York: Harper & Row, 1964.
Wezel, P. *The naughty bird*. Chicago: Follett Publishing Company, 1967.
Winter, P. *The bear and the fly*. New York: Crown, 1976.

We thank Elaine Belfield for compiling these lists.

Suggested Readings

Clay, M. *What did I write?* Auckland, New Zealand: Heinemann, 1975.
   This well-known book is a detailed, highly readable, and amply illustrated analysis of
   young children's earliest writing. Clay demonstrates that mere "scribbles" are rich
   sources of information about children's developing knowledge of written language.
Holdaway, D. *The foundations of literacy.* Sydney, Australia: Ashton Scholastic, 1979.
   The shared book experience between teacher and children is at the center of Holdaway's literacy program for early childhood. In this text, he provides readers with
   both a theoretical rationale and detailed, practical suggestions for teaching children to
   read by involving them with books.
Paley, V. *Wally's stories.* Cambridge, MA: Harvard University Press, 1981.
   As a kindergarten teacher, Vivian Paley regularly taped and transcribed her children's
   discussions and conversations. The resulting transcripts provide the bulk of her book,
   allowing readers a front-row view of young children's thinking and talking. Paley is a
   model observer and responder to children, and the conversations themselves reflect
   the intertwined cognitive, linguistic, and sociolinguistic aspects of classroom life.

CHAPTER 7

Six- to Eight-Year-Olds: Interacting Through Text and Talk

Introduction

Ms. Betts: Let's pretend Arthur lost his glasses on another day. What else might have happened if he couldn't see? . . . I know. Arthur visited a farm where he saw a little puppy. "Hello, dog," he called, "Oink, oink," said the dog.

Children: It's a pig!

Ms. Betts: Mm mmm. It's a pig. Wasn't that silly? Now, what else might have happened to Arthur? Can you tell a story?

Melinda: If he was walking he might bump into a tree.

Ms. Betts: Oh, no! And then what happened?

Melinda: He got a headache.

Tanya: When he meant to go to school, he went to the grocery store and act like it was school.

Ms. Betts: Oh, really? Did he sit down and think he was going to be taught a lesson? (Tanya nods.) Oh, I bet he felt silly. So he couldn't see where he was going so he accidentally went to the grocery store instead of school.

Cynthia: Um, he was going to the store and . . . um, and while he was walking . . . um . . . he couldn't—he didn't know where the supermarket was so, um, instead of going to the supermarket, he went to somebody's house. And he went and stole—he got some of their furniture. Then they went—and he paid for it at their house.

Ms. Betts: And they just wondered what he was doing, didn't they? They said, "This isn't a store!"

Ms. Betts had read *Arthur's Eyes* (M. Brown, 1979) to her first graders and then had the children narrate their own funny tales. In the children's storytelling, we see evidence of their varying ability to narrate. Certain children told only one event; others linked events, explaining cause/effect relationships. We note also the naturally occurring complex sentences as the children explained that:

If he was . . .

When he was . . .

While he was . . .

Instead of . . .

Ms. Betts responded to all the stories, encouraging her children to extend plots, to imagine characters' feelings and reactions, and to add dialogue.

Later that day the children dictated "Arthur" stories to Ms. Betts. Their stories incorporated more feelings, reactions, and dialogue than the earlier stories had. Again Ms. Betts interacted with her young narrators:

Chris: (dictating) Instead of going to school, he went to a house. He sat down and said, "Give me some work."

Ms. Betts: (repeats and writes his words) Now watch what happens here, Chris. I have to use quotation marks 'cause he's talking. . . . I have to go over on the back of the page. . . And then what happened?

Chris: Arthur rode his bike.

Ms. Betts: Let's stay on the same story, Chris. What happened after he said, "Give me some work."

Chris: The people said, "We have not got none. This is not a school."

Ms. Betts: (repeats and writes his words)

Chris: He said, "Oh, I'm sorry."

Ms. Betts and her class demonstrate primary grade children's growing ability to communicate in both oral and written language. In this chapter, we observe that developing competence across a range of situations in which first and second graders communicate.

In these early grades, children's activities are increasingly structured. In addition, they are asked to use language to explore increasingly more abstract ideas. In this chapter, we turn first to children's oral communication within typical primary grade activities. We focus primarily on peer conversations within structured classroom tasks and on teacher-led discussions. We also include here sections on sharing time, a typical structured oral language activity of the primary grades, and on teacher-planned activities which center children's attention on the varieties of English spoken around them; in this latter section, we address particularly teachers whose children speak nonstandard English. We then consider children's written language communication, focusing particularly on the reading and writing of stories. As in previous chapters—although we focus first on oral communication and then on written—the separation is for organizational purposes only, talking, listening, reading, and writing are mutually supportive tasks.

Becoming Skillful Oral Communicators

Ms. Martin's second graders have been preparing for International Week. They have learned the story "The Little Red Hen" in Korean. Ms. Martin explains to them that "after we tell the story in Korean, we'll tell it in English." The following conversation then occurs:

Charles: English! Who's gonna teach us English?

Darin: Yeah. That's what I wanna know. Who's gonna teach us English?

Jake: Yeah.

Johann: (Johann is from South Africa) You already know English—that's what you speak.

Charles: I do!?! I speak English!?! (said with amazement and a touch of pride)

As Charles demonstrated, language is not an object of contemplation for young children; it is an instrument of use. Teachers help children become skillful users of language by creating situations in which talk can occur, by observing their children's growing competence, and by interacting with them in ways which encourage use of a range of language purposes.

Sharing circle

One of those purposes is to share personal experiences with others. Primary grade classrooms commonly have a daily time in which individual children formally talk to their classmates. They may bring in an object from home to share, or they may simply talk about a recent event. The sharing task is to focus on a topic which will be interesting to others and to present ideas in a clear, engaging manner.

Consider sharing time in Ms. Cook's classroom in a rural Georgia school. Since it is close to Halloween, Ms. Cook has asked the children to describe a scary experience that they have had. The responses vary greatly in fluency, clarity, and style. For example, Clint stands up and says only "out in the dark," while Fred tells this elaborate tale:

> One time I was out there in the woods. I was out there with my BB gun at nighttime. So anyway, I heard something up there eerie flying around my head. I looked there and there was a bat up there flying around. I went back in the house and got a flashlight and went up there and shine' it at things flying around my head. So anyway, I shined the light back over there, and I saw an owl, his eyes shining, and I cut it back off. . . Boy! I took off back through the yard.

There are also children like Janie, who speaks very softly; Jeff, who rambles from topic to topic, never really settling on one idea; and Carrie, who finds it difficult to listen to her peers—she squirms on the rug, tracing designs with her finger.

Ms. Cook responds to the children's stories. She asks for elaborations: "Clint, I wonder, were you alone in the dark? What were you doing?" She requests clarifications: "What do you mean by. . . ?" And she provides summarizing remarks: "Bats and owls in the night *are* scary." In addition, Ms. Cook encourages the other children to listen and ask questions of the speakers about anything they didn't understand or are curious about. In this way, the child-speakers receive feedback on the clarity of their sharing and their listeners gain practice in attentive, critical listening and in seeking out needed information.

For children like Carrie, who find it difficult to attend in this situation, Ms. Cook might find that small group sharing is helpful as each child is closer to the speaker and in addition has greater opportunity to participate. Small group sharing may also help those who are reluctant to speak in large group situations.

While Ms. Cook served as leader during sharing time, children may conduct their own oral sharing, cooperating with and responding to each other. For example, in the classroom observed by Michaels and Foster (in press), children successfully managed sharing without any direct adult assistance. A teacher-appointed group leader assumed the responsibility for allotting turns to share and for making sure that children "behaved." Certain children used their turns to share information—facts—as did Paul who talked about his rocks:

> They're um they're a kind of rock that's white and they have a little salt, in 'em. . . .
> I'm going to go around here because those people didn't get to see 'em.

Others, like Rene, shared personal stories:

> Then uh, and in midnight, . . . ac—actually it was like two o'clock in the morning I
> heard a scratch again, and I went to the same room and it was just a little, little baby
> rabbit with his mo—with one mother, and he was SO cute and, . . . I let THEM out.

The listening children responded to all sharers with questions and comments, at times searching for more information (e.g., "Do salt rocks taste like salt?") or requesting clarification (e.g., "Why did your dad say, um, we'd better close the windows because . . . we opened the windows because it was *cold*?").

Michaels and Foster point out that successful sharers are those children who monitor their audience, making adjustments in their topic or style, perhaps seeking comments and questions from their listeners. On the other hand, "boring" sharers are less sensitive to their audience and are likely to be told by them, "That's boring." Thus, the children are actually assessing and fostering each other's ability to be an effective communicator. In the next section we discuss peer learning in greater detail.

Talking with peers

> Jason: I'd like to visit the Greek Parthenon.
>
> Charles: Parthenon! I live on Parthenon St. (said with sincere amazement, perhaps because Parthenon is not a particularly attractive part of town).
>
> Jason: No, the *Greek* Parthenon.
>
> Charles: Huh?
>
> Jason: It's in Greece.
>
> Charles: Greece!?!

Talking with peers is a natural learning activity for children, just as it is for adults. In this section we stress two types of peer interactions of particular relevance to the school situation—didactic and collaborative talk.

The following interaction between Springli and Peter illustrates a didactic situation, in which one peer seeks assistance from another:

> Peter: Springli. . . Springli.

Springli: What?

Peter: If I want to say *I,* do I, in the middle of a section, do I put a lower case or a capital?

Springli: Capital.

Peter: OK.

Researchers, such as Wilkinson and Dollaghan (1979), have emphasized the skill involved in such interactions. Children seeking information must be able to get the attention of a peer, they must know which peers are most likely both to have the needed information and be willing to give it, and they must clearly state what information is needed. Children vary in their ability to get assistance from peers; children's difficulty in this area may limit their ability to participate fully in classroom learning activities.

As with the seeking of information, the giving of information also involves considerable skill. The tutor may need to focus the tutee's attention on the task, to give information clearly, and to monitor the tutee's performance, giving the necessary feedback. At times, the tutor must balance assisting others with securing enough time for his or her own work:

Peter: Eva, do you know how to spell—just a second, (rereading his paper) "Snails; I got some snails out of the aquarium and I"—how do you write *am*?

Eva: Erase this (referring to some scratch-outs on Peter's paper).

Peter: OK. (Although Peter willingly begins to erase, Eva takes the eraser from him and begins to erase for him. After about a minute she gives the eraser back to Peter.)

Eva: Can you erase it 'cuz I need to get busy?

Peter: OK.

Certain children are capable of doing more than simply giving information; they can model assistance strategies used by their teacher. Similarly, some children are supportive of their peers; others are less patient, at times resentful of their teacher-role.

Ms. Dean, a first grade teacher, experienced many of the successes and, also, the difficulties which confront teachers who wish to structure didactic talk settings in the classroom. She wanted to provide individual help for certain children who needed extra support in learning to read. However, she found that there was more involved in pairing the children than simply matching a more with a less proficient reader. Robert, the best reader in the classroom, appeared bored during the activity. He stared into space as his partner Andrew read, responding only to Andrew's direct requests for needed words. In contrast, Melissa appeared to enjoy the task. She put her arm around John as he read, frequently praising him; "You did real good on that page." When John ran into trouble, she adopted Ms. Dean's own instructional strategies: "Read it [the sentence] again 'n see if you can guess what that word is. . . It's the same word as this one—you read it over here on this page. . . "

In order to foster didactic talk, teachers may explain directions for a particular assignment to one child who, in turn, explains the assignment to a group of peers (Cazden, et al., 1978). The peer-run sharing circle discussed in the previous section is another situation in which children, as experts on a particular topic, are required to share their knowledge with others. In both these situations, the "teacher's" students are encouraged to ask questions in order to clarify or gain further information.

Throughout the day, children interact collaboratively as well as didactically; that is, they work together, without teacher guidance, to accomplish particular tasks. In such interactions, children must listen and respond clearly to each other. They negotiate roles, since all cannot lead nor can all follow. The playground provides a rich context for collaborative talk, as illustrated in the following incident.

A group of primary grade children were playing on the hanging bars. They designed a game in which two children would begin to cross at opposite ends of the bars, passing each other in the middle. The pairs who successfully negotiated this feat were those in which at least one child planned verbally who would do what, taking into consideration their respective skills. For example, Jan was unsure of herself on the bars; as Jan and her partner Krissie approached the middle, Jan called out, "Krissie, you go to the side [bars] and I'll stay on the bars." Clint and Tina, however, met in the middle, neither one speaking. Finally, Clint grinned sheepishly and dropped off the bars, and Tina crossed to the other side.

To foster collaborative talk, teachers may design clearly focused activities for small groups. When completing such tasks, children may listen to each other more carefully and explain their meanings to each other more clearly than in casual conversation. Note the complex language and thinking and the precise word choice in the following anecdote:

Two first grade boys are trying to build a boat from small plastic blocks that will float in the water:

Andy: This one don't float too good. Looks like a water boat.

Jeff: I think we need more weight on this side.

Andy: I mean how to. . .

Jeff: Look at this man. I think we need some more weight. . . Our house is going to be drownded! In the middle of the ocean! Help! We're drowning! I know what's the matter. We got too much weight on the back. That's what I think. We got too much weight on the back. . .

Andy: It's partly because of this chimney and these, man.

Jeff: We got too much weight on the back. I need something for weight on the front.

Andy: I'm putting real much weight on the front and back, see? Got a lot of weight on the front and back. Here's where the back's going to be. . . (Pinnell, 1975, p. 320).

In planning such collaborative small groups, teachers have traditionally considered only academic achievement as the basis for grouping. However, if we consider one of our goals to be that of increasing children's ability to interact effectively with their peers, then other criteria for grouping become important. Effective small groups (those in which children interact cooperatively to fulfill their common purpose) may be formed based on common interests or friendship patterns. Children's interests are revealed through various expressive activities, not only through informal conversations, but also through the stories they write, the pictures they paint, the themes they enact in their play. Children's friendship or interactional patterns are revealed through careful teacher observation. To assist them in organizing their observations, teachers may use a checklist, similar to Figure 4–1 in Chapter 4. Such a checklist may be particularly helpful in documenting the interactions of children who appear to be "shy" or "loners." During those times of the day when children are playing or working independently, teachers can note the frequency with which, and with whom, a particular child speaks.

In a public school in which the second author worked, we used such observations of children's interests and interactions to guide the formation of small groups to stimulate collaborative talk between monolingual Spanish and monolingual English speakers. My partner teacher, Ms. Rios, was originally assigned to teach my 6- to 7-year-old monolingual English class Spanish, while I was to teach her monolingual Spanish class English. We became concerned about our teaching effectiveness. Our children spoke their new language only to their respective language teacher; they spoke their first language with each other. Thus, the children were actually speaking more Spanish than English in my "English" class, and the reverse was true for her "Spanish" class. We decided to abandon our separate language lessons. Guided by the work of Wong Fillmore (see Chapter 2), we assigned each child in my room a partner from Ms. Rios's room. We asked the children to speak Spanish in Ms. Rios's room and English in my own. In this way, we hoped that the children would teach each other. We planned varied activities, focused on a theme (e.g., "Animals," or "Transportation"), for the small groups. Each lesson began with a large group activity, such as a discussion, film, or book-sharing. Then the children worked in their group as we circulated among them, stimulating and extending their talk.

Through trial and error, we identified certain factors which were essential to effective groups. First, pairing children led to more interaction between Spanish and English speakers than did forming larger groups. In the larger groups, the children tended to interact primarily with others who shared their first language. Second, the most successful pairs were those children who had displayed a liking—or at least a tolerance—for each other, for example, by wanting to sit next to each other or by playing together on the playground. Third, effective group activities were those that required collaborative talk for their completion. Looking at story books or painting pictures were not successful talk-stimulators as the children did not have to speak to each other in these situations. On the other hand, dramatic play or constructive tasks, such as building blocks (if we asked the children to build a construction together), were successful. Not all activities worked equally well with all children. However, by observing both children's preferred activities and their preferred partners, we did achieve the desired hum (and, of course, the intermittent shouts) of busy, involved children talking.

Teacher-led discussions

Certainly, at times we want our children as a group to come together and talk. In the previous chapter, we discussed the difficulty young children may have in participating in such large group discussions. The skillful teacher interacts with her children in order to clarify and extend their thinking and, simultaneously, their language. In addition, her interaction helps them to become effective discussants, who are able to participate in the collaborative exploration of a topic.

In addition to these general goals, the teacher will have specific goals for individual children. In any classroom, the teacher will notice the children who, in large group discussions, are reluctant to talk, those who speak very softly or who rely heavily on gesture and verbal fillers (*oh yeah, well, you know*). On the other hand, she will observe those who are reluctant to yield the floor to their peers; who blurt out ideas when others are talking; or who carry on small conversations with nearby peers, rather than attend to the larger group effort.

In the following discussion, Ms. Martin demonstrates various teacher strategies for working toward both these general goals for classroom discussions and particular goals for individual children. She displays as well her abilities to observe and listen, which are necessary to effectively achieve those goals. She follows up her questions to individual children with questions designed to extend their thinking ("Why. . . ?") or to clarify their language ("What do you mean by. . ."). She not only initiates and extends discussion topics, she allows the children to initiate topics as well; she intertwines their comments into the ongoing cooperatively constructed discussion:

Ms. Martin has been reading a biography of Helen Keller to her group of mixed-ability second graders. She is beginning a class discussion of recently read chapters:

Ms. Martin: What was Helen Keller like as a little girl?

Charles: She was mean.

Ms. Martin: Yeah—she had a temper, didn't she? And how did her parents deal with that?

Jake: They spoiled her.

Ms. Martin: What do you mean by "spoil?"

Jake: They let her have all the things she wanted.

Ms. Martin: Why did they do that?

Shawna: 'Cuz she was blind and deaf.

Tony: She couldn't even see.

Ms. Martin: Yeah, they felt sorry for her. They didn't know quite what to do with Helen.

Jeanna: She didn't like the baby sister in the crib.

Mark: Yeah.

Jeanna: And she didn't even know the baby was in there.

Ms. Martin: What did she call the thing that was in the crib?

All: It.

Ms. Martin: She said, "I don't like it," but she couldn't express that to her parents—she couldn't *say*, "I don't like it."

Shawna: The teacher said it was a baby.

> Ms. Martin: So finally when her teacher, Ann Sullivan, came to live at the Keller home, she began to communicate.

Notice how Ms. Martin does not parrot the children's remarks but, rather, incorporates what they say into a coherent discussion. She also asks open-ended questions which allow several children to respond with different answers to the same question. Both these techniques allow the children to share responsibility for shaping the evolving discussion:

> Ms. Martin now reads an article written by Helen Keller to her children. In the article, Ms. Keller describes what she would like to see if given three days of sight. Ms. Martin stops periodically as she reads to discuss the article with her children, focusing particularly on unusual words or phrases:
>
> Ms. Martin: Helen wants to see the "small simple things." What does *simple* mean?
>
> Will: The easy things.
>
> Barry: Things like a pencil and pen.
>
> Ms. Martin: If this [holding up a worksheet] is simple work, it means it's easy to do, but what about simple things?
>
> Children: Pictures . . . chairs . . . flowers . . . butterflies . . . rugs . . . books.
>
> Ms. Martin: (nodding) She doesn't want to see the real expensive things, Charles. (Charles has been drawing designs on his article.) Maybe you've got a brand new videotape player that costs $2000. She's not interested in these things. She wants to see the simple things. Maybe a flower pot. What else in your home is not really important, but you like it a lot?
>
> Charles: Football.

In the above excerpt, we also see Ms. Martin helping her children to explore relatively abstract ideas, ideas which cause them to reflect together on their own experiences, their own simple things.

Ms. Martin also assists the children in becoming attentive, critical listeners who are capable of summarizing major ideas:

> Ms. Martin: Let's think over the ideas we've discussed today. What have we talked about?
>
> Curt: About Helen Keller.
>
> Ms. Martin: What did she write about?
>
> Curt: About what she'd like to see.
>
> Ms. Martin: And, in this article by Helen Keller, what are some of the things she mentioned? What would she like to see?
>
> Children: Her dogs, baby.

> Ms. Martin: (touching a finger for each idea listed) her dogs, a baby. . .
>
> Jake: take a walk in the woods
>
> Ms. Martin: She wanted to see the beauty of nature in the woods. . .

Finally, Ms. Martin urges the children to carry the ideas discussed home with them—to continue to reflect upon and make personally meaningful ideas discovered in interaction with others:

> Ms. Martin: When you walk home today—or when you ride home, look for the little things, the simple things. Don't let your eyes be lazy. Don't just get in the car and sit there. Make a list of the things you see. Write them down, and tomorrow morning, we'll share what we saw; we'll read our lists.
>
> Jeanna: When it rains and it stops, you can see rainbows in the street.
>
> Ms. Martin: You don't have lazy eyes, Jeanna, if you can see the rainbows in the street.

In sum, Ms. Martin has used the process of discussing a topic with her children to promote growth in varied areas simultaneously. As she urged the children to clarify and extend their ideas, they responded by clarifying and extending (making more precise and more complex) their language as well. In addition, through her responses to their contributions, she allowed them to use language to shape the evolving discussion. Cognitive, linguistic, and sociolinguistic skill were all in evidence.

Highlighting variation in language

Many of the children we've discussed in this book have been speakers of nonstandard English. As we noted in Chapter 4, we do not view the early childhood years as the appropriate time to formally teach standard English. However, teachers can create situations in which children adopt roles which may, quite naturally, lead children to use more formal, and more standard, English. For example, allowing children to adopt the role of television reporters as they interview an interesting adult, such as the local policeman, can lead to the use of standard English sentence patterns or pronunciations (Haley-James & Hobson, 1980), as can assigning particular children to take teacher roles and explain directions for classwork to peers.

Ms. Raney, who teaches in rural Georgia, discusses with her children the contrasting speech of the different people in their community.

Her children refer to standard English as "how they talk on the TV." Ms. Raney creates situations in which the children use their TV voices, for example, interviewing adult workers in the school or taking the roles of characters in the books she shares with them. To see the dramatic style changes many children are capable of, compare the following two samples of eight-year-old Alex's speech. In the first, Alex is describing a picture:

> Dat cah right dere goin' ta hit da cub [curb] 'n dat cah right dere goin'
> ta hit da ho'se 'n dat cah right dere goin' to hit da do-ug [dog] 'n
> dat other cah goin' te try ta' go to the rescue the do-ug—gonna' try
> 'n go 'n get da do-ug 'cuz he don't want dem ta hit da do'ug cuz it's
> his do-ug. (Ms. Raney asks what the cars are traveling down.) A road. . .
> a skreet.

In the next sample, Alex is taking the role of the donkey in a play, "The Breman Town Musicians," read by Alex, Ms. Raney, and a small group of peers:

> Dog: Good morning.
>
> Donkey: Good morning. Where is your—where's your Mastah?
>
> Dog: I'm running away from her.
>
> Donkey: That's funnah. I'm runnin' away from mine. For many years it's been nothing but work work work. Now that I'm old and tired, he wants to get rid of me. . . Where are you going?
>
> Dog: I'm just running. Where are you going?
>
> Donkey: I'm goin' to Breman. I have always like the music of the Breman Street bands. I thought I might join one of them. I still have a pretty good voice. Why don' you join me? . . . You could play in—a drum with your tail.
>
> Narrator: A cat comes by.
>
> Donkey: You have a very sad face this morning. What's the matter?

The written samples do capture the phonological shifts in Alex's language, for example, the changes from *dat* to *that, da* to *the, skreet* to *street, goin'* to *going*. However, they do not fully convey the articulation changes. In the first sample, Alex spoke in a casual style, deleting the endings of many of his words. In the second he adopted a more formal style; he spoke his words crisply, carefully, exaggerating the pronunciation of particular words (*street*) and word parts (*ing*). Alex clearly illustrates that, with the assistance of a knowledgeable teacher who creates varied contexts for talk, children can display remarkable flexibility in language use.

Ms. Raney keeps audiotaped records of her children's ability to vary their language across situations. She records each child in an informal situation—such as, with Alex, describing a picture—and then records the child in a more structured situation in which the child is asked to assume a role other than ''student.'' The tapes are not only valuable documentation of one aspect of children's communicative competence, they are also effective tools for illustrating to other adults who work with the children (a) the tentativeness that must accompany any judgements about a child's ''verbal abilities,'' and (b) the effect of a child's use of nonstandard English on adults' judgements of the child's competence; the Alex in the first sample may cause a teacher to judge him very differently than would the Alex in the second sample.

Here we should point out that—although we've discussed these activities with particular reference to children who speak nonstandard English—all children must, of course, become increasingly sensitive to the dynamic interplay between speech and social situation. Thus, creating situations in which children step out of student or peer roles and become actively engaged in alternate roles is essential to both assessing and fostering all children's communicative competence. In the following tall-tale play, written and acted out by second-grade middle-class children in a Texas public school, we see evidence of these children's ability to change their style of language, particularly in their choice and pronunciation of words, as they adopt roles. In fact, one child uses exaggerated features of southern regional dialect as she becomes Pecos Kevin's ''li'l ol' wife'':

Scene One (setting: a classroom)

Jeanna: Well, you would not believe what happened to my classroom the other
(Teacher) day. I just have to tell you about it! Why don't I just show you. (She
turns away from the audience and begins teaching her ''class.'' She
looks around the classroom and begins to smell something funny.) Puh!
What is that smell? Can y'all smell that?

Bret: Yes, that smells awful!
(Student)

Ashley &
Aaron: Yuk! It stinks in here!
(Students)

Jeanna: Ook, that smells like a skunk.

Ashley: Look! There it is!

Aaron: Eek! Help!

Bret: I'll go get my bebee gun.

Jeanna: Now Mark, we don't have things like that at school; they are dangerous. I have an idea. We need Pecos Kevin.

Ashley: I'll call for him. PECOS KEVIN, PECOS KEVIN, WE NEED YOU!

(In pops Pecos Kevin with his wife following behind him.)

Kevin: I'm Pecos Kevin, here to save the day. (All behind the stage say, "DA, DA.")

Marci: Don't mind me. I'm just Pecos Kevin's li'l ol' wife.

Jeanna: Pecos Kevin, you've got to do something about that awful smell in here.

Kevin: Sure, I can do anything.

Marci: Well of course he can; he's my husband.

(Exit Kevin and Marci.)

Scene Two (Setting: Pecos Kevin's ranch)

(Marci is washing and hanging up clothes.)

Kevin: Honey, I'm going to find something to get the smell out of that classroom with. (Kevin rides off.)

Marci: Oh, dear! He forgot to kiss me goodbye. (She gets on horse and rides after her husband.) Sugar Plum, Sugar Plum, wait, wait!

(Kevin looks around and then falls off his horse into a lake.)

Marci: Oh, dear! I hope he does not drown.

(Kevin is gasping for air.)

Kevin: This sure is a strange smelling lake.

(Up pops Jake.)

Jake (Giant Pickle): I'm a giant pickle, and you are in Pickle Lake.

Kevin: Now I have an idea! I'll use the giant pickle to get the skunk smell out of the schoolhouse.

Jake: Sure, I wouldn't mind at all.

Marci: Oh, Sugar Plum, I knew you would come up with a good idea.

In their play, "Pecos Kevin" and his peers not only demonstrated their oral communicative competence, but they highlighted as well their competence in written language. They wrote a sophisticated narrative, with an engaging beginning, a logical chain of events organized around a central problem, and a satisfying conclusion. Their choice of both the play's topic and the varying language styles ("Yuk, it stinks in here," "Sugar Plum, Sugar Plum . . .") were designed to amuse and interest their second grade peers. As writers, they are more skillful communicators than the children we introduced in Chapter 6.

Up to this point, we have discussed children's increasing skill at using language to participate fully and effectively in classroom life. The

In each of the following situations:	Situations						
	Informal Interactions				Formal Interactions		
	with peers	with teachers	with other adults in school settings	in drama, role-playing activities	in small group activities	in sharing time	in large group activities
Does the child willingly participate orally?							
Does the child listen attentively to others?							

Are the child's contributions
  –relevant to the topic?
  –responsive to others?							

Does the child ask questions or request needed assistance?							
Does the child speak fluently, with apparent ease?							
Does the child speak audibly? too loudly?							
Does the child use nonstandard forms?							
Does the child demonstrate an ability to change language style (word choice, pronunciations), particularly in role-playing activities?							

Figure 7–1 Checklist for observing children's use of oral language

questions in Figure 7–1 may assist teachers in observing and documenting this growth. We now turn our attention from children's growing oral
competence to their increasing skill as written communicators.

Refining the Written Language System

Springli has been trying to spell wheel. She asks, "Does *wheel* end
with two letters at the end? The same two? I know it seems like it's one
but sometimes it's two.

"Yeah," laughs her friend Trace. "Why don't you just put two?"

"Looks like it to me," agrees Springli, and she adds the *l*, making *well (wheel).*

For Springli, Trace, and many of their first grade peers, the global
exploration of written language's sound, appearance, and function has
been refined into a concern with precisely how the written language
system works. The skillful teacher aims to keep their exploration of the
workings of that system firmly embedded within functional language
use—the listening to, reading, writing, and talking about meaningful,
involving experiences. In the following sections, we consider ways of
assessing and fostering children's refinement of the receptive and expressive aspects of literacy.

Responding to literature

Seeking out books. By observing children's interactions with
books, parents and teachers gain insight into their children's interest in
literature. For example, Ms. Seely, a first grade teacher, had never seen
Andrew read through an entire book. He would repeatedly pick one up,
settle on the rug, look at a few pages, then return to the shelf and pick
up another. His friend Robert, however, would browse through the
books until he found one which seemed to appeal to him. Often, he
would then read the book from cover to cover. (Like adults, Robert
would sometimes decide that the book he had selected was not really
what he had in mind, and he would select another.) Ms. Seely asked
Robert and Andrew to select a book and read it together. She told them
that they could share their selected book with the class. With Robert
taking the lead, the boys browsed through several books, discussing
their appeal (focusing particularly on the topic, the illustrations, and the

length) before selecting one to read. Andrew was thus involved in a more thoughtful selection procedure.

Responding to books in various ways, at various times. As we do with the younger children, we watch for evidence of children's responses to stories and poetry in their own creations—in their talk, dramatic play, art, writing. Missy, who lives in Georgia, drew a picture of Cinderella and then dictated this story to her teacher:

> I found Cinderella at the ball when I went there. I said "Hey" to Cinderella. Me and Cinderella danced with the princes.

As we read Missy's story, we sense that, in Cinderella, she has found a friend.

In Becky's independently written story, we find, not a particular character, but a style of writing. Becky enjoyed Maurice Sendak's (1963) *Where the Wild Things Are*. Recall Sendak's story ("And when he came to the place where the wild things are they roared their terrible roars . . . till Max said "Be Still!" and tamed them . . . and they were frightened and called him the most wild thing of all. . ."). Now read Becky's story aloud and see if you can hear Sendak's rhythmical, flowing style:

> Lucy and Snoopy. Lucy and Snoopy went to a park. Than snoopy saw a prtty pappy. And snoopy is going to put his clothes in his prtty pappy [puppy's] closet. And they lived in Micky Mouse ['s] house and they were mad all of they [them]. And Charley Brown said stop. And they stoped. And they lived in the house and they won't be made [mad]. And Mickey Mouse and his girl wrer kissing.

Teachers may develop both children's positive attitudes toward, and their appreciation of, literature by planning activities for extending books. Teachers do not need to plan follow-up discussions or activities for all books that they share with their children. The pleasure of hearing (and rehearing) a well-written story or poem is an end in and of itself. Nonetheless, in providing for varied ways of responding to books which children particularly enjoy, teachers are allowing individual children diverse ways of giving meaning to the language of books. In translating verbal symbolism into a painting or a dance or a dramatic reenactment, children may find personal meaning in the story. Provision for such activities seems particularly important for the child who shows the least interest in listening to or spontaneously responding to stories. The finding of personal meaning in literature is the ultimate motivator for reading.

This process of finding meaning in literature is illustrated by the responses of a group of first graders to Lucille Clifton's (1976) *My Friend Jacob*. As their teacher read, several children whispered to peers sitting near them, "Are you my friend?" Two little girls put their arms around each other, leaning their heads together. After the reading, the children drew pictures of their own friends; they also dictated or independently wrote compositions about friends. Shane's composition seems to capture the essence of young children's friendships:

My Friend

My friend's Name is Jon. He shares his crayons with me. When we are outside we race together. He sits next to me during Math.

In addition to encouraging personal satisfaction and enjoyment of literature, extending activities involve children directly with aspects of literary structure. Settings are recreated in dioramas or murals, characters are translated into puppets, and plots are retold, reenacted, or continued as children create new scenes for vivid characters. In the next section, we will focus on one type of extending activity, retelling stories.

Retelling stories.   Children reveal their understanding of the structure of narrative literature in their attempts to retell stories. In the following incidents, children are retelling a folktale entitled "Salt," which they have heard only once. The three retellings, by kindergarteners, second graders, and a sixth grader respectively, illustrate developmental differences; they differ in the number of major events recalled, in the accuracy of the sequencing of events, and in the inclusion of logical links between events. In addition, they differ in the nature of the children's language, that is, in the fluency of the telling, the complexity of the sentences used, the precision of word choice, and the amount of story vocabulary maintained. Finally, the retellings differ in the amount of teacher support needed by the children.

Kindergarten

Teacher: Now, who would like to start telling the story? John? OK.

John: He had a big mustache grow and his mittens on the nose.

Teacher: Right. But what happened first? Do you remember what happened first in the story? Joseph?

Joseph: Ivan—um—his two brothers—uh—

John: Was going across the sea.

Joseph: Was going across the sea. And—uh—Ivan followed um.

Teacher: Right. Do you remember what happened next? . . . John.

John: Uh—then he found Ivan—a lot of salt and he shift them in the sea. And then he traded the salt for gold and then he went to the—first he went to the king and then he put the salt in the stuff and then—

Teacher: Do any of you girls remember what happened after that? After he put the salt in the food. Teresa?

Teresa: Then he made the king happy.

Second Grade

Teacher: Who would like to start out? Tommy? OK.

Tommy: His father had had this boat and Ivan wanted . . . Ivan wanted a boat so he could go out and his father said if you went out you would get your head chopped off out in the sea and then Ivan was out there floatin' and—and—uh—what was the second brother's name?

Teacher: Vasil.

Tommy: Vaseline and . . .

Teacher: Fodar

Tommy: Fodar was out there too. And he—

Gregg: . . . wind come up . . . And then the wind came and blew—

Rocky: North and south . . . of Ivan . . . away and he . . . landed on this dumb looking island, with this dumb looking giant.

Tommy: And he found the salt and he told his men to throw all the wood and stuff out and then he loaded up the salt. . .

Sixth Grade

Teacher: Um—what do you remember happens at the beginning of this story? Cheryl?

Cheryl: This merchant had three sons, Ivan, Versalas, and Fodiere. And their . . . the three brothers' father gave them a ship but he didn't want to give Ivan one because he thought he was a fool playing the madeline so he saw how much Ivan wanted a ship so he gave a ship with a cheap, cheap cargo—beans and everything—and Ivan set out in the sea with his brothers. And they stayed for a day or two and he was blown off course to uh island of salt. And he took all the salt and put it on the ship and he went to an island and he sold it to the king (Zidonis, et al., Note 1).

The kindergarteners in the above retelling had more difficulty than did those discussed in Chapter 6, who were retelling more familiar tales. These kindergarteners were not able to remember or sequence the major events, nor did they provide characters' motivations, the logic behind the action. The actions recalled were linked by a series of *and's*. The children required the teacher's support to retell what they did of the story.

In contrast, the second graders began at the beginning and collectively remembered more major events, although they too provided few details or explanations. Again, the recalled events were linked with *and's*.

It is only with Cheryl, the sixth grader, that those of us unfamilir with the folktale begin to grasp the nature of Ivan's great adventure. She provided the necessary details and explained the logic of the story, revealing that logic, in part, through the use of alternatives to *and: but, because, so*. Cheryl told the story fluently, needing no help from the teacher; her own sense of how a narrative should flow supported her retelling.

Forming concepts about literature. In addition to their growing sense of the structure of narrative, young children are also developing an appreciation of the nature of literature itself. The ability to step back from literature, to view it as an ordered creation of the human imagination, develops gradually. For example, children initially view imaginative stories as events which may actually have occurred long, long ago (Applebee, 1978). In a similar fashion, they may not grasp the non-literal meaning of poetic or figurative language. Further, their reactions to stories and poems may be related to their personal feelings about the literature's topic or their judgements about its "truthfulness"; that is, is it indeed something that could happen?

In the following evaluations of poetry by first and second graders, we sense this growing concept of literature. The children were read the poem "December Leaves" by Kaye Starbird (1963), in which fallen leaves are described as "cornflakes that fill the lawn's wide dish." They were asked, first of all, if they liked the poem and, then, why they liked it. Here are some of their reactions:

> My brother's birthday is in December and I don't like my brother so I don't like the poem.
>
> [I like it.] I like December and the snow.
>
> [I don't like it.] I don't like Christmas—I like Hannukkan instead.
>
> [I don't like it] because I have to rake leaves and I don't like them.
>
> [I don't like it.] Leaves can't make cornflakes.
>
> [I don't like it.] I don't think leaves are brown all the time like cornflakes. . .

Certain children, particularly the second graders, gave evaluations based on an appreciation of the poetry as a work of art:

> I like the poem—it's soft.

I could see the leaves and snow in my mind.

I liked the part where she said it filled the "lawn's wide dish" because the idea was funny.

I liked the description of snow as sugar. (Fisher, Note 2)

Teachers and parents can help children develop their understandings about literature. They can cause children to manipulate the structure of the story (e.g., "What do you think would have happened if Baby Bear had come home alone and found Goldilocks?"). In addition, teachers may plan to present stories with similar types of characters, plot structures, or themes over a period of a few days; then children can compare the books. For example, they can discuss how two characters or two stories are alike or different. When asking children to make such comparisons, teachers have the books physically present to give the children concrete support for their thinking. Even if children are not able to formally discuss the similarities of particular types of characters, plots, or themes, they may evidence their growing understanding of literature in their own story tellings, dictations, and writing. Consider, for example, this description of a dragon written by Chris, a second grader:

There once was a big green dragon who could breath fire and he was scaley and was realy speanded indead. he could do tricks. He could fly in the air. for his wings were strong. He lived in a big wet muddy ucky cave.

Certainly dragons who are "realy spleanded indead" are found only in the worlds created by books.

Becoming independent readers

In Chapter 6, we described young children's initial attempts to read various forms of print, including traffic signs, magazines, children's books, and their own dictated writing. Such forms of reading continue in the primary grades, although reading from reading textbooks has traditionally received the greatest amount of teacher attention. In this section we consider ways of assessing children's growing ability to read—to make sense of text—in a variety of meaningful contexts for a variety of purposes.

Reading homemade books. Children may compose their own homemade books by dictating stories to their teachers. Teachers may also make homemade books; these books are often composed of strong rhythmic language patterns. Ms. Dods combines both techniques. She has her first graders complete their own books by, first, illustrating textless books and, then, dictating words to complete a simple, rhythmical language pattern. The pattern will help the children to predict the text. For example, here is a child's book entitled *My Family:*

Here is my *Mommy.*
She is *walking my dog.*

Here is my *baby.*
He is *sleeping in bed.*

(The italics indicate the sections of the text which were dictated by each child.)

In addition to individual books like Ms. Dods, Ms. Luchs has the children complete class-sized "big books" (Holdaway, 1979). Ms. Luchs takes a pattern from a children's book or from a well-known rhyme; she has the children compose new lines. For example, here is a section from her class book *Brown Bear, Brown Bear, What Do You See?* (Martin, 1970), which was completed after a field trip to the zoo. Each child contributed to the book by dictating the needed words to Ms. Luchs and then drawing a large illustration of an animal to cut out and paste into the class book:

Tiger, Tiger, what do you see?
I see a *giraffe* looking at me.

Giraffe, Giraffe, what do you see?
I see *all the kids* looking at me.

Big books can also be made by enlarging the text of participation books (see Chapter 6). The children can read along with the teacher predicting and participating in the reading.

In the previous chapter, we discussed the observations which teachers could make to assess children's growing command of written language. For example, is the child able to read along with the teacher, predicting what the text says? Do the child's dictations sound like the formal language of books, rather than the informal language of everyday talk? Does the child evidence understanding of directionality? Of voice/print match? Here we continue that discussion. We consider ways of assessing the child's increasing precision in matching text and talk, focusing on observable behaviors which suggest progress.

Initially, when children read their stories, their reading is fluent, like their speech. They are relying primarily on language cues, their sensitivity to and memory for language patterns, in order to read. As children begin to tackle the visual aspects of written language, their reading slows down; they may begin to read in a word-by-word fashion (Clay, 1979b). For children who are just beginning to read, then, word-by-word reading is a sign of progress. In addition to the deliberate pace of the reading, children may begin to self-correct in their attempt to read the precise words that were written. Self-correction indicates that the child is no longer simply inventing a meaningful text; he or she is attempting to accurately match text and talk.

As children begin to attend to the visual aspects of print, teachers interact with them, focusing their attention on recurrent patterns of letter/sound correspondences, words, or word phrases:

Hey, this word *went* is in your story a few times. Can you find it?

Mom starts like Melissa's name, doesn't it? What other words in your story start like *Mom*? Do you think *muffin* would start like Mom if we wrote it?

How come you changed your mind and read this word as *Dad*, not *Mom*? . . . Right, it starts with a *D*. That was good thinking.

When children begin to read, they may only be able to read particular words in set print contexts. For example, they may be able to read "Happy Birthday," but unable to read *happy* in "I am happy today."

In using terms such as *word, letter,* and *sound,* teachers should be aware that many young children are confused over these concepts. Children's understanding of them grows slowly as they learn to read (Clay, 1979b). Framing the word or letter being focused on with one's hands or with a window card may assist children in attending to a particular segment of text.

McDonnell and Osburn (1978), relying on the work of Clay, have developed a checklist to assess children's early efforts to match talk and print. The checklist, shown in Figure 7–2, focuses on both the child's use of the language cues (e.g., the story's meaning) and the visual cues (e.g., directionality, voice/print match) available in print, and on the degree to which the child integrates both types of cues. It should be noted, though, that a weakness in any one area does not indicate a need for a particular lesson in, for example, directionality; these skills cannot be effectively taught separate from the act of reading. Rather, a weakness indicates a need for more exposure to, and interaction about, reading and writing.

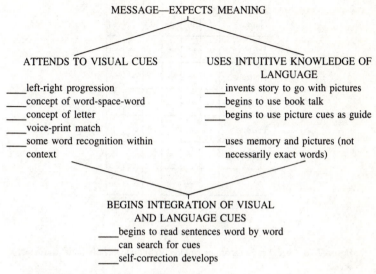

Figure 7–2 Checklist for recording children's use of print's language and visual cues

In addition to checklists which focus on general reading strategies, checklists can be used to note progress within one type of cue system—sound/symbol skills. For young children, the first sound/symbol associations to be used are initial consonants. An example of a checklist for initial consonants is shown in Figure 7–3. Teachers may assess this skill by asking the child to recognize from a group of letters, or to write, "the letter that begins _____." When sound symbol skill is assessed in this way, the teacher must still observe the child's reading of text in order to judge whether or not the child can use letter/sound cues when reading. The child may be able to perform the isolated task without an awareness of how that skill relates to the reading task.

To both assess and foster children's ability to use letters to figure out unknown words, the teacher can create cloze activities. For example, the teacher may leave gaps or put tabs over words in the "big books," in stories projected on the overhead, or in individual children's books. The teacher leaves out or covers up predictable words; in some cases she lets the initial letter of the word "peek out" as a clue. For example, the following story could be projected on the overhead for children who had worked with the sounds of *f,d,* and *s*: Dee and Susie went to the pond. The d____ were swimming. The f____ were croaking. The s__ was shining. Dee and Susie put their f___ in the water. But then the clouds

Children's Names	f	m	c	d	j	s
Jesse	✔	✔	✔	—	—	—
Andrew	+	+	+	—	—	+
Amy	—	—	—	—	—	—
Freddie	+	+	+	✔	✔	+
Ruth Ann	+	+	+	+	+	+
Joe	—	—	—	—	—	—

+ child knows
✔ child sometimes knows
— child does not know

Figure 7—3 Checklist for recording children's ability to identify initial consonant sounds

moved __. Away went the d____. Away went the f____. Away went the s__. And away went D__ and S____.

Developing flexible strategies for making sense of text. As children achieve the necessary voice/print match and become more fluent readers, they may use a variety of strategies, involving both language and visual cues, for making sense of text. The most successful young readers are those who are able to make flexible use of alternate strategies (Clay, 1979b). By listening to children read and attending particularly to their errors or ''miscues,'' teachers can assess their children's ability to make use of different sources of reading cues. Goodman and Burke (1972) have created a diagnostic tool *The Reading Miscue Inventory* to assist teachers in analyzing children's use of reading cues. The inventory focuses teachers' attention on questions similar to these:

Miscue Type

What type of miscue did the child make? Did the child substitute one word for another? Did the child omit a word? Or, did the child simply stop and wait for assistance?

Language Cues

Did the child's miscue fit syntactically into the sentence context? That is, was it an appropriate part of speech (e.g., did the child substitute a noun for a noun or a verb for a verb)?

Did the child's miscue fit semantically? Did it make sense in the sentence? Did it make sense considering the text as a whole?

Visual Cues

Was the child's miscue graphically similar to the actual word? That is, is its spelling similar to that of the printed word?

Dialect

Was the child's miscue a reflection of the child's dialect?

Self-Correction

Did the child attempt to self-correct the miscue?

The following anecdotes illustrate possible child strategies and possible teacher responses. In all cases, the teacher is reluctant to intervene if the child's miscue does not change the text's meaning. When the teacher does intervene, she attempts to keep her cueing brief. Both these behaviors help children to keep their focus on the sense of the text. Further, in responding to their students, the teachers are modeling effective strategies which the children may eventually use themselves:

Tanya reads her text as follows (Tanya's deviation from the text is written above the slashed word:)

swimmed
Bobby swám in the water.

Tanya's teacher does not correct Tanya's reading. Tanya still "regularizes" irregular verb forms in her speech; Tanya decoded the print into her own meaningful oral language. If Tanya, whose speech contains many features of Black dialect, had made a dialect-related deviation, as in

have
He hás a good time,

the teacher also would not have intervened.

As Fred reads, he often stops and looks at his teacher, waiting for her to tell him each unknown word. His teacher waits a few seconds, keeping her eyes focused on the text. If Fred still does not attempt the word, she asks him to go back a sentence and reread, so that he can "think about what word would make sense." She also often directs his attention to the initial consonant: "It starts with a *p*, Fred."

Dave's miscues frequently make no sense in the context of the sentence. In this case he read:

now
This is a néw ball.

His teacher responds, "A *now* ball, Dave? That doesn't make sense. . . That's it, a *new* ball."

Effren's miscue suggests that he is making little use of sound/symbol correspondences. As his error would affect his understanding of the entire story, his teacher intervenes at a natural break in the text. "Effren, you made a good guess here, but it's not quite right. Take a look at the word again. It's almost like *make*. . . That's it, *snake*.'' Effren's teacher helped Effren to compare the unknown word to a known one with a similar word part, here a similar phonogram.

In addition to the illustrated strategies, here are two which are particularly useful for children who are just beginning to tackle the visual cues of text. Both personal observation and the literature (Holdaway, 1979) suggest that they are spontaneously used by many young children. The first is for the child to simply ask for the identity of the unknown word. This is the strategy often used by preschoolers who teach themselves to read in the home. The other strategy is to identify the word by recalling or actually finding the word in another, more familiar context:

(Child is reading.) *The ball is* . . . (recalling word in another print context)

Come here, Sally—*here. The ball is here.*

In order to identify children's reading strategies, the teacher must allot time for listening to individual children read. Ms. Marshall, a first-grade teacher, pairs her children and has "partners" read together. Ms. Marshall has several partners sit on her classroom rug and read quietly to each other. She circulates among the children, listening to each child read a page or two. As she listens, she makes notes on the child's reading behaviors. Figure 7–4 contains sample notes.

In this discussion, we have focused on specific strategies children use for decoding text. But making sense of text involves more than decoding. It involves relating the read-about experiences to one's own lived experiences. In the next section, we focus on children's involvement in the evolving story itself.

Responding to reading. In reading, as in listening, children actively construct meaning as their own background of experiences interacts with the incoming information. To comprehend, then, children must be involved in the story; they must have some interest in and purpose for reading (for example, to gain information, to be entertained, to satisfy a curiosity or an emotional need). Our goal for young readers is to assist them in becoming thoughtful readers who actively respond to text, that is, readers who predict future developments, reason about characters' motivations and reactions, and relate the story to their own experiences, perhaps changing their current thinking in some way.

Children may spontaneously offer evidence of their comprehending;

Name	Date	Book (initials), page	Notes
Tanya	2/23	OW6, pp. 100-1	fluent; good use of context
	2/25	OW6, pp. 114-5	fluent, no problems
Efren	2/24	OW6, p. 104	OK, does not appear to be applying consonant blend sounds we've studied
Fred	2/23	NF, p. 89-91	Great! beginning to use context clues
	2/25	NF, p. 98	OK--problems with medial vowel patterns (pan/pin)
Angel	2/24	NF, p. 30	lots of word recognition problems--no fluency; book may be too hard. Check tomorrow.

Figure 7–4 Grid showing sample notes on children's reading behaviors

they may orally predict, reason about, or relate their own experiences to the story. Others may be prompted to do so by teacher questioning. In the following interaction, first graders confidently think aloud about a story they are reading together, and their teacher displays genuine interest in and acceptance of their comments. In addition, the teacher leads her children to predict and reflect on the story's content and, also, on their own responses to the story; she doesn't merely have children recall facts from the story; but she reasons with the children about those facts:

The children are reading a story silently. (Many young children read "silently" by reading orally in a quiet voice.) The story, in a preprimer, is about a man with a magic hat (Early, Cooper, & Santensanio, 1979). The man, Mr. Fig, and his friends Rabbit, Turtle, and Mouse are flying over a pond in Mr. Fig's car. Suddenly, Mr. Fig loses his magic hat and, alas, the car crashes into the pond.

Erbey: (spontaneously as he reads, to no one in particular) It's just like the General Lee, I think. (The General Lee is a car on the television show "The Dukes of Hazzard.")

As the children finish the page they're reading, Ms. May, their teacher, asks: What horrible thing has happened?

Victor: The hat flew away.

Ms. May: Yes the hat flew right off his head, didn't it? Why did that happen?

Erbey: Because the car was going so fast that the hat flew off.

Tanya: Oh. They gotta go down beside that cat. (In the illustration, there's a cat on the ground—a cat that had tried earlier to eat Mouse.)

Erbey: They better watch out for that cat.

Ms. May: How do you think that cat made Mouse feel:

Children: Mad . . . sad (*Mad, sad,* and *happy* are typical responses of young children to questions about feelings. Ms. May probes:)

Ms. May: How would you feel if you were a mouse?

Missy: I'd get mad and run . . .

Ms. May: Well, let's see if something really bad happened.

(The children read on into the story silently; then Ms. May asks:) Now what's happened? Where's the car?

Erbey: That car went in the water.

Ms. May: Why didn't the car keep flying in the air?

Erbey: Because he took his hat off.

Victor: He said it was magic but nobody's magic no more.

Ms. May: Right. Nobody's magic anymore because—because what was the magic thing he had?

Tanya: The magic hat, and that's gone.

Ms. May: The magic hat is gone, and he doesn't have any magic.

Tanya: If the hat gets wet, it probably won't have any magic.

Ms. May: I never thought about that before, but you may be right.

(In the final section of the story, Turtle saves Rabbit, who cannot swim. In the illustration, Rabbit is sitting on Turtle's back.)

Erbey: Why is Rabbit happy?

Ms. May: Well, she's happy on that page. That's a good question. Why do you think?

Missy: Because she got a ride on the turtle.

Ms. May: She was saved—she got a ride on the turtle.

Erbey: But over here [on the next picture] she's sad.

Ms. May: Yes, she is. Why do you think she's sad over here?

Tanya: Because Mr. Fig still doesn't have his hat.

The active reasoning evident in the above interaction contrasts with the following discussion. In this discussion, second graders have read a story about a little boy, Evan, who has taken a job at a grocery store in hopes of earning enough money to buy a pet turtle. The children talk only in response to the teacher, Ms. Barber, who asks primarily recall questions:

Ms. Barber: Who can tell us why Evan was feeling proud and happy? Lonnie?

Lonnie: He knew he was going to get his turtle.

Ms. Barber: No. He didn't know he was going to get his turtle yet. Monica.

Monica: 'Cause he was helping a lady carry out her groceries and he got a dime?

Ms. Barber: Just one dime? How many, Laura?

Laura: He had two dimes.

Ms. Barber: He had two dimes, and that's why he was proud and happy.

Both Lonnie and Monica offered ideas that could have been explored in relation to why Evan felt proud and happy. Certainly, their responses suggest inferential thinking—reasoning about—their reading, rather than merely recalling what was literally stated. While distinguishing between inference and stated fact is a legitimate goal, rejecting all answers but the most literally correct is a questionable practice. Certainly it would seem to hamper the development of the active, spontaneous reasoning evident in Ms. May's group. Listening to the children's answers, searching for clarifications and elaborations of their reasoning, would—from the point of view of the developing language learner—be the more effective strategy.

In the preceding teacher-guided discussions, the children were responding to stories. In contrast, in the following interaction, the children are reading an informational selection. The teacher has asked her second graders to read and find out interesting facts about animals:

Robbie: I never knew there was an ant that looked like a leaf.

Ms. Lee: Why would he look like a leaf?

Robbie: Because he probably eats leaves and makes his nest out of them.

Jenny: 'Cause maybe some big bird would come and try to eat him and he would pretend like he was a leaf.

Dean: With his wings put together he looks like a leaf.

(Ms. Lee discussed the concept of camouflage. She asks them to remember times they saw something camouflaged.)

Jenny: One time I saw a little bug and it landed somewhere on a leaf and I looked all over but I couldn't find it.

Robbie: When the Americans fought the Germans they used kinda plants on top

> of their Army hats so they could hide inside the planes and shoot at
> them.
>
> Ms. Lee: That's interesting. Did you know that the Army and the Air Force and
> other people who used planes camouflaged them by putting white on the
> bottom?
>
> Robbie: Oooooooh, because of the sky—the sky is white.
>
> Ms. Lee: Mmmmmm. They'd look like clouds.
>
> Ruthy: Yesterday I saw something move on a leaf. I tried but I couldn't find it
> because it was camouflaged. It looked like a leaf. It started moving
> everytime I touched it—

And so Ruthy and her peers make connections between read-about and
lived experience. Their talk illustrates well the careful shaping of language ("I tried, but I couldn't find it because it was camouflaged") that
results from the desire to share an experience with others.

In the preceding discussions, the children demonstrated comprehension by their talk. There are other ways of demonstrating comprehension of text. If the purpose of the reading is to uncover the directions for
a new game, then successfully playing the game is a demonstration that
one has comprehended. If the purpose is to learn how to bake a type of
cookie, then an edible product is a sign of comprehension. Similarly, if
the purpose is to be entertained, then eagerly reading regularly in a self-
chosen book is evidence of comprehension. The point here is that there
are a variety of purposes for reading; the way in which the children
respond to the text is dependent upon their purpose for reading.

Reading for a variety of purposes is part of being communicatively
competent. Children, like adults, may scan to find today's menu or the
needed entry in a reference book. They may carefully work their way
through a series of directions to complete an art project. They may
quickly find the "good ones" in a joke book or slowly savor a well-
loved tale. Clearly, teachers must provide a variety of contexts, not only
for oral language use, but for written language use as well.

Reading in an appropriate graded reader. Most teachers use an
instructional reader for part of their reading program. Teachers may use
language experience stories and children's literature for instructional
purposes; they then use graded readers for children's independent reading, thus providing the children with short, simple stories which they
can read quite easily on their own.

In selecting appropriate books for individual children, an informal
reading inventory (Betts, 1946) can be helpful. This procedure involves

having children read passages from texts of different degrees of difficulty. For example, the child may read from a preprimer, a primer, and a first reader-level text. The teacher selects the text in which the child can read a passage fairly fluently, missing no more than three to six words per hundred, and can recall independently or through questioning the major parts of the selection. The reasoning behind the inventory is that the child must be able to use the sense of the text to figure out any unknown words. If the text is too difficult, the child will no longer have a language context (semantic and syntactic cues) to support the reading. In other words, the print will make no sense.

Although an informal reading inventory procedure has been successfully used by many primary grade teachers to place children in graded materials, it should be noted that many factors influence the difficulty of any particular story or book, including the predictability of the text's language; whether or not the story has been previously read to the children; the number of unfamiliar words; the familiarity of the concepts presented in the story to the individual child; the child's interest in the selection, which may be affected by both the topic and the function of the reading itself (e.g., Is the child deciphering a map during a scavenger hunt or merely reading an assigned selection?); the physical layout of the text itself (e.g., the size of the print, the amount of print per page). Because the readability of any particular text is affected by so many factors, there is no reason to confine children's reading to any one kind of text. Children can read a variety of texts for a variety of purposes.

Writing: Growth in Independence

One evening, Mrs. Booth, mother of 6-year-old Bridget, noticed a note paper taped to the cat's drinking bowl. Curious as to why the paper was on Tabby's bowl, she squatted down and read:

Dear Tabby
I love you very very much.
Love Bridget

Like Bridget, children in the early primary grades become increasingly sophisticated writers. By observing children as they write and by regularly saving samples of the children's work, teachers can observe their young writers' progress. Observation of progress is dependent, though, on an understanding of writing as a developmental phenomenon. In this section, we illustrate typical developmental features of young children's writing as revealed in activities within the primary grade classroom.

One primary grade teacher, Ms. Cory, begins the school year by assessing her children's writing behaviors. On the first day of school she passes out journals to her first graders and asks them to write however they can. The resulting writing reflects the diversity of approaches to writing described in Chapter 6: some children write alphabet letters, hoping that they've communicated, others confidently write their *ABC*'s, while still others write well-known words, such as names of mothers, fathers, brothers, and sisters. Ms. Cory circulates around the room, asking the children about their work and, in many cases, writing the children's comments. For example, under Brandon's *Jeanne*, Ms. Cory wrote "Jeanne is my sister."

From the very beginning of the school year, certain first graders will independently write sentence-length or longer messages by inventing spellings (a technique we will discuss in detail later on in this chapter). Others depend on spelling assistance from teachers, peers, and various print resources in the room; these resources may include wall charts of word categories (e.g., color, number, and size words) and personal dictionaries in which requested words or words from the children's basals are recorded. In addition, before drawing and writing on a topic, the children may brainstorm words, which the teacher then lists on the board.

Spelling presents a major difficulty, in part, because of children's difficulty in grasping the phoneme-grapheme relationships which allow invented spelling to occur. In addition, during the early school years, children are commonly intent on "getting it right," and, thus, may be initially reluctant to guess. However, spelling is neither the only nor the major difficulty young children may have in writing. To illustrate potential successes and problems, we consider an early writing session of Ms. Wilson's first graders.

After reading and discussing friends, Ms. Wilson asked the children to draw and write about their friend. The children's efforts reflected the difficulty of the writing task. The children had to plan their message, which was, initially at least, a single sentence, remember the whole message, break it down into sections, encode sections, decide which sections of their message had been written and which had not, and, also, decide how to find out the spellings of sections which they could not encode. We will observe the varied strategies children used for carrying out this complex task.

Certain children simply drew their friend and then copied words listed on the board with no particular intended message. Ms. Wilson talked to these children, helping them to assume control of their own written message:

> "What do you want to say about your friend, Russell?"
>
> "I want to say, 'I like my friend Kyle.'"
>
> "OK. How do you write *I*, as in 'I like my friend'?"

And, together, Ms. Wilson and Russell wrote his message.

Ginny asked Ms. Wilson, "How do you spell, 'My friend is my brother.'?" Ginny had taken control of the message she wished to write, but she was unable to segment that message into words. Ms. Wilson wrote *my* on an index card and told Ginny, "There's *my*. What's the next word you need? My . . . ? *Friend*, that's right. Can you find the word on the board? What does it start with?" After Ginny had located the word *friend*, Ms. Wilson wrote that word on an index card. Ms. Wilson continued the strategy of having Ginny identify needed words. She wrote each word on a separate card to help Ginny see the process of segmenting an oral sentence into written words. Although Ginny successfully wrote her sentence, her later reading reflected her difficulty with segmenting language, specifically, with voice/print match:

$$\begin{array}{c c c c c}
\text{My} & \text{friend} & \text{is} & \text{my} & \text{brother} \\
\uparrow & \uparrow & \uparrow & & \uparrow \\
\text{My} & \text{friend} & \text{my} & \text{broth} & \text{er}
\end{array}$$

Whereas, Ginny wrote words which she later did not read, Kevin and Kelly both "read" words which they had not written. Kevin, using both visual memory and the words written on the board, wrote this text:

MyfriendloveKevinChristopher

He read this, "My friend love Kevin love Christopher"; he wrote *love* only once, but read it twice. Jan wrote, "My friend Kelly," which she read as "My friend is Kelly," inserting the linking verb orally. In a manner similar to Kevin and Jan, young writers often omit grammatical endings (e.g., possessives, plurals) and function words (e.g., prepositions) in their written sentences, although they insert them orally.

Lack of one-to-one correspondence between talk and text may occur in the final copy despite the child's understanding of the oral/written relationship. In the painstaking writing process, children may lose the original meaning or structure of their message. The longer and more complex the message, the greater the possibility of error. To illustrate, consider Scott's production of Figure 7–5. Scott wrote primarily by copying words from the board and from visual memory. After he wrote each word, he reread the text, apparently to see which word should be written next. In the first version of his composition, Scott wrote: "My friend is my dog His name Brandy." Upon rereading his completed paper, Scott noticed that *is* was missing. "I've got it wrong," he remarked, pointing to the *is* in *His*. He then erased the *is* (from *His*) and put it after the word *name*.

For many young children, then, writing is a complicated, challenging task. Beyond planning and refining their messages, a difficult enough task for us as adults, children deal with memory, muscle control, spelling, and, most critically, the whole concept of how written and oral language relate in our writing system. In the next section, we examine the writing of young children who were beginning to exercise a

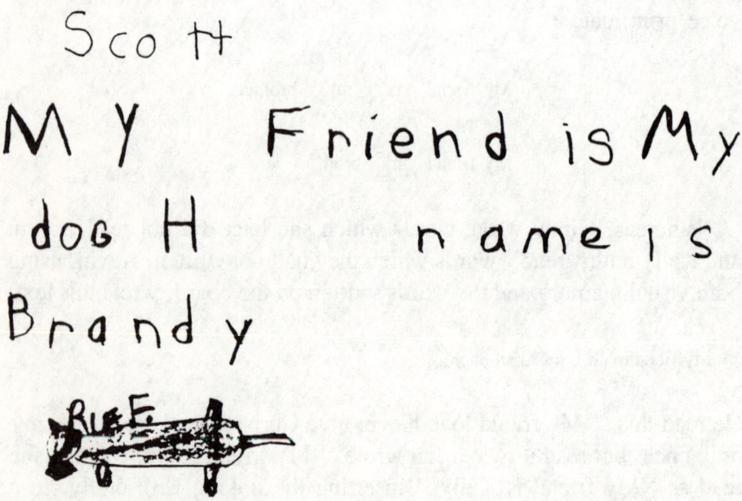

Figure 7–5 Scott's product: "My friend is my dog. His name is Brandy."

more confident control over this unwieldly process, children who were finding their written voices.

Expressive writing. Initially children's independent writing may be confined to well-known words or contained within repetitive sentence structures (Clay, 1975; McCaig, 1981). That is, children can rearrange a limited set of words or substitute words into a well-known pattern. The following excerpts from a first grader's diary illustrate a structured writing technique:

> September 13 I like to write in my diary.
>
> September 15 I like rabbits.
>
> September 16 I like to play with my hamster.
>
> September 17 I like dogs.

Later in the year, however, his diary entries become grammatically more complex and, at the same time, took on an easier, talk-like style:

> June 9 Me and Jordie cot a moth Tuesday.
>
> June 7 I got some guns in they are kapguns.

(Amarel, 1980, pp. 14–15)

A similar change in style can be seen in the following first graders' writing. The compositions on the left were written in October, those on the right, in February:

Derrick:	Look at the mummy and the ghosts.	My Mother and father can take me out when it is Valentines. My brothers like to go too peeza inn. They leve me seven pezza.
Tina:	Go away ghosts and witches and bats and pumpkins and mummy.	I like my uncle because he throws me in the air and gets me candy when I see my cousins I give them some of my candy and that is sharing.
Ruth Ann:	Dick said Look at the pumpkin. Boo Jane said Sally.	Sally is wasing her car so is Father and Father needs the wather hose. Sally is going to cry because Father wont let her yous the wother hos.

When young children's writing assumes this talk-like style, teachers know that the children have made the connection between their own talk and writing—they have found their written voice. The children's later writing style can be referred to as expressive. Britton (1970) uses this term to refer to writing which sounds like, and is based on, sustained speech; Britton refers to it as "written down speech." In expressive writing, children appear to be representing their experiences for themselves; their writing is often intelligible only to someone who knows as much about their topics as the child-authors.

As children's writing becomes more expressive, it may also contain more errors. The children are taking new risks, expressing more complex ideas, trying more complex grammatical structures, and attempting their own spellings rather than relying on teacher or on reference lists. The errors are signs, then, of progress. To illustrate, Derrick's sentence, "They leve me seven pezza," is not completely comprehensible—but, then, it represents a more complex idea than the earlier occurring "Look at the mummy and the ghosts" ("My brothers don't eat all their pizza; they leave seven pieces for me."). In addition, the later composition is "expressive" of Derrick's own thoughts—he is representing his experiences as much for himself as for anyone else, and, for Derrick, the sentence is meaningful.

Consider also Tina's compositions. Her first piece is perfectly punctuated—her second is not. But putting one period at the end of one sentence is much simpler than deciding where, in the midst of all the ideas expressed in the second composition, one should put periods. Ruth Ann's compositions also reflect the error that comes with progress. The second of her two pieces seems to indicate a deterioration in spelling ability. But, in the first composition, Ruth Ann copied words from her basal reader and from Halloween word lists displayed in the room. In the second, Ruth Ann assumed greater control of the encoding; her spellings reflect her own growing experience with the sound/symbol relationships of our alphabetic language. We take a closer look at spelling in the following section.

Invented spelling. In the preceding chapter, we met 5-year-olds who were inventing spellings. In the early grades, most children begin to invent their own spellings, basing these spellings on their current hypotheses about how our alphabetic writing system works. Initially, invented spellings may omit vowels, as in *CT (cut), CP (cup), MN (moon),* and *prtty (pretty).* As children progress, vowels begin to appear, reflecting children's own perceptions of sound/symbol associations and, also, their overgeneralization of well-known patterns (Forester, 1980; Read, 1971). The following spellings illustrate these strategies:

groe (*grow*)	— overgeneralization of pattern
bea (*be*)	— overgeneralization of pattern
wie (*why*)	— overgeneralization of pattern
sum (*some*)	— phonetic analysis
brot (*brought*)	— phonetic analysis
chot (*chart*)	— phonetic analysis

Children's spellings may also reflect their visual recall of a part of a word's pattern (e.g., the letters but not the exact order), as in *gril* (girl). Other spellings may be traced to homophones (*to, too, two*) or to word ending rules (*makeed, rideing*).

As in oral language development, children's spelling errors reveal their progress. As a first grade teacher, the second author would study her children's compositions, noting any new developments. If possible, she filed papers containing significant changes; for example, a child who had previously been reluctant to guess invented a spelling; another began to use *ing* and *ed* suffixes. In this way she documented their developing sophistication in spelling.

Peer interaction during writing. As children analyze spellings, they can be of assistance to each other. In fact, certain children may require support from their peers if they are to persist in the difficult writing task (Dyson & Genishi, 1982).

The following interactions illustrate this helping process:

Min: How do you spell *mean*?

Tambrea: *Mean*?

Min: *Mean, mean* (elongating the *ea*)

Tambrea: *M–T . . . M–Y . . .*

Min: *Mean . . . mean* (elongating the word's pronunciation)

Tambrea: *Mean*?

Min: /m/ /ee/ /n/

Tambrea: *M–Y–N*

Min: *M–Y*?

Tambrea: *M–Y–N . . . N*, you know, in *nothing . . . N . . . N*

It is not of critical importance that the help given is not completely accurate; what is important is that the children are supporting each other's efforts to make sense of the confusing spelling process.

In listening to children's interactions during writing, teachers may note that, although spelling concerns may be the dominant topic, the children respond also to the meaning of each other's work, especially if that is the teacher's dominant way of responding to writing. Listen to a few comments from Mr. Robert's first graders:

> Hey, John's got a funny one! I read it.
>
> Read Krissy's. She's got a good one.
>
> I know a good title for that, John: "Animal Friends."
>
> Tell me what yours says.

Such comments are positive signs of progress for primary grade teachers. They signal that children are focusing on writing as the communication of meaning, despite the effort and attention which spelling commands. In addition, the comments suggest children's awareness of the audience's role in the writing process. This is significant because young children are generally considered egocentric, writing primarily for themselves with little thought given to their potential audience.

Writing stories and poetry. As we have discussed, when young children begin writing with a degree of fluency, their writing is expressive: the writing reflects the child's own speech and appears to be, primarily, writing for oneself. In the following piece, Tina seems to be writing to think through a painful personal experience:

> When I came home my friend said let's play. And I brot my ball out. And my baby got it. I got anuthr ball. The ball that my baby had my friend got it. And the ball is my ball and my friend said it was his. I told my mother what happen. And she let him have it. It made me sad. I ran to my room and cried cried. And when my daddy came from work I told him. And he is going to buy me a ball.

Tina's piece has the characteristic use of *and,* typical of the oral and written language of many 6-year-olds. Tina's switching from past to present tense is another common characteristic of young children's expressive writing (Smith, Goodman, & Meredith, 1976); it seems as if the memory of the past experience is so vivid that it is happening in the present.

As children gain control over written language, and as teachers provide varied situational contexts for writing, children develop increasing skill in creating more formal literary works—poetry and story. To use Britton's (1978) terms, their writing fulfills a poetic function—it takes the form of a coherent, ordered design—a work of art.

We began this chapter by observing Ms. Betts and her class tell and write stories with settings, characters, plots, and themes. The children's stories were more developmentally advanced than those compositions in which they described or reported on a personal event. Martin (1971), who studied primary grade students in England, reported a similar observation. Her students' stories were longer than anything else they wrote (such as personal news or science reports). They used more sophisticated language structures: in addition to *and's* and *then's*, they needed *he said's, because's, might be's,* and *but if's*. Because the stories dealt with possibility rather than reality, many children felt freer to express their desires and fears; like dramatic play, story writing allowed them to verbally explore new areas of experience. Finally, story writing led the children to use formal literary elements: their stories often began with "Once upon a time" or "Once there lived"; they frequently used repetition of event or situation in their stories, a technique common to children's literature. The following two compositions by Becky, a first grader, illustrate these potential differences between types of written products. The first piece is a personal news report, the second a story written in response to a picture:

> You know teacher I get roses at my house. I got two roses. One of our roses is fulling off. Our roses petals are fulling down.

> Sally said? move out of my way. So I can see Tv. Charle Brown did not listen. Sally said? move. If I say [move] one more time you will get in trouble. If I move will you make me some popcorn. Sally said? oK. And then thay were happy.

We have considered differences that teachers may note in comparing written language in story writing with that used in other types of writing. Looking within one type of writing situation, teachers may note characteristic developmental behaviors in children's compositions (Fisher, Note 3). As growth in composition skill occurs, changes occur in these behaviors. The following stories, written by primary grade children, illustrate these characteristic behaviors:

> The boy is sweating and sweating. (See Figure 7–6.)

> *Robin, kindergarten*

Cleaning Up

> A Women had 2 boys. But the boys makeed a mess. She had to clean up. She did not like to clean up But She liked her boys. In the room They had checkers and Books and a trucks and colors and shoes. The end.

> *Ruthy, grade 1*

Figure 7–6 Robin's product: The boy is sweating and sweating

Me and My Flying Machine

I will make my FLYing MACHIN First! I will Find pieces of wood next. Third, fly time. I will go to Cherrokee Indian land. then I'll go home. The next morning I take off again. I will go to dinasaur land. It would be fun. I like Dinasaur land. Then I will go to dragon land. They spit out fire. It can hurt you. So be careful. I like you a lot so be careful.

Today I'll go to Africa. I met a Arab. He was nice. I asked him something. He said mallatchas. I couldn't understand him.

Know it's time for me to go home.

Jake, second grade

It is human in the past I found the boon in the grass Then in pick it up and cleen it out and I hade to get the hart out and I dug and dug and dug and I do not no what it is something is talking and the voice was tlaking to me!

Will, second grade

In story writing, as in all areas of development, the basic trends are from the simple to the complex, the general to the specific, from an orientation around the self to a consideration of other points of view, and from the concrete, here-and-now to the abstract and the possible. These general trends are illustrated in the above stories.

Simple to complex. Many young children's first stories are essentially a listing of statements about a particular topic (Sowers, 1979). Robin's story is basically a statement about her drawing: ''The boy is sweating.'' Ruthy's is a series of statements about a magazine picture. Both Jake's and Will's involve the development of an event or a series of related events. Of these four stories, Will's has the most sophisticated plot line in that the story does have a central problem (the difficulty of unearthing and cleaning the bone), builds logically to a climax, and leaves the resolution of the story to the reader's imagination. A conventionally developed story is not typical of early primary grade story writers. Such a story consists of a setting, an initiating event, an internal response, an attempt, a consequence, and a reaction, as in this simple story:

> *Setting:* Once there was a big gray fish named Albert. He lived in a big icy pond near the edge of a forest.
>
> *Initiating Event:* One day, Albert was swimming around the pond. Then he spotted a big juicy worm on top of the water.
>
> *Internal Response:* Albert knew how delicious worms tasted. He wanted to eat that one for his dinner.

Attempt: So he swam very close to the worm. Then he bit into him.

Consequence: Suddenly, Albert was pulled through the water into a boat. He had been caught by a fisherman.

Reaction: Albert felt sad. He wished he had been more careful.

(Stein, 1979, p. 265)

The second author has noted that, in her first grade classroom, presenting the children with pictures depicting potential conflicts and then discussing potential resolutions can have an impact on the sophistication of children's plots. Ms. Betts, the first grade teacher introduced in the beginning of this chapter, has similar success by posing problems for her first graders to solve in writing. For example, one day Ms. Betts discussed the problems of "Mr. Clumsy" (Hargreaves, 1980) with her children. She asked them what might happen if Mr. Clumsy visited their school. What problem might Mr. Clumsy create? What would they do? Here's Melinda's story:

Mr. Clumsy at [Melinda's school]

One day we were going to lunch and we were having spaghetti. He took his fork and got all tangled up. It took all the people in the class. I had to watch him all the time. The End.

General to specific. With development, children begin to refine and embellish their written stories. In Robin's, as in many young children's stories, the drawing conveys more of the story than the actual text does. Ruthy details the mess in the room with a listing of objects, but the nature of those objects (e.g., their appearance, how they were arranged in the room) is not given. Both Jake and Will provide more explicit pictures of the events in their stories. The detail naturally leads to longer, more complex sentence structures. Jake uses adjectives to describe the various lands he is traveling to. Will details in part through the use of prepositional phrases ("in the past," "in the grass"). However, Will provides specifics primarily by describing in horrifying detail the process of removing the heart; he even conveys, through text and through punctuation, the emotions of his imagined character: "I do not no what it is something is talking and the voice was tlaking to me!"

In considering this trend, we again wish to point out that children's stories are a result, not only of their level of skill, but also of the quality of the interaction with teacher and peers that has surrounded the writing. For example, Jake's piece originally read:

I will make my FLYing MACHIN First I will Find pieces of wood next Third fly time I will go to Cherrokee Indian land then I'll go home. The next morning I take off again.

Jake's teacher first asked questions to clarify Jake's meaning. Certain of these questions quite naturally involved mechanics (i.e., punctuation):

Is it "First I will make my flying machine" or "First I will find pieces of wood"? What are you doing first? Well, how will your reader know that *first* goes with *flying machine* and not with *pieces of wood*? . . . Right, you need a period after the end of your first sentence, after *first*.

Where is your flying machine going to go next?

At this point, Jake explained that he was going to go to dinosaur land. A peer remarked that dinosaurs blew out fire, which led to a discussion of the differences between dragons and dinosaurs. Another child remarked that dinosaurs were where the Philippines was, which led to an inspection of the globe and a discussion of the differences between distance in time and distance in space. Notice that, in his composition, Jake went to another country, Africa, as well as to another time, dinosaur land. Talking with his teacher and his peers led to a more detailed, more thoughtful composition.

Beyond the here and now, beyond the self. Primary grade children's writing is, as we have stressed, primarily self-expressive. Here, then, we look for evidence of the children separating themselves from their stories. Neither Robin, Ruthy, Jake, nor Will appear to be a consistent observer to the evolving story. However, we do find evidence of the children's considering another's point of view. Ruthy points out that mother "did not like to clean up. But she liked her boys." Jake notes that the Arab answered his question in a foreign tongue ("mallatchas") which he could not understand. Will's story portrays the emotions of his character (himself?) when faced with the talking bones. His piece also seems to be constructed with an awareness of his potential readers—he builds the tension, culminating in the climactic "and the voice was tlaking to me!"

In both stories with developed plots—Jake's and Will's—the children are dealing within the realm of the possible, but find it difficult to maintain their stance; they switch tenses, finally ending in the immediate present, completely involving themselves in their own stories.

Again, the questions and reactions of teacher and peers to the evolving story affect the nature of the resulting product. Children can be helped to take an evaluative approach to their writing; in other words, they can be helped to achieve some distance from their own work. One teacher, Mary Ellen Giacobbe, does this through writing conferences. She explains:

> During a writing conference, the child reads the piece. I retell the story giving the writer the opportunity to say, "Yes, that's the way it is," or "No, you don't understand." I do not interfere by giving my ideas. Instead, I ask questions that enable the writer to rethink the content. "What do you think about your story? What is the best part? Why? Are there any other details that you can add? What are you going to do next with this piece of writing." The writer then has the choice to rewrite or not to rewrite. (Caroselli, 1981)

In addition to analyzing children's story writing for evidence of developmental trends, teachers can also note signs of imaginativeness and creativity. The story itself may be constructed in an unusual way—teachers may note the striking use of punctuation, a catchy title, a plot with an interesting twist, or engaging dialogue. Or, the choice of individual words—or the ideas themselves—may be novel. The following piece, written also by Will, illustrates many aspects of creativity:

> On Thursday Jed hit me in the eye and he hit me in the foot ouch he hit me MOM in the leg OUCH you hit me in the leg EEEEE You will get hit with a belt OUCH Jed quit OUCH you OUCH I am going to tell Mom. Mom OUCH Jed hitting me with stick Ouch Ouch he hit me in the face Jed quit hitting Will.

Although story writing is the dominant part of young children's poetic writing efforts, children who read, listen to, and respond to poetry (for example, through choral readings or interpretations through movement) will write poetry as well. Certainly traits identified as revealing creativity—the unusual structuring of language, the novel idea, the intense concentration on and illumination of one experience or emotion—are the substance of creating poetry. The following poems were written by two first graders after they had heard Shel Silverstein's (1981) poem "What If." Both children's poems evidence a grasp of the poetic form used in Silverstein's poem, a concentration on one experience, and, in addition, the effective use of humor. Note also the careful sequencing of ideas in each poem:

> What if I saw a
> big bubble

What if I was in
a bubble

I wish I was in a
big big bubble

What if the bubble popped!

by Lee

What if Bobucke [Bo Duke] ask me to
marry him

What would I say

I would say yes Bo honey!

What if he forgot to come
I Would do something very bad

by Amanda

Writing throughout the day. Becoming able to use written language for varying social purposes is part of what it means to be communicatively competent. Thus, teachers, parents, and other caregivers may watch for writing purposes which arise naturally in the course of the school day. For example, as part of social studies or science projects, children can record observations of classroom animals or plants, conduct surveys and record results, write letters of various types, make posters, compose announcements. One primary grade classroom raised plants to sell for Mother's Day. The class "borrowed" money from their teacher to make the initial investment (to purchase seeds). The children planted the seeds in a small dirt plot outside their classroom. They recorded weekly observations of their plants' growth. When the plants were of sufficient size, the children repotted them, using recycled materials (juice cups from the cafeteria). Then the children composed announcements and made posters for the coming plant sale. Finally, they decorated the plants with colorful ribbons and added gift tags (popsicle sticks, stuck in the dirt, which read "Happy Mother's Day") and, of course, price tags. After the sale, the children paid off their loan, pocketed a quarter apiece profit, and used the remainder to purchase needed classrooms materials. In the course of this experience, the children not only learned a great deal about the business world, they also used oral and written language for a variety of real purposes.

This type of writing—writing to get things done—is referred to as transactional writing (Britton, 1978). The purpose of much of this writing is to convey information. As adults—in our own informational writing—we limit personal or emotional reactions; this is not true of young children. As discussed previously, young children's writing is primarily self-expressive; this "personal-ness" is evident even in their nonpersonal compositions. Young children's personal comments in informational writing allow children to relate new information to their own developing views of the world.

Belinda and Derrick, two first graders, wrote reports which are clearly expressive in nature. Belinda wrote this composition during a study unit on plants:

> We are trying to grow a flower.
> Mine is not grow yet.
>
>   Belinda

And here is Derrick's, written during a study unit on neighborhood animals:

> I saw two rabbits inside my yard. They were looking at me and I liked them. And I got them for a pet and I got two pets now. I saw two more and they did not like me and I got mad and they came back to me. And when my mom came home she liked them.

In the following two compositions by 7-year-olds, we see an increasing amount of objective information. Yet, Mary, whose writing contains a personal reaction, seems to have been more involved in her learning experience (a survey on the class's animal preferences) than Yvonne was in hers (an experiment on the nature of air):

> From my graph I can tell that there are 13 people who like dogs, there are 3 people who like cats. There are 3 people who like rabbits. There is 1 person who likes guinea pigs. there are 0 people who like hamsters. I think it is a sheme for hamsters Because they are such nice creahs
>
>   Mary

> All about air . . . We put lit paper in a Jar and we put a piece of cardboard underneath the Jar and we put another Jar underneath the other side and the smoke rises.
>
>   Yvonne
>   (Martin, 1971)

Teachers may respond to informational writing by functioning as an interested reader, asking the children questions to clarify the intended communication. Talking with children about their writing helps develop the needed sense of audience. Consider what questions you might ask 8-year-old Frank, who has written on the subject of pet care:

You take the old stuff out and you put the new stuff in.

In addition to informational writing, children can write letters to varying audiences: to each other, to teacher, to parents, to other adults within the school. . . . A class mailbox can become a central part of the classroom (Florio, 1979). First letters may contain only the name of the addressee, the sender, and few well known words (e.g., "I like you," or "LOVE"). The teacher may plan class letter-writing activities for such purposes as thanking, inviting, persuading, requesting, and consoling; such activities help children develop a concept of what letters are for.

At home, children can write letters to cousins, Grandmas and Granpas, aunts and uncles, and friends who have moved away. As a first grade teacher, the second author received the following letter from a child who moved from Texas to Washington:

> Dear Teacher say Hi to all The class and how are you Teach Say Hi to melissa and amy we went to see The spase needle and rode on The monrail TraiN hope you write Back soon This is all For now your student
>
> Ruth Ann

Journal writing is another form that daily writing may take. Teachers may give each child a notebook and ask the child to write in the book each day. The daily writing provides an easy method of maintaining a record of each child's development as a writer; the teacher can study the children's journals for spelling patterns, dominant writing functions (e.g., recording personal news or narrating stories), development of writing conventions, including both mechanics (e.g., spelling and punctuation) and aspects of story structure (e.g., developing plots or dialogue). In addition, the journals allow teachers insight into the daily lives of their students. Note the following series of journal entries by Becky, a first grader:

> My mother is makeing a tepee for me to play in it. My aunt she gos to the town. Do our mother lets you go. No she don't.
>
> My brother broked my tepee win I was playing in my tepee. And then he laughed at me. My mother she said, "You go in.
>
> The boy on the seesaw is a scared are you a scared? Yes I am my brther is not a scared. Everyone is a scared. But except my broher.

While Becky seemed to be exploring her conflicting feelings about her brother, her classmate Ruben appeared to be adopting the amused-older-brother stance toward his:

> I like my baby brother because he is going up on my bed and he pees in my bed because he drinks water too much

> My brother wakes me up in the middle of the night because he is scaared.

As Becky and Ruben were concentrating on their brothers, JB was thinking about food:

> I eat tortillas all the time at my Grandmothers house. I love tortilles do you? I really do?

Getting it "right."   Although we have discussed young children's spelling, our focus has been primarily on the purposes for which children write. The mechanics of writing, including legible handwriting and conventional spelling, punctuation, and capitalization, are skills which are secondary to the communication of meaning; children's skill in these areas improves with use.

The developing ability to punctuate is illustrated in this chronologically arranged series of compositions by Becky, some of which have appeared earlier in this chapter. The first composition, written in January of Becky's first grade year, reflects a confusion of the question mark with the quotation mark. By the end of the school year, Becky had mastered the question mark and was beginning to use quotation marks correctly:

> Sally said? move out of my way. So I can see Tv. Charle Brown did not listen. Sally said? move. If I say one more time you will get in trouble. If I move will you make me some popcorn. Sally said? oK. And then thay were happy.

> Let's go swiming "I am going to drown YOU!" said "Charley Brown. Sally said, "help me," said Sally.

> My brother broked my tepee win I was playing in my tepee. And then he laughed at me. My mother she said, "You go in.

> The boy on the seesaw is a scared are you a scared? Yes I am my brother is not a scared. Everyone is a scared. But except my broher.

In reading Becky's third composition, you may have noted Becky's past tense form "broked." Many 6-year-olds are still acquiring the irregular past verb forms. In addition, Becky had learned English in the kindergarten—her first language was Spanish. Thus, we may expect that she may be working out the irregularities of the English language at a later age than would a native English speaker. As with first language speakers, her teacher was accepting of Becky's efforts to learn the rules of the English language. Fluent young writers, like Becky, draw on oral language for the substance of their writing; thus, we cannot expect them to write differently from the way in which they speak.

Becky's teacher did not red-pencil Becky's grammatical mistake. In fact, she did not mark Becky's paper at all, a useless procedure. Rather, through folders containing samples of Becky's work, anecdotal records, and checklists (see Figure 7–7), her teacher was able to document Becky's progress in these areas. The checklist was particularly useful in grouping Becky with children who had similar needs for small group instruction. Becky's teacher also edited Becky's work *with* her in an individual conference when there was a reason for such editing, for example, a story to be "published" for the classroom library (i.e., a story to be printed into a cloth bound book), a letter to be sent, an announcement to be posted. In such editing sessions, Becky's teacher began by having Becky read her work out loud; Becky, like many children, would often independently note words which had been left out or misspelled. Her teacher then asked questions to clarify both content and mechanics: "Becky, you've got two sentences here. Read them out loud and see if you hear where you pause—that's where the period goes."

Ms. Nash, a second grade teacher, made a writing "checklist" on

Names	Begins sentence with a capital letter	Ends sentence with a period	Ends question with a question mark	Uses commas in a list	Uses apostrophes in contractions
Diane	✓+	✓+	✓+	✓+	✓
Efren	✓	✓	✓	✓	✓
Robert	✓+	✓+	✓	-	-
Ruth Ann	✓	✓	✓+	-	-
Becky	✓+	✓+	-	-	✓

Key: ✓+ always
 ✓ sometimes
 - random or never

Figure 7–7 Checklist for recording children's use of the conventions (mechanics) of written language

the inside cover of her children's writing folders (folders in which they kept all written work). Each child was to proofread his or her own work for the skills listed on the checklist. The following is an example of the type of checklist Ms. Nash used:

Jesse's Writing Checklist

I put a period at the end of every telling sentence.

I run fast.

I put a question mark at the end of every question.

Can you run as fast as I can?

I start every sentence with a capital letter.

Running is my favorite sport.

Spelling Checklist

I checked for these words:

The

can't

don't

were

to—I go to school.

too—Mary goes too.

two—That makes two of us.

Summary

In the elementary school grades, children encounter an increasingly structured world. School activities take place within particular social settings, including large group discussions, small group sessions, peer-to-peer dialogues. To help children participate effectively in school, we must foster their ability to use language effectively in a variety of talk contexts. The academic aspects of school cannot be separated from the social or from the linguistic. In this chapter, we discussed ways of assessing and fostering children's ability to function in these varied school contexts for talk.

Children grow in their control over written language as well as oral language in the early elementary school grades: the global approximations of the functions and forms of written language discussed in Chapter 6 are shaped and refined. We discussed benchmarks of progress in this refinement process. To assist children in gaining control over the written language system, teachers become sensitive observers. Careful observation assists teachers in identifying and building upon children's current levels of functioning. As we discover the children's concepts of written language's functions and forms, we support and extend those concepts, helping children become full-fledged participants in the literacy conventions we all share.

Reference Notes

1. These excerpts were taken from Frank J. Zidonis *et al. Instructor's guide to the language of children protocol materials on oral language acquisition.* Columbus, OH: The Ohio State University, pp. 70, 74, 77.
2. We are grateful to Carol Fisher for sharing these samples of children's language with us. Fisher, along with M. Natarella, has studied young children's poetry preferences. See: Fisher, C. and Natarella, M. Of cabbages and kings, or, What kinds of poetry young children like. *Language Arts,* 1979, *56* (4), 380–385.
3. In organizing this section, we were influenced by the clear discussion of developmental trends in writing in C. Fisher and A. Terry. *Children's language and the language arts.* New York: McGraw-Hill, 1982.

Suggested Readings

Clay, M. *Reading: The patterning of complex behavior.* Auckland, New Zealand: Heinemann, 1979.

Clay believes that reading failures can be prevented by teachers who are sensitive and skillful observers of young children's reading behaviors. To this end, Clay's text, based on her own extensive research, provides finely detailed, well-illustrated descriptions of young children learning to read and practical assessment guidelines for teachers.

Galloway, C. M. (Ed.). Communicating with young children. *Theory into Practice,* 1979, *18* (4).

This journal issue provides readable and well-documented articles about children's oral communication. The articles focus on children from a range of age levels and ethnic backgrounds and, in addition, include samples of children's talk gathered in both home and school contexts.

Gilmore, P., and Glatthorn, A. A. (Eds.). *Children in and out of school: Ethnography and education.* Washington, DC: Center for Applied Linguistics, 1982.

This book is a good resource for further information concerning research on children's interactions in varied contexts. Written primarily for researchers, it is a description and analysis of current ethnographic work. The collected articles provide a thorough and well-documented discussion of the rationale behind and current trends in research on children's use of language in society.

Graves, Donald H. *Writing: Teachers and children at work*. Exeter, NH: Heinemann, 1983.

Graves' book is designed to help teachers with children's writing. Using data collected in his three-year study of writing development, Graves describes teachers and young writers interacting in classrooms. Especially relevant for our purposes are Graves' helpful suggestions for documenting children's writing progress.

Rosen, C., and Rosen, H. *The language of primary school children*. London: Penguin Education, 1973.

The Rosens' books is based on a 2-year project designed to sample the oral and written language of British children in primary school classrooms. The many illustrations of children's talking and writing demonstrate fully how children use language to make sense of their daily lives.

CHAPTER 8

Summing Up

The pages of this volume have been filled with images of the child as communicator in order to help you appreciate, foster, and assess language in the early childhood years. In this brief chapter we summarize procedures for assessing children's language, principles for fostering and assessing language, and the nature of language development in young children.

The essentials of informal assessment are the observant ear and eye. To aid in remembering and assessing what you notice about children's language we suggested the following:

1. Hand-written anecdotes are an effective and easy way to record individual children's interactions or utterances. They can be unsophisticated, brief, or elaborate for purposes of assessment and planning.

2. Because spoken language consists of fleeting sounds, the audiotape recorder is a valuable means of preserving speech. Audiotapes assure more careful study of what children say and, thus, fairer and more accurate judgments of what they can say and do.

3. Observation forms and checklists help record participants' names, the nature of the activity, and nonverbal context, particularly while you audiotape.

4. Assessment forms and checklists help document specific aspects of children's spoken or written language. These are time savers that are most useful when you modify them to suit your own situation, needs, and interests.

5. Some methods developed by others, for example, the Berko test and Clay's test for the child's concepts about print, are included. These lead to a fuller understanding of children's own rules and thoughts about spoken and written language.

6. You can also document progress by keeping selected audiotapes, transcribed segments of talk, captioned artwork, and children's written products. For parents and teachers such items over time can be the most meaningful records of change and progress.

Procedures for assessment are meaningless if there is no productive language in center or classroom to observe and assess. We, therefore, presented principles for fostering and assessing language that underlie programs noted for talk-filled interactions. First, the physical and social situation affects the kind of language participants use; language changes as features of the situation change. To encourage children to use different kinds of language, we provide varied situations and activities for them. Second, language fulfills many functions. Within situations and activities children will use language to inquire, to solve problems, to provide information, as well as to make friends, disagree with someone, be creative, or assert their own importance. Third, we should expect and accept variation in functions and forms of language. We expect variation in function: children use language to make requests, joke, be insulting, and so on. We should also expect variation in form. Children may make mistakes from the adult viewpoint as their rules are developing, or they may use nonstandard forms that others in their families and social groups use. Especially in the early childhood years, acceptance of a child's forms and functions is necessary to support growth in language. Fourth, since language changes according to the situation and the speaker's purpose, assessment of a child's language is not accomplished through one or two tests, whether they focus on forms or functions. Observing the child in many interactive situations—in varied activities, with different interlocutors—leads to the most valid assessment.

The development of language is one of the child's most spectacular accomplishments. Like other aspects of development, it begins at birth and continues throughout the lifespan. As children learn forms and functions of communication, they proceed from general to specific, global to refined, concrete to abstract. The cries in the first days of life become differentiated so that caregivers later distinguish a hungry cry from a lonely cry. Two-word utterances are modified and expanded so that by age 5 or 6 children combine two or more ideas in one sentence, using rules as sophisticated as those their parents know. Where forms lacked endings, inflections like *-ed* and *-ing* eventually appear; *walk* is refined to become walk*ed* or walk*ing*; "Mary walk?" becomes, "Is Mary walking?" Simultaneously, the functions that the forms serve increase, most often in interaction with engaging people or things.

Many of the young child's utterances hinge on action and on the concrete, the here-and-now. Objects, activities, and people provide the scaffolding for early communication and talk. Over time the scope of what language refers to widens to include the past and future, the there-and-then. The classroom context affords opportunities to begin to free language from context, so that the child depends more on words only to communicate. Written language, which can represent and record our experiences, is often abstract, removed from familiar human contexts. Early childhood teachers ease the transition from the familiar to unfamiliar, the spoken to written. When children are very young, many uses of spoken language blend together as teachers provide varied, generally concrete, experiences in day care and preschool settings. Teachers encourage children to use language for familiar and increasingly varied functions. As children enter kindergarten and the primary grades, teachers help the child to see the connections between what is said and what is written in more prescribed and directed ways. Still the aspects of language and language arts are integrated. In the teaching process adults respect each individual child's style of learning and expression.

Through these pages, we have involved you in the study of child language. We have made many suggestions and so have added to your tasks as a caregiver or teacher. We are aware that there are days in center or school that are too full for even the quickest assessment of a child's language. But on those days, perhaps you will hear and appreciate an interesting or unique use of language that would have gone unnoticed before.

We opened this volume by stating our perspectives on language and language acquisition. We close by putting language in perspective. As we presented examples of children's language and emphasized the importance of fostering and assessing it, we kept productive—spoken and written—language in the foreground. As the child develops, language remains in the foreground, particularly in school contexts. Eventually, however, it becomes most significant as a remarkable tool that we manipulate to help us think, learn, and interact in satisfying ways with others. As a tool, we value it not for its own sake but to the extent that it facilitates learning and living. The activities in our examples allow teachers to assess children's communicative competence and allow children to develop competence as they adapt their language for a range of purposes and situations. The ultimate aim, then, of these activities and assessment strategies is a person with his own communicative style who uses his language to be a confident and effective participant in life.

References

Almy, M., & Genishi, C. *Ways of studying children*. New York: Teachers College Press, 1979.

Amarel, M. The teacher as observer. Occasional paper, Right to Read Office. Harrisburg, PA: Department of Education, 1980.

Anderson, B. *Acquisition of English as a second language and its relationship to linguistic input: A case study of a 4-year-old Japanese speaker*. Doctoral dissertation, in progress, The University of Texas at Austin.

Applebee, A. N. *The child's concept of story: Ages two to seventeen*. Chicago, IL: University of Chicago Press, 1978.

Asch, S. E., & Nerlove, H. The development of double function terms in children: An exploratory investigation. In B. Kaplan & S. Wapner (Eds.), *Perspectives in psychological theory: Essays in honor of Heinz Werner*. New York: International Universities Press, 1960.

Barnes, D. *Language, the learner, and the school*. Harmondsworth, England: Penguin, 1969.

Barrett, M. D. Distinguishing between prototypes: The early acquisition of the meaning of object names. In S. Kuczaj, II (Ed.), *Language development (Vol. I): Syntax and semantics*. Hillsdale, NJ: Erlbaum, 1982.

Bates, E. Peer relations and the acquisition of language. In M. Lewis and L. A. Rosenblum (Eds.), *Friendship and peer relations*. New York: John Wiley & Sons, 1975.

Batherman, M. *A row of crows*. New York: Holt, Rinehart, and Winston, 1973.

Bemelmans, L. *Madeline*. Harmondsworth, England: Penguin, 1977.

Berk, L. E. *An analysis of activities in preschool settings (Final report)*. Washington, D. C. National Center for Educational Research and Development, November 1973. (ERIC Document Retrieval No. ED 099131).

Berko, J. The child's learning of English morphology. *Word*, 1958, *14*, 150–177.

Betts, E. *Foundations of reading instruction with emphasis on differentiated guidance*. New York: American Book Co., 1946.

Bissex, G. *GNYS AT WRK: A child learns to write and read*. Cambridge, MA: Harvard University Press, 1980.

Black, J. Formal and informal means of assessing the communicative competence of kindergarten children. *Research in the Teaching of English*, 1979, *13*, 49–68.

Bloom, B. S. (Ed.). *Taxonomy of educational objectives: The classification of educational goals* (Vols. 1 and 2). New York: David McKay Company, 1956.

Boehm, A. E., & Weinberg, R. A. *The classroom observer: A guide for developing observation skills*. New York: Teachers College Press, 1977.

Bowerman, M. The acquisition of complex sentences. In P. Fletcher and M. Garman (Eds.), *Language acquisition*. Cambridge, England: Cambridge University Press, 1979.

Britton, J. *Language and learning*. Harmondsworth, Middlesex, England: Penguin, 1970.

Britton, J. The composing process and the functions of writing. In C. R. Cooper and L. Odell (Eds.), *Research on composing: Points of departure*. Urbana, IL: National Council of Teachers of English, 1978.

Brown, M. *Arthur's eyes*. Boston: Little, Brown, 1979.

Brown, R. *Psycholinguistics*. New York: Free Press, 1970.

Brown, R. *A first language: The early stages*. Cambridge, MA: Harvard University Press, 1973.

Brown, R., Cazden, C., & Bellugi, U. The child's grammar from I to III. In J. P. Hill (Ed.), *Minnesota symposium on child psychology* (Vol. 2). Minneapolis: University of Minnesota Press, 1969.

Bruner, J. S. The ontogenesis of speech acts. *Journal of Child Language*, 1975, *2*(1), 1–20.

Bruner, J., & Feldman, C. F. Where does language come from? *The New York Review of Books*, June 24, 1982, *29*(11), 34–36.

Bussis, A. M., Chittenden, E. A., & Amarel, M. Collaborative research. In S. Madeja (Ed.), *The teaching process and the arts and aesthetics*. (Third yearbook of research in arts and aesthetics education). St. Louis, MO: Cemrel, 1978.

Carle, E. *The very hungry caterpillar*. New York: World Publishing, 1969.

Caroselli, M. Romance precedes precision: Recommended classroom teaching practices. In S. Haley-James (Ed.), *Perspectives on writing in grades 1–8*. Urbana, IL: National Council of Teachers of English, 1981.

Cazden, C. B. Four comments. In P. Gilmore and A. A. Glatthorn (Eds.), *Children in and out of school*. Washington, D. C.: Center for Applied Linguistics, 1982.

Cazden, C. B., Bryant, B. H., & Tillman, M. A. Making it and going home: The attitudes of black people toward language education. In C. B. Cazden (Ed.), *Language in early childhood education* (Rev. ed.). Washington, D. C.: National Association for the Education of Young Children, 1981.

Cazden, C. B., Cox, M., Dickinson, D., Steinberg, Z., & Stone, C. "You all gonna hafta listen": Peer teaching in a primary classroom. In W. A. Collins (Ed.), *Children's language and communication*. Hillsdale, NJ: Erlbaum, 1978.

Chall, J. *Learning to read: The great debate*. New York: McGraw-Hill, 1967.

Chomsky, C. *The acquisition of syntax in children from 5 to 10*. Cambridge, MA: MIT Press, 1969.

Chomsky, N. *Aspects of the theory of syntax*. Cambridge, MA: MIT Press, 1965.

Clark, E. V. What's in a word? On the child's acquisition of semantics in his first language. In T. E. Moore (Ed.), *Cognitive development and the acquisition of language*. New York: Academic Press, 1973.

Clark, M. *Young fluent readers*. London: Heinemann, 1976.

Clay, M. *Emergent reading behavior*. Unpublished doctoral dissertation, University of Auckland, 1966.

Clay, M. *What did I write?* Auckland, New Zealand: Heinemann, 1975.

Clay, M. Early childhood and cultural diversity in New Zealand. *The Reading Teacher*, 1976, *29*(4), 333–342.

Clay, M. *The early detection of reading difficulties: A diagnostic survey with recovery procedures*. Auckland, New Zealand: Heinemann, 1979(a).

Clay, M. *Reading: The patterning of complex behavior* (2nd ed.). Auckland, New Zealand: Heinemann, 1979(b).

Clay, M. *Sand (Concepts about Print Test)*. Auckland, New Zealand: Heinemann, 1979(c).

Clifton, L. *My friend Jacob*. New York: Viking, 1976.

Cook-Gumperz, J. Persuasive talk—the social organization of children's talk. In J. Green and C. Wallat (Eds.), *Ethnography and language in educational settings*. Norwood, NJ: Ablex, 1981.

Cook-Gumperz, J., & Gumperz, J. From oral to written culture: The transition to literacy. In M. F. Whiteman (Ed.), *Variation in writing*. Hillsdale, NJ: Erlbaum, 1981.

Cross, T. G. Mother's speech adjustments: The contribution of selected child listener variables. In C. E. Snow and C. A. Ferguson (Eds.), *Talking to children: Language input and acquisition*. New York: Cambridge University Press, 1977.

Cross, T. G. Mother's speech and its association with rate of linguistic development in young children. In N. Waterson and C. E. Snow (Eds.), *The development of communication*. New York: John Wiley, 1978.

Doake, D. Preschool book handling knowledge or book experience and emergent reading behavior. Paper presented at the International Reading Association Preconvention, Atlanta, Georgia, May 1979.

Doke, L. A., & Risley, T. R. The organization of day-care environments: Required vs. optional activities. *Journal of Applied Behavior Analysis*, 1972, *5*, 205–420.

Durán, R. P. (Ed.). *Latino language and communicative behavior*. Norwood, NJ: Ablex, 1981.

Durkin, D. *Children who read early: Two longitudinal studies*. New York: Teachers College Press, 1966.

Dyson, A. Haas. *A case study examination of the role of oral language in writing processes of kindergarteners*. Unpublished doctoral dissertation, The University of Texas at Austin, 1981.

Dyson, A. Haas. The emergence of visible language: Interrelationships between drawing and early writing, *Visible Language*, 1982, 16(4), 360–381.

Dyson, A. Haas, & Genishi, C. "Whatta ya tryin' to write?": Writing as an interactive process. *Language Arts*, 1982, *59*(2), 126–132.

Early, M., Cooper, E., & Santensanio, N. *Magic afternoon*. Preprimer 3 of the *Bookmark Reading Program*. New York: Harcourt, Brace, Jovanovich, 1979.

Eisenberg, A. R., & Garvey, C. Children's use of verbal strategies in resolving conflicts. *Discourse Processes*, 1981, *4*(2), 149–170.

Erickson, F. Classroom discourse as improvisation: Relationships between academic task structure and social participation structure in lessons. In L. C. Wilkinson (Ed.), *Communicating in the classroom*. New York: Academic Press, 1982.

Ervin, S. M., & Miller, W. The development of grammar in child language. In U. Bellugi and R. Brown (Eds.), The acquisition of language. *Monographs of the Society for Research in Child Development*, 1964, *29* (1, Serial No. 92).

Ervin-Tripp, S. M. Activity structure as scaffolding for children's second language learning. *Sociolinguistic Working Paper* No. 100. Austin, TX: Southwest Educational Development Laboratory, 1982.

Ervin-Tripp, S., & Mitchell-Kernan, C. (Eds.). *Child discourse*. New York: Academic Press, 1977.

Ferreiro, E. What is written in a written sentence? A developmental answer. *Journal of Education*, 1978, *160*(4), 25–39.

Ferreiro, E. The relationship between oral and written language: The children's viewpoints. Paper presented at the International Reading Association Preconvention, St. Louis, May 1980.

Fillmore, L. W. *The second time around: Cognitive and social strategies in second language acquisition.* Unpublished doctoral dissertation, Stanford University, 1976.

Fillmore, L. W., & Ervin-Tripp, S. Sources of individual differences in second language acquisition. Report of project sponsored by National Institute of Education, 1979.

Florio, S. The problem of dead letters: Social perspectives on the teaching of writing. *Elementary School Journal,* 1979, *80*(1), 1–7.

Florio, S., & Clark, C. The functions of writing in an elementary classroom. *Research in the Teaching of English,* 1982, *16*(2), 115–130.

Forester, A. D. Learning to spell by spelling. *Theory into Practice,* 1980, *19*(3), 186–193.

Fosburg, S., Singer, J. D., Goodson, B. D., Warner, D., Irwin, N., Brush, L. R., & Grasso, J. *Family day care in the United States: Summary of findings* (Vol. 1). Washington, DC: U.S. Department of Health and Human Services, 1981.

Freedman, P. A comparison of multi-age and homogeneous age grouping in early childhood centers. In L. G. Katz (Ed.), *Current topics in early childhood education* (Vol. 4). Norwood, NJ: Ablex, 1982.

French, L., & Nelson, K. Taking away the supportive context: Preschoolers talk about "then and there." *The Quarterly Newsletter of the Laboratory of Comparative Human Cognition,* 1982, *4*(1) 1–6.

Garvey, C. Some properties of social play. *Merrill-Palmer Quarterly,* 1974, *20,* 163–180.

Garvey, C. *Play.* Cambridge, MA: Harvard University Press, 1977.

Garvey, C., & Hogan, R. Social speech and social interaction: Egocentrism revisited. *Child Development,* 1973, *44,* 562–568.

Genishi, C., & Di Paolo, M. Learning through argument in a preschool. In L. C. Wilkinson (Ed.), *Communicating in the classroom.* New York: Academic Press, 1982.

Georgia Department of Human Resources. *Rules and regulations for group day care centers,* 1974.

Gleason, J. B. Do children imitate? *Proceedings of the International Conference on Oral Education of the Deaf* (Vol. 2). June, 1967, 1411–1448.

Gleason, J. B. Fathers and other strangers: Men's speech to young children. In D. Dato (Ed.), *Developmental psycholinguistics.* Washington, DC: Georgetown University Press, 1975.

Gleason, J. B., & Weintraub, S. Input language and the acquisition of communicative competence. In K. E. Nelson (Ed.), *Children's language* (Vol. 1). New York: Gardner Press, 1978.

Golden, M., Rosenbluth, L., Grossi, M., Policare, H., Freeman, H., & Brownlee, E. *The New York City infant day care study.* New York: Medical and Health Research Association of New York City, 1978.

Goodman, Y., and Burke, C. *The Goodman-Burke reading miscue inventory.* New York: Macmillan, 1972.

Graves, D. An examination of the writing processes of seven-year-old children. *Research in the Teaching of English,* 1975, *9*(3), 227–242.

Graves, D. *Balance the basics: Let them write.* New York: Ford Foundation Report, 1978.

Graves, D. Research update: Writing research for the eighties: What is needed. *Language Arts,* 1981, *58*(2), 197–206.

Graves, D. Research update: How do writers develop? *Language Arts,* 1982, *59*(2), 173–179.

Graves, D. *Writing: Teachers and children at work.* Exeter, NH: Heinemann, 1983.

Griffin, P. How and when does reading occur in the classroom? *Theory into Practice,* 1977, *16*(5), 376–383.

Grossman, A. S. More than half of all children have working mothers. *Monthly Labor Review,* 1982, *105*(2), 41–43.

Haley-James, S., & Hobson, C. D. Interviewing: A means of encouraging the drive to communicate. *Language Arts,* 1980, *57,* 497–502.

Hall, M., Moretz, S., & Statom, J. A study of early writing. *Language Arts,* 1976, *53* (5), 582–585.

Halliday, M. A. K. *Explorations in the functions of language.* London: Edward Arnold, 1973.

Halliday, M. A. K. *Learning how to mean.* London: Edward Arnold, 1975.

Hamilton, J. L., & Stewart, D. M. Peer models and language acquisition. *Merrill-Palmer Quarterly,* 1977, *23*,(1), 45–55.

Hargreaves, R. *Mr. Clumsy.* Los Angeles: Price, Stern, Sloan, 1980.

Harkness, S. Aspects of social environment and first language acquisition in rural Africa. In C. E. Snow and C. A. Ferguson (Eds.), *Talking to children: Language input and acquisition.* New York: Cambridge University Press, 1977.

Harste, J., Burke, C., & Woodward, V. Children's language and world: Initial encounters with print. In J. Langer and M. Smith-Burke (Eds.), *Reader meets author/Bridging the gap.* Newark, DE: International Reading Association, 1982.

Heath, S. B. Questioning at home and at school: A comparative study. In G. Spindler (Ed.), *Doing the ethnography of schooling: Educational anthropology in action.* New York: Holt, Rinehart and Winston, 1982(a).

Heath, S. B. What no bedtime story means: Narrative skills at home and school. *Language in Society,* 1982(b), *11,* 49–76.

Hickman, J. A new perspective on response to literature: Research in an elementary school setting. *Research in the Teaching of English,* 1981, *15*(4), 343–354.

Hildreth, G. Developmental sequences in name writing. *Child Development,* 1936, *7,* 291–302.

Holdaway, D. *The foundations of literacy.* Sydney, Australia: Ashton Scholastic, 1979.

Howe, C. *Acquiring language in a conversational context.* New York: Academic Press, 1981.

Hutt, C. Exploration and play. In B. Sutton-Smith (Ed.), *Play and learning.* New York: Gardner Press, 1979.

Hymes, D. Introduction, in C. Cazden, V. John, and D. Hymes (Eds.), *Functions of language in the classroom.* New York: Teachers College Press, 1972.

Irwin, D. M., & Bushnell, M. M. *Observational strategies for child study.* New York: Holt, Rinehart, and Winston, 1980.

Karmiloff-Smith, A. Language development after five. In P. Fletcher and M. Garman (Eds.), *Language acquisition.* Cambridge, England: Cambridge University Press, 1979.

Kernan, K. T., & Blount, B. G. The acquisition of Spanish grammar by Mexican children. *Anthropological Linguistics,* 1966, *8* (9), 1–14.

Keyserling, M. D. *Windows on day care:* A report on the findings of the National

Council of Jewish Women on day care needs and services in their communities. New York: National Council of Jewish Women, 1972.

King, M. Evaluating reading. *Theory into Practice,* 1977, *16*(5), 407–418.

Kroll, B. M. Antecedents of individual differences in children's writing attainment. Manuscript. Iowa State University, (n.d.).

Labov, W. *Language in the inner city: Studies in the black English vernacular.* Philadelphia, PA: University of Pennsylvania, 1972.

Labov, W. The logic of nonstandard English. In F. Williams (Ed.), *Language and poverty.* Chicago: Markham Publishing, 1970.

Lamb, M. E. The development of mother-infant attachments in the second year of life. *Developmental Psychology,* 1977, *13,* 639–649.

Lindholm, K. J. Bilingual children: Some interpretations of cognitive and linguistic development. In K. E. Nelson (Ed.), *Children's language* (Vol. 2). New York: Gardner Press, 1980.

Maclure, M., & French, P. A comparison of talk at home and at school. In G. Wells (Ed.), *Learning through interaction: The study of language development.* Cambridge: Cambridge University Press, 1981.

Martin, B. *Brown bear, brown bear.* New York: Holt, Rinehart, and Winston, 1970.

Martin, N. What are they up to? In A. Jones and J. Mulford (Eds.), *Children using language.* London: Oxford University Press, 1971.

Martínez, M. F. *Young children's verbal responses to literature in parent-child story time interactions.* Unpublished doctoral dissertation, The University of Texas at Austin, 1983.

Masur, E. F., & Gleason, J. B. Parent-child interaction and the acquisition of lexical information during play. *Developmental Psychology,* 1980, *4*(5), 404–409.

McCaig, R. A district-wide plan for the evaluation of student writing. In S. Haley-James (Ed.), *Perspectives on writing in grades 1–8.* Urbana, IL: National Council of Teachers of English, 1981.

McDonnell, G., & Osburn, B. E. New thoughts about reading readiness. *Language Arts,* 1978, *55*(1), 26–29.

McLaughlin, B. *Second-language acquisition in childhood.* Hillsdale, NJ: Erlbaum, 1978.

Mehan, H. The structure of classroom events and their consequences for student performance. In P. Gilmore and A. A. Glatthorn (Eds.), *Children in and out of school.* Washington, DC: Center for Applied Linguistics, 1982.

Mehan, H. "What time is it Denise?": Asking known information questions in classroom discourse. *Theory into Practice,* 1979, *28*(4), 285–294.

Michaels, S., & Foster, M. Peer-peer learning: Evidence for a kid-run sharing time. In A. Jaggar and T. Smith-Burke (Eds.), *Kid-watching: Observing the language learner.* Urbana, IL: National Council of Teachers of English, in press.

Miller, P. J. *Amy, Wendy, and Beth: Learning language in South Baltimore.* Austin, TX: The University of Texas Press, 1982.

Nelson, K. Structure and strategy in learning to talk. *Monographs of the Society for Research in Child Development,* 1973, *38* (1–2, Serial No. 149).

Nelson, K., & Gruendel, J. M. At morning it's lunchtime: A scriptal view of children's dialogues. *Discourse Processes,* 1979, *2,* 73–94.

Nelson, K. Individual differences in language development: Implications for development and language. *Developmental Psychology,* 1981, *17,* 170–187.

Ninio, A., & Bruner, J. S. The achievement and antecedents of labelling. *Journal of Child Language*, 1978, *5*, 5–15.

Paley, V. *Wally's stories*. Cambridge, MA: Harvard University Press, 1981.

Parke, R. D. Perspectives on father-infant interaction. In J. D. Osofsky (Ed.), *Handbook of infant development*. New York: John Wiley, 1979.

Parten, M. B. Social participation among preschool children. *Journal of Abnormal and Social Psychology*, 1932, *27*, 243–269.

Philips, S. U. Participant structure and communicative competence: Warm Springs children in community and classroom. In C. B. Cazden, V. John, and D. Hymes (Eds.), *Functions of language in the classroom*. New York: Teachers College Press, 1972.

Piaget, J. *The construction of reality in the child*. New York: Basic Books, 1954.

Piaget, J. *The language and thought of the child* (3rd ed.). London: Routledge and Kegan Paul, Ltd., 1959.

Piaget, J., & Inhelder, B. *The psychology of the child*. New York: Basic Books, 1969.

Piestrup, A. M. Black dialect interference and accommodation of reading instruction in first grade. *Monographs of the Language-Behavior Research Laboratory*, No. 4. Berkeley, CA: University of California, 1973.

Pinnell, G. S. Language in primary classrooms. *Theory into Practice*, 1975, *24*(5), 318–327.

Plessas, G., & Oakes, C. Prereading experiences of selected early readers. *The Reading Teacher*, 1964, *17*, 241–243.

Read, C. Preschool children's knowledge of English orthography. *Harvard Educational Review*, 1971, *5*, 5–15.

Read, C. *Children's categorization of speech sounds in English*. Urbana, IL: National Council of Teachers of English, 1975.

Rhodes, L. I can read: Predictable books as resources for reading and writing instruction. *The Reading Teacher*, 1981, *34*(5), 511–518.

Robinson, H. B., & Robinson, N. M. Longitudinal development of very young children in a comprehensive day care program: The first two years. *Child Development*, 1971, *42*, 1673–1683.

Rosen, C., & Rosen, H. *The language of primary school children*. Harmondsworth, Middlesex, England: Penguin, 1974.

Ross, H. S., & Goldman, B. M. Establishing new social relationships in infancy. In T. Alloway, L. Krames, and P. Pliner (Eds.), *Advances in communication and affect* (Vol. 4). New York: Plenum Press, 1976.

Rubenstein, J. L., Howes, C., & Boyle, P. A two-year follow-up of infants in community-based day care. *Journal of Child Psychology and Psychiatry*, 1981, *22*(3), 209–218.

Sanders, N. M. *Classroom questions: What kinds?* New York: Harper & Row, 1966.

Saville-Troike, M. The development of bilingual and bicultural competence in young children. In L. G. Katz (Ed.), *Current topics in early childhood education* (Vol. 4). Norwood, NJ: Ablex, 1982.

Schachter, F. F., & Strage, A. A. Adult's talk and children's language development. In S. G. Moore and C. R. Cooper (Eds.), *The young child: Reviews of research* (Vol. 3). Washington, D. C.: National Association for the Education of Young Children, 1982.

Scaife, M., & Bruner, J. S. The capacity for joint visual attention in the infant. *Nature*, 1975, *253*, 265–266.

Schieffelin, B. B. Getting it together: An ethnographic approach to the study of the development of communicative competence. In E. Ochs and B. B. Schieffelin (Eds.), *Developmental pragmatics*. New York: Academic Press, 1979.

Scribner, S., & Cole, M. Cognitive consequences of formal and informal education. *Science,* November 9, 1973, *182,* 553–559.

Sendak, M. *Where the wild things are.* New York: Harper & Row, 1963.

Shultz, J. J., Florio, S., & Erickson, F. Where's the floor? Aspects of the cultural organization of social relationships in communication at home and in school. In P. Gilmore and A. A. Glatthorn (Eds.), *Children in and out of school.* Washington, DC: Center for Applied Linguistics, 1982.

Shure, M. B. Psychological ecology of a nursery school. *Child Development,* 1963, *34,* 979–992.

Silverstein, S. *There's a light in the attic.* New York: Harper & Row, 1981.

Slobin, D. I. *Psycholinguistics* (2nd ed.). Dallas, TX: Scott-Foresman, 1979.

Smith, E., Goodman, K., & Meredith, R. *Language and thinking in school.* New York: Holt, Rinehart, and Winston, 1976.

Smith, F. *Understanding reading* (2nd ed.). New York: Holt, Rinehart, and Winston, 1978.

Snow, C. E., Dubber, C., & De Blauw, A. Routines in mother-child interaction. In L. Feagans and D. C. Farran (Eds.), *The language of children reared in poverty: Implications for evaluation and intervention.* New York: Academic Press, 1982.

Snow, C. E., & Ferguson, C. A. (Eds.). *Talking to children: Language input and acquisition.* New York: Cambridge University Press, 1977.

Sowers, S. Young writers' preference for nonnarrative modes of composition. Paper presented at the Fourth Annual Boston University Conference on Language Development, Boston, MA, September 1979.

Starbird, K. *Don't ever cross a crocodile.* Philadelphia, PA: Lippincott, 1963.

State Advisory Committee on Child Care Facilities, Texas Department of Human Resources. *Minimum standards for day care centers,* 1980.

Stein, N. L. How children understand stories: A developmental analysis. In L. Resnick and P. Weaver (Eds.), *Theory and practice of early reading* (Vol. 2). Hillsdale, NJ: Erlbaum, 1979.

Stern, D. *The first relationship: Infant and mother.* Cambridge, MA: Harvard University Press, 1977.

Sylva, K., Roy, C., & Painter, M. *Childwatching at playgroup and nursery school.* Ypsilanti, MI: The High/Scope Press, 1980.

Teale, W. H. Parents reading to their children: What we know and need to know. *Language Arts,* 1981, *58*(8), 902–912.

Teale, W. H., Estrada, E., & Anderson, A. B. How preschoolers interact with written communication. In M. L. Kamil (Ed.), *Directions in reading: Research and instruction,* Thirtieth Yearbook of the National Reading Conference. Washington, D. C.: National Reading Conference, 1981.

Tizard, B., Cooperman, O., Joseph, A., & Tizard, J. Environmental effects of language development: A study of young children in long-stay residential nurseries. *Child Development,* 1972, *43,* 337–358.

Tolstoy, A. *The great big enormous turnip.* New York: Franklin Watts, 1968.

Torrey, J. Learning to read without a teacher: A case study. *Elementary English,* 1969, *46*(5), 550–556, 658.

Tough, J. *Talking and learning.* London, England: Ward Lock Educational, 1977.

Vandell, D. L., & Mueller, E. Peer play and friendships during the first two years. In H. C. Foot, A. J. Chapman, and J. R. Smith (Eds.), *Friendship and social relations in children*. New York: John Wiley, 1980.

Viorst, J. *Alexander and the terrible, horrible, no good, very bad day*. New York: Atheneum, 1972.

Vygotsky, L. S. *Mind in society*. Cambridge, MA: Harvard University Press, 1978.

Wells, G. *Learning through interaction: The study of language development*. New York: Cambridge University Press, 1981.

Whiteman, M. F. *Reactions to Ann Arbor: Vernacular black English and education*. Arlington, VA: Center for Applied Linguistics, 1980.

Wilkinson, L. C. (Ed.). *Communicating in the classroom*. New York: Academic Press, 1982.

Wilkinson, L. C., & Dollaghan, C. Peer communication in first grade reading groups. *Theory into Practice*, 1979, *28*(4), 267–274.

Zepeda-de-Kane, F. *Young children's drawing as related to basic communication skills*. Gainesville, FL: P. K. Yonge Laboratory School, University of Florida, 1980.

Zidonis, F. (Ed.). *Instructor's guide to the language of children protocol materials on oral language acquisition*. Columbus, OH: The Ohio State University, n.d.

Author Index

Italic page numbers indicate complete bibliographic citations.

A

Almy, M., 80, 111, *246*
Amarel, M., 39, 225, *246, 247*
Anderson, A. B., 39, *253*
Anderson, B., 126, *246*
Anno, M., *187*
Applebee, A. N., 209, *246*
Asch, S. E., 15, *246*

B

Barnes, D., 25, *246*
Barrett, M. D., 13, *246*
Bates, E., 70, *246*
Batherman, M., 165, *246*
Baum, W., *187*
Bellugi, U., 10
Bemelmans, L., 49, *246*
Berk, L. E., 93, *246*
Berko, J., 11, 135–138, *246*
Betts, E., 220, *246*
Bissex, G., 40, *246*
Black, J., 106–107, *246*
Bloom, B. S., 116, *246*
Blount, B. G., 138–141, *250*
Boehm, A. E., 80, *246*
Bonne, R., *186*
Bowerman, M., 14, *247*
Boyle, P., 64, 70, *252*
Brazelton, T. B., *60*
Briggs, R., *187*
Britton, J., 228, 235, *247*
Brown, M., 190, *247*
Brown, R., 10, 11, 19, 86–87, 88, *247*
Brownlee, E., 64, *249*
Bruner, J. S., 8–10, 13, 37, *247, 252*

Brush, L. R., 63, *249*
Bryant, B. H., 72, *247*
Burke, C., 31, 214, *249, 250*
Burton, S., *186*
Bushnell, M. M., 80, *250*
Bussis, A. M., 39, *247*

C

Calkins, L. M., 35
Carle, E., 157, *186, 187, 247*
Caroselli, M., 234, *247*
Carroll, R., *187*
Castaneda, A. M., 116
Cazden, C. B., 10, 25, 72, *89, 134,* 195, *247*
Chall, J., 27, *247*
Charlip, R., *186*
Chittenden, E. A., 39, *247*
Chomsky, C., 15, *247*
Chomsky, N., 9, 10, *247*
Chukovsky, K., *134*
Clark, C., 34, 36, *249*
Clark, E. V., 13, *247*
Clark, M., 28, 29, *247*
Clarke-Stewart, A., *89*
Clay, M., 30, 31, 33, 34–35, 38–39, 163, 164, *188*, 212, 214, 225, *241, 247, 248*
Clifton, L., 207, *248*
Cole, M., 19, *253*
Cook-Gumperz, J., 22, 36, *248*
Cooper, E., 217, *248*
Cooperman, O., 64, 65, *253*
Cox, M., 195, *248*
Cross, T. G., 16, 67, *248*

Subject Index